THE LOST WORLD OF QUINTANA ROO

Michel Peissel

THE
LOST WORLD
OF
QUINTANA ROO

ILLUSTRATED

1963

E. P. DUTTON & CO., INC. • NEW YORK

To My Parents

CONTENTS

ILLUSTRATIONS

PHOTOGRAPHS

Following page 84

Beside this lagoon stands the Mayan temple of Yochac, seen in the
background
Señor Mesos before his hut
Top of the pyramid at Puha
The author at temple of Yochac
The small oratory at Matanceros
The author at Matanceros
Pablo Canche
A house in the Indian village of Tulum
The stone head that protects the corn at Pablo Canche's *milpa*
A family of the village
The main pyramid at Chunyaxche
Palace entrance at Chunyaxche
The tall pyramid at San Miguel de Ruz
The palace at Chamax—on it the three smugglers
Red hand prints on the interior wall of the palace at Chamax

Following page 148

Oval Mayan temple at Recodo San Juan
In search of the temple of Tupak
   Chuc hewing a way through tangled vegetation
   Wading through a swampy lagoon
The temple of Tupak

MAPS AND DIAGRAMS

ACKNOWLEDGMENTS

I am greatly indebted to and would like to thank all the inhabitants of the Quintana Roo coast who so kindly helped me on my journeys. I would also like to thank all those persons who patiently advised me before my departure and upon my return. In particular I would like to thank Dr. Ignacio Bernal and Señor Carlos Pelissier for having introduced me to the Mayan civilization and Dr. John O. Brew for having kindly allowed me to fathom the depth of my ignorance in Mayan archaeology at the Peabody Museum of Harvard. I am particularly grateful to Dr. William R. Bullard, Jr. for having gone through my manuscript and thus revealed how much more I still have to learn on the archaeology and history of Yucatán.

For their generous hospitality I would like to thank Señor A. Mesos, Señor Jorge Gonzales, Mr. Ilya Chamberlain, the French Vice Consul in Belize Mr. Melhado, and especially I thank Pablo Canche for having revealed to me his world—that of the Quintana Roo jungles.

To Marie Claire de Montaignac, who shared the hardships of my second journey, I owe most of the merit this book may have.

M. P.

THE LOST WORLD OF QUINTANA ROO

I

Devils of Tepoztlán

The day after my arrival in Mexico I was hustled into the back seat of a small gray car and invited by my newly acquired friends to take my first look at the country.

This was Mexico, the land that lurid posters and weary professional tourists had described to me as one of fire and death. A land of exuberance, they had called it, and of many other trite qualities. All this had nevertheless made me come to see for myself.

Through an introduction scribbled on a small, dirty piece of paper I had met some friends who rather reluctantly, as is often the case when a foreigner crashes into the privacy of a home, had invited me on a picnic.

We drove down the Paseo de la Reforma, whose modern buildings and bordering parks recalled the fact that Mexico City is not only capital of the nation but a mighty city of four million inhabitants and international fame. We then sped on through Lomas de Chapultepec, the fashionable residential district whose flowered villas shelter thousands of wealthy foreigners who seek asylum, often either political or matrimonial, in Mexico.

I was off to Tepoztlán, a place whose strange name was to be the first of many I was to learn while in Mexico, and which, like such names as Coatzacoalcos and Teotihuacán, suggests a strange poetical beauty hidden under a harsh and complicated Indian origin.

I had come to Mexico with no particular purpose save to spend pleasantly the six months that lay between my entering graduate school and my completion of a dreary six months as trainee in a bank on Wall Street. After the rush of life in New York the calm beauty of Mexico seemed overwhelming. And as our small car took to Mexico's only superhighway, I relaxed to enjoy the scenery as it passed by my shatterproof window on the world. Ironically enough, the only good highway in Mexico, instead of joining major cities or industrial centers, serves Mexico's two largest luxury resorts, Cuernavaca and Acapulco. There is nothing surprising in this, for Mexico is still an aristocratically run country, and the pleasures and interests of a few come before the desire to improve the economic condition of the masses, who have long been brought up to accept in silence their lot—simple pleasures and hard work.

Had I known how far the eighty-mile run to Tepoztlán was to take me, I would probably have declined the invitation to the picnic, and if I could have had the eyes of a prophet I would have seen stretching on beyond the four lanes of the highway narrow, dark jungle paths leading endlessly into the unknown. . . .

Tepoztlán, often called the most beautiful village in Mexico by those who live there, is also known as the "valley of the devils." Its tiny huts of dried earth bricks are staggered on terrace-stepped streets that surround the main church. They are overshadowed by the looming specter of the Aztec pyramid which stands on the edge of a sheer, pinnacle-like cliff, one of the many that border the valley of Tepoztlán, shading it from the full force of the sun and of civilization. Inhabited by a people of its own—the Tepostecs —Tepoztlán, with its own language and customs, and even its own type of musical instrument, is a world of its own. In much the same way, I soon found out, Mexico is entirely composed of innumerable different worlds which really meet only in the green or gray smudges of international atlases. It was in Tepoztlán that I fully realized that Mexico was a country yet to be fully explored.

I immediately felt greatly attracted to the country, and my

enthusiasm was amply exploited by Gustav Regler, the writer we
had come to visit in Tepoztlán. Gustav Regler, well known as a
cynic and for his profane and ironical books on the sixteenth century, is also one of the men who know Mexico the most thoroughly.
His book called A Land Bewitched has acquired world fame.

Regler lived in a beautifully modernized pink and bright blue
peasant house in Tepoztlán, situated at the gates of what had once
been his paradise, a magnificent villa that he had built in the
same way Axel Munthe built San Michele. It was a villa composed
of odds and ends gathered around the world and put together
according to the plans of a dream, a dream that was to make Gustav Regler a king, in accordance with which his old villa had
been crowned by a regal-looking tower. But like the devil to whom
Regler had often been compared (and for whom he liked to be
taken), he had, through involved circumstances, been banished
from his paradise and now lived beyond its gate.

A man quite so fascinating I had never met, and Gustav Regler
had no trouble firing my imagination about Mexico and setting
alight in me a small fire for exploration and adventure that had
almost been extinguished by the rigors of student life and docile
resignation.

In this sense Gustav Regler was responsible for what was to
happen to me during what I had planned to be a peaceful stay in
Mexico. The narrow window of the small gray car had not been
so narrow after all, and had led by way of the four-lane highway to
Gustav Regler and onto a path that was going to cost me all but
my life.

Coming from the dreary streets of New York's financial district,
barely rid of my banker's uniform, and hardly out of touch with
the bitter music of the ticker tape, I found that Tepoztlán with its
devil, Regler, had an overwhelming effect on me. Conscious of my
weakness, the devil had small difficulty in taking control of me.
Gustav Regler, as I left for Mexico City that evening, when the
picnic baskets were empty and the day began to look sour, took

me aside and, with a charming grin, offered me three small statues of some pre-Hispanic culture of Mexico.

"I hope," he said, "that when you leave Mexico you will be able to tell which of these three objects is a fake and which is authentic."

The next day, seated in a *limousina*, the Mexican half-breed of locomotion which is a cross between a small bus and a taxi, I sped along the same highway to Cuernavaca, the summer capital of Mexico. The beauty and restful lower altitude of this spot had already led to its selection by Cortez himself as the seat of his summer palace. There, leaving the tourist-crowded streets, I hopped onto what could be described as the miracle Ford—a local bus that goes to Tepoztlán. This bus, like all Mexican buses, is, I believe, one of the greatest tributes to modern science that exist. For here is the real steam horse, the man-made engine taking upon itself tasks that only thinking beings should be asked to assume. Mexican buses are usually some forty years old and carry forty people more than the authorized number, plus forty pigs that at some chance stop have been piled on top of the already sagging vehicle. They are truly a wheeled miracle. The gears, if any, are automatic and seem to change to the rhythm of alternate prayers and oaths as the driver, seated before a shrine of the Madonna which obstructs most of his view through a usually cluttered windshield, if not an opaque one, goes through the various rites of driving, a curious ceremony imprinted with elements of Christianity on a base of profanity.

The bus, as it was pretentiously called, careened over a road that would have been a scandal even in the wheelless Aztec empire. Few or no foreigners seem to ride this means of conveyance, and mine was the only white face among the many pairs of dark eyes and long shiny pigtails interwoven with red ribbons that decorated the rigid faces of the Indian women who were the majority of the passengers.

I had made up my mind the day before and decided to settle in Tepoztlán. I was greeted again by Gustav Regler, who, as he expounded his interpretations of Dante, paused to introduce me to a near neighbor. Alan Ball—which wasn't his real name—was a man in his early forties whose unforgettable face showed at the same time the ravages of a disheveled life and the poetic creases of a clown. He was nearly bald, with a long, narrow forehead accentuating a healthy nose whose original luster seemed, and in fact was, unnaturally reddened by much drink, much worry, and a consistent nervous twitch. An artist at heart and a writer by profession, Ball had landed in Tepoztlán after a rather tortuous and difficult tour of the United States dispensing knowledge as the driver of a "bookmobile"—a library on wheels. I never was able to grasp fully the elements of the rather strange career of this man, British, aristocratic, and bearing the great name of one of England's historic heroes, his great-grandfather. Despite his large straw hat, his few sober hours, and his altogether bohemian appearance, Ball was a great wit, a man of knowledge and culture. He impressed me very much, and he was a friend of Regler; I was only twenty, and had not met anyone like him.

Since I was in search of a house or lodging in Tepoztlán, Ball generously invited me to live in his house provided I paid the rent. At the time, the arrangement seemed profitable to me, and I warmly accepted. Only too delighted at being able to stay in Tepoztlán, I was not in the slightest concerned by the fact that the house in question had but two rooms and no water, and was also the abode of a friend of Ball's whom I shall call Jack Hanson. This equally delightful and confidence-inspiring character was currently engaged in the trade of making sandals and mosaics, having recently lost his job as Javanese cook in a Mexican restaurant. This was of little concern to me, seeing that Hanson spoke Ottomine and a handful of other Indian dialects fluently, and was an artist. But the strangest feature of my two hosts was that, in addition to their both being penniless, they had the same physical features— the same profile and receding hair, the same nose with the same glow. Such a resemblance in two individuals so different, so weathered by life's ravages, seemed to me unbelievable, and this particularly delighted me in spite of the rather frightening realization that I was to support, on my small income, two men bound to be hungry and in fact nearly always thirsty.

The day I settled in Tepoztlán I was lost forever to the prospect of a peaceful stay in Mexico. And listening to Hanson speak of his experiences among the Ottomine Indians, a tribe known for its rather brutal savagery, I decided that my vocation lay in exploring the country myself.

Tepoztlán was of sufficient interest to attract my attention for the first month of my stay. And the drinking habits of my two lodgers forced me into numerous contacts with the rather taciturn and reserved Indians of Tepoztlán, contacts that were, if not entirely anthropological, nevertheless intimate. They consisted mostly in explaining in rather poor Spanish to drunken Indians that my rather more drunken friends had meant no offense and that "a knife was better in a sheath than in someone's back"—an appropriate adage of dark Chinese origin. I was successful in this, for neither Jack Hanson, Alan Ball, nor myself came to any harm.

Despite the rather dissipated tenor of our lives in Tepoztlán, I was to learn a great deal, particularly about the local inhabitants, rarely known to mix with white people, but who, out of sympathy and through our common drinking trouble, became quite open toward me, the "good boy of the two red-nosed devils."

To these rather summary anthropological débuts, I was able to add through numerous visits to Mexico City and through the kind assistance of Gustav Regler and Señor Ignacio Bernal, the curator of pre-Hispanic monuments in Mexico City, more information about the ancient civilizations of Mexico, especially the fierce Aztecs who had conquered central Mexico and whose monumental if not refined art had superimposed itself upon the many more artistic but less military cultures which they had conquered.

I had been brought up in England, and in the temperate lowlands of Hertfordshire had craved exoticism and felt frustrated that the wildest animal I had seen at the age of twelve was a white-breasted badger. I felt that now was my opportunity to fulfill my childhood dreams of living adventurously in the "real tropics."

One night on the veranda of our small house I was looking at a map of Mexico with Ball, and together we formed a plan. We discovered a vast, barren, white expanse on the map that bore the beautiful name of Quintana Roo, and we immediately decided to go there. And since the name "Quintana Roo" called for something to balance it, we named our expedition "Quintana Roo-Darién," the Serranía del Darién being a barren, inaccessible, and little-known mountain range stretching south of the Panama Canal and along the Colombian border.

We lost little time in our preparations, and a few days later Ball returned from Mexico City with a sheaf of writing paper bearing the heading "Expedition Quintana Roo-Darién" printed in dark blue ink in Gothic characters.

I now have no doubt that this letterhead was most instrumental in what was to happen. This printing pushed me over the dangerous cliff that separates reality from wild dreams.

The next month was spent concentrating on living up to that title. I began to investigate seriously the words "Quintana Roo-Darién." We decided that ours would be an expedition by sea; we would start from the coast of Quintana Roo and make our way by native craft down to the Darién coast. I do not know today how sincere Ball was in all these plans, and if later I was to be bitterly disappointed by the fact that he had apparently never thought seriously of the project, I cannot help but feel grateful that he lent me, if only temporarily, his backing, for that is what put me on the road to adventure.

Quintana Roo is a territory of Mexico, one of the three political subdivisions of the Yucatán peninsula—that thumblike projection of Mexico that closes the Gulf of Mexico south of Florida. I learned that the Yucatán peninsula also included the province of Campeche and the province of Yucatán, a small triangle whose base is the northern coast of the peninsula and whose summit is wedged between Campeche and Quintana Roo. Unlike most other parts of Mexico, Quintana Roo, being so sparsely populated, has not the full rank of a province but is a territory without local government, and comes under the jurisdiction of the capital; it is a Territorio Federal of Mexico.

In vain I searched for someone in Mexico to tell me about this territory. It soon became evident that the name Quintana Roo was as unknown and exotic to Mexican ears as the Upper Congo to those of Icelandic fishermen. In short, Quintana Roo was the unexplored haven that I had always dreamed of.

A detailed map of Central America showed that our proposed route would take us down what could be considered the most savage coast of the American continent, the Atlantic shoreline of Central America, down the barren coast of Quintana Roo to the relatively uninhabited littoral of British Honduras, into Guatemala, then to Honduras and the famed Mosquito Coast in Nicaragua. This was the first part of the American continent to be seen and explored by Christopher Columbus, whose tracks we would follow all the way down to Darién and Colombia. In all, it would be a run of a thousand miles.

Seeing that little could be done in Mexico to obtain precise details of the areas we expected to visit, we limited our study there to the people we would first encounter in Quintana Roo, at the same time securing from the British Embassy assurance that we could enter British Honduras without trouble. At the Embassy we were told that no visas were required for French citizens like myself, or for British subjects. The courtesy toward French citizens was a result of an agreement between France and England to facilitate the flow of tourists in Europe, and this agreement extended to the British colonies. However, I discovered later, while I was in jail, that this had not yet come to the knowledge of the local British Honduras authorities.

As for penetrating Guatemala from British Honduras, we were informed that this would be more difficult, since the two countries were almost at war; already comic battles were being fought on postage stamps. The stamps of Guatemala nearly always bear the slogan *Belice es Nuestro* (Belize is ours). Belize is the capital of British Honduras, and the name by which the colony is generally known.

But we had little time to bother about the intricate political situation of the countries we were to cross, for we had yet to find a means of going down the barren coasts we planned to explore.

Ball for some reason decided that I should go ahead to the capital of the province of Yucatán, Mérida, from where I could begin material preparations and possibly obtain more precise information on Quintana Roo. For his part he would stay in Tepoztlán awaiting my word for him to join me.

Before setting out for Mérida, I gathered in Mexico City all the information I could on the ancient Mayan civilization that had once covered the Yucatán peninsula, most of British Honduras, Guatemala, and a fair bit of Honduras proper.

The Mayan civilization, I found out, was probably the most sophisticated culture of pre-Columbian America. Among all the great pre-Hispanic civilizations of the American continent, the Mayas developed the most advanced form of writing—strange glyphs capable of recording historical facts, glyphs that even today are but partly understood. The mystery of their writing is but one of the many which still surround the Mayas. One of the most intriguing of these mysteries is why the ancient Mayas suddenly abandoned their greatest cities, such as Palenque in Mexico and Tikal in Guatemala. The sudden disappearances and reappearances of the Mayas, and the vastness of their cities—many of them including thousands of buildings—which they abandoned in perfect condition to the groping vines and ill effects of the rain forest, are among the most enigmatic aspects of this culture.

The Mayas were probably the greatest builders of the ancient inhabitants of Central America. They left thousands of temples and palaces spread all over what was their domain, the principal cities being Palenque, Tikal, Copán, Uxmal, and Chichén-Itzá, strange places whose pyramids, towers, and palaces still stand today as silent testimonial of the great Mayan civilization.

The Mayas today are one of the largest groups of Indians in the American continent whose dialects belong to the same language family. In Guatemala and Yucatán there are still nearly two million of these descendants of the ancient temple builders, the greatest number living in the Yucatán peninsula in the provinces of Yucatán and Campeche, although there are also some in Quintana Roo. Mayan is more widely spoken in Yucatán than Spanish, and many books are written, in modern characters, in Mayan, which is also taught in schools.

I learned that the peninsula of Yucatán has always considered itself independent from Mexico, and the Yucatecans, as they are called, had often tried to gain their freedom, even attempting to join the short-lived Texas republic. In April 1958, when I set out, there were no roads connecting Yucatán with central Mexico, and apart from planes the only means of communication was by the Ferrocarriles del Sur Este, a small, prehistoric railroad line that wound through the dense jungle of the Isthmus of Tehuantepec to the state of Campeche.

The first leg of the trip was therefore to be a minor expedition in itself, seeing that the train took three days to cover some five hundred miles. I decided to visit on the way the city of Palenque, situated halfway along the railroad line.

April is the peak of the hot season in Mexico. And with the heat and dry weather around Tepoztlán the Indians were setting fire to the forests and woods; night and day forest fires raged. When they died out the arsonists would go and collect the burned wood to sell as charcoal to the innumerable street peddlers of tortillas and other cooked foods who cluster on the sidewalks of the poorer districts of Mexico. Thus each night, as our preparations reached their end in Tepoztlán, Ball and I would sit on the terrace of our small house, lit by the tragic glow of the great forest fires eating away at the woods above our heads, closing in upon the valley of the devils.

We had purposely bought no equipment in Mexico City, thinking it would be wise to acquire any material we needed in Mérida where I could take a close look at the climatic and physical difficulties we would be up against.

Therefore, with a small suitcase I boarded a modern bus in Mexico City, the most rapid means of reaching Coatzacoalcos, the railway head of the Ferrocarriles del Sur Este.

As I descended south through Puebla toward Coatzacoalcos, the weather became hotter and the scenery more tropical—vast dried-up fields strewn with clumps of palm trees, which gave the only shade against the burning sun.

There being only three trains a week, and the dates of their departure being, apparently, held secret by the Mexican Government, when I arrived in sun-baked, foul-smelling Coatzacoalcos I was obliged to take a train that stopped in the middle of nowhere, at a place called Teapa. There I must wait two days to go twenty miles to the small station of Palenque, or continue direct through to Campeche. I decided to risk it, thinking that a little experience in out-of-the-way places could do me no harm seeing that I was totally uninitiated in any of the physical, moral, and intellectual abilities expected of the explorer I hoped to be.

I boarded the famous train, with a cluster of Indians dressed in blue-jeans-type trousers, rolled up to below the knees, revealing their thin ankles and large bare feet. Most of them wore, slung at their belts, machetes, the three-foot-long knives so necessary for survival in the jungle. As we puffed our way toward the Yucatán peninsula I could take a look at the great rain forest. This was the first time I had seen a jungle. For years the word had conjured up mysteries for me, and I saw the jungle of my childhood dreams populated by creepy creatures, gigantic snakes, and all the other horrors that Kipling had revealed to me through the dry, unexotic lips of my old Nanny. I was not to be disappointed, for if no snakes jumped into the train, I could nevertheless imagine them lurking behind the giant mahogany trees, the coconut palms that swished past the windows of the train as we clattered at fifteen miles an hour through the green vegetation. Occasionally parrots would rise with a deafening noise above the trees, and I could hear many "jungle noises" during the innumerable stops we made in the middle of nowhere. Mosquitoes seemed happy enough on the train to stay with us; my face became covered with spots.

Finally we came to Teapa, right in the middle of the railway line—a bustling jungle town, the center of the local mahogany camps, and, from all appearances, an open city. The station is eight miles from the town, and when I inquired whether I could spend the night at the station, I was told that a man had been killed there a week before. I therefore took a tumble-down bus to the town. Inside the bus, instead of the usual small shrine to the Virgin of Guadalupe that one finds in every bus in central Mexico, I found that this one was covered with profane words and oaths painted on the dirty panels. The town proved to be no better than the bus, and seemed a mixture between a Far West nightmare and a foreign occupation. Every healthy-looking man wore a gun or two in his belt and looked like a murderer; as for the unhealthy poorer people, they looked like rebellious slaves with dangerous machetes. I was told that the men with pistols were the *dueños* (the owners) or the *encargados* (the supervisors) of the various work camps in the jungle; as for the workers, they were for the most part ex-convicts imported from the dregs of Vera Cruz, Mexico's largest seaport. In my rather civilized attire and without guns, pistols, or machetes I wondered where I fitted into the rather grim picture that Teapa presented. I soon concluded, nowhere, when I tried to find a hotel for the night. . . .

"Where is a hotel?" I asked a small group of machete-swinging men standing on the steps of the church, which had been turned into a cinema. I had looked at no man in particular, not wanting to start a fight lest my question be misunderstood. No reply came, but as I stood not knowing whether to try elsewhere or to repeat my question, one of the meaner-looking of the crowd stepped toward me. "Gringo no good, ha ha!" he screamed, and with the rest of the men I laughed, looking like a fool. I turned away and decided to ask an old woman for the simple information I wanted. But this did not work, for as I approached her she hastened on and soon I had to abandon the chase for fear of causing a scandal. By this time I had made myself so conspicuous that all my movements were carefully followed by hundreds of frightening eyes. Fortunately someone volunteered to ask me what I wanted, and soon I was looking over our hotel room. I say "our," for there were six beds in the windowless room and evidently I was to share this communal affair with five others. Hiding my luggage under the bed and hoping for the best, I decided to take a long night's rest and went to sleep immediately.

The next day I was blind, thanks to the collaboration of two mosquitoes. Decidedly jungle towns were not for me, so I set out in a truck encountered somewhere on the square, toward Villa Hermosa. There I knew I could charter a small plane to fly to Palenque.

I was a passenger of Tabasquenio Airways, and I must admit that "once a passenger, never a passenger again." At the airstrip a Mexican child explained to me that he had decided not to be a pilot because the week before Lopez had died "over there." He pointed to the electric lines near the airstrip, whose parallel cables still showed the ill effects of Lopez's accident. I then boarded the only surviving plane owned by the company. Soon I was in the air, seated next to an Indian pilot, a charming man whose pleasant face began to show anxiety as the plane slowly dipped toward the ground starting a nose dive that would have been fatal had I not realized in time that my anxiety had brought me to press with all my strength on the foot pedal of the dual controls. The plane was duly straightened out; we flew past a few scraggy fields and over the rolling green waves of the rain forest. Here I could see the lay of the land and look at the jungle in comfort. Such a mass of vegetation is quite a spectacle. From the air it looks now like green sea swells, now like bread fungus bubbling out of the earth, with occasionally the ghostly branches of a dead tree sticking out as a landmark. At one point the forest opened up revealing a small clearing with two thatched-roof huts, the only sign of life for miles.

I thanked heaven that the Quintana Roo-Darién expedition was to be by sea, and more than ever I admired those who battle on foot through the giant mushroomy forests of the world's jungles. I saw no jaguars from the plane, but I imagined them treading slowly over thousands of poisonous snakes—a vision as terrible as any I could summon up.

I had little time to alarm myself further, for soon the pilot put the plane into a wide turn and beyond wing-tip I took my first look at Mayan ruins as the great city of Palenque loomed into sight. Majestic, awe-inspiring, white and gray buildings perched upon a green shelf overlooking the same endless jungle as that which tumbled down the mountain that loomed over the city.

Such a sight in such a barren and god-forsaken spot left a deep impression on me. And if ruins usually have a grand and romantic charm, those of Palenque are unique and stupefying in their unexpected presence in a sea of hostile forest. There before me stood the mystery of the centuries, of a civilization dead and gone yet still strangely present and reflected in the grandiose buildings that proclaim a pride and glory that is no more. Such sights are the material of deep reflections. Here, I felt, began a world so strange to me that its beauty and grandeur were unspoiled by the contingencies of my own mind, a civilization that had the unalterable strength of those who have departed and therefore cease to be affected by man and existence.

I had chosen to come to Palenque to initiate myself into the study of the Mayas; little did I know that Palenque would be the first chapter of a long-lasting passion.

Now every year thousands of tourists crowd the city of Palenque despite its isolation and its inaccessibility. In April it was so hot that there were no tourists on my arrival; the Palenque I saw was one of heat and emptiness. I was almost alone to contemplate the beauties of the ancient city, alone save for four men—a carpenter, a mason, a potter, and a poet.

In the small village of Santo Domingo del Palenque, some five miles from the ruins, there are two or three taxis. Cars are brought in by the railroad, and the taxi drivers have the strange custom of looking to the sky for prospective clients. They rushed in a cloud of dust to my landing place and were waiting for me, but I was soon to learn that this pleasant welcome was very expensive. I had to stay three days in Palenque before the arrival of the next train that would take me farther on to Yucatán, but I had not the slightest idea of where I could spend the night. By now, after Teapa, my blazer was looking shabby and my eyes were still orientalized by the ill effects of the two mosquitoes that had done such a perfect and painful job of closing them in Teapa.

"To the ruins," I said to one of the drivers. And soon I was jogging in the vast back seat of my limousine, gathering dust rapidly but at the same time enjoying the restful position of having my feet up on the folding seats behind the driver.

On the way up the road toward the ruins the car came to a grinding halt and to my dismay four barefooted young Indians got in; this rather dirty and unwanted addition to my expensive taxi drive was easier to accept when one of the young men offered me a drink from a dirty old bottle. I warmly accepted what my stomach was later to reject, and tasted the local drink with a dubious smile. Was it really gasoline? I do not know. The young men were the first Mayan Indians I had met. Of pure Indian stock, they had stunning black eyes, delicately sheathed in perfect swan-like lids marked with two graceful pleats. Their hair was straight, with a warm luster and a dark brown shade. Their skins were golden, as seen on suntanned Europeans. Of small stature, their wrists and ankles were delicate but sturdy and their chests slightly too large to be graceful. Their bare feet and ankles were so worn and hardened by walking through the rough undergrowth that it seemed that they were wearing ankle-high boots, where their skin had chafed and calloused, taking on a darker brown shade.

No sooner were our passengers in than they were out, and under the torrid midday sun I rode in state down a grandiose avenue bordered by four tall pyramids whose golden-white stones shone with incredible force in the bright light.

Soon I was standing among the ruins, listening to the silence as it slowly replaced the drone of the disappearing limousine.

Nothing is more awe-inspiring than the ruins of the American continent, for unlike those of Greece and Egypt they are so devoid of historical recollection, so strange to our occidental culture, that they reflect something which at first it is impossible to grasp. I stood repeating the banal phrases, "Greater than the pyramids of Egypt," and "Is it possible that men lived here to build these places?"

I could easily have made the mistake of the first archaeologists to see Palenque, who for many years attributed these buildings to the Greeks or Egyptians in disbelief that they could have been built by any other people.

But the jungle around me, and the strange architectural features of the buildings, reminded me that I was not in Greece or on the edge of the Nile. What lay before me was made by men on the American continent during the time when Byzantium was falling and Gaul still in the chaos of post-Roman rule. This was a world of its own, a world that I could not yet understand.

All these considerations were not enough for me to forget the rather material facts that (a) I was out on an expedition, and not a tourist, and (b) my suitcase was not in its proper place in the middle of the ruins. I had no bed for the night and was five miles away from the village, so I should start thinking fast about the immediate future.

At that moment I met a man. He was around fifty, bald, stripped to the waist, wearing a pair of shorts and sandals; perspiration trickled down his elegant brow. His distinguished features contrasted with his rather scanty attire, which nevertheless was certainly more appropriate to the circumstances than my gray flannels and blue blazer which had suffered so much during the past few days. Who was the more surprised at whom I do not know, but I suspect it was I.

I did not know then that the man was a poet. Later, after leaving Palenque, I was told he was Mexico's greatest poet, a mystic, and respected by all. For in Mexico as generally in Latin America, poets come before presidents, revolutions, and even the Church. The poets stand out as gods who command the people; great poets have been the pillars around which the history of Latin America has been written.

In many ways, as Gustav Regler had opened my eyes to Mexico, Carlos Pelissier in the anonymity of my ignorance and his pair of shorts was to reveal to me the Mayas, their art and civilization.

It so happened that Carlos Pelissier was staying at the Campamento Archeologico, a small house situated a few yards from the ruins which had been constructed to serve as shelter for visiting archaeologists. Dr. Pelissier was at Palenque to erect a museum. He kindly invited me to stay with him for the days I was to spend at Palenque.

Soon I was abandoning my blazer in the small white room given to me at the Campamento, and shortly ate the first of many extraordinary meals I would have at Palenque.

If the meals were extraordinary it was due to the great simplicity and intelligence of Carlos Pelissier. For here was an educated man, all but a genius, living with three other men, all artisans, the potter, the carpenter, and the mason. These three men were building under his instructions the small museum to house the objects he had chosen among the thousands which had been found during the years of excavation at Palenque.

Strangely enough, in accordance with Mexican tradition, titles were used in conversation. And if Carlos Pelissier was known simply as Señor, he never failed to call his companions Maestro, the title given in Mexico to full-fledged artisans. His conversation was so enlightening and tactful that his three associates, despite their crude upbringing and simple origins, lived up to the distinguished sophistication of Señor the poet. And apart from minor barbaric eating habits the men were so transformed as to appear of the same stuff as the educated man.

There was something so medieval and so unreal about this quartet that I could not help imagining myself in Europe at the time of the building of the great cathedrals, at the table of a noble landlord eating with the artisans and discussing the erection of a Gothic *domum domini*.

During my three days' stay at Palenque there were no tourists there, and I was alone among the ruins, often accompanied by Carlos Pelissier, whose enlightening comments and acute and sensitive observations brought alive for me the great buildings that had earlier escaped my understanding. Through him I learned not only the history of the old city but also how to look at ruins, and note what were the important things to observe.

Palenque was the hub of Mayan archaeology and study. Despite its isolation it had been the first large Mayan city to be discovered. The city became known in 1773 when Indians gave its location to a priest who then visited it and drew up a report. Later the site was viewed by a Spanish soldier accompanied by an Italian architect, Antonio Bernaconi. They carried out a rather destructive archaeological survey. The site was also brought to the attention of King Charles III of Spain (the archaeologist and patron of the excavations at Pompeii), who ordered that all finds at Palenque were to be preserved to illustrate the *Historia Antigua de America*.

The modern history of Palenque covers nearly two hundred years, a time during which visitors to the city included such strange personalities as Count Waldeck, who in 1832 made drawings of the city slightly falsified to give the impression that the structures had been built by the Phoenicians or Romans; this common error regarding Palenque was rectified only in 1840, when what could be called the founders of modern Mexican archaeology came to the city. They were the New York lawyer John Lloyd Stephens and his companion, the artist Frederick Catherwood. The faithful drawings of this artist were so precise that today they are still used for reference instead of photographs. Many of the stelae and hieroglyphs which he drew have now been destroyed but they can nevertheless be studied because of his work.

Archaeologists are still discovering new and exciting facts about Palenque. In 1951, Dr. Alberto Ruz l'Huillier, the famous archaeologist, when he was restoring some of the buildings, discovered that the floor of the small temple that crowns the largest of the pyramids was drilled with small holes. Using these as holds with which to raise the stone slabs, he discovered a stairway leading to the heart of the pyramid; at the foot of the stairway, some sixty feet down from the summit and nine feet below the surface of the earth, he came upon a large stone slab blocking the stairway. Before it were six skeletons of Mayas that had been set there to guard the door which protected the most amazing of Mayan finds, the tomb of a nobleman covered by a five-ton slab of stone, delicately carved and engraved with hieroglyphs. All around the body, which was covered with jade necklaces and pearl ornaments, many pieces of pottery were found intact. This was the most elaborate tomb to be discovered inside a Mayan pyramid, and had evidently been built at the time the temple was constructed, rather than later as had been the case elsewhere.

The study of dates found on the numerous carved slabs in Palenque, which can be read since they were deciphered by a newspaper editor in Virginia who had never seen a Maya, shows that Palenque was erected in the fifth and sixth centuries A.D. and was abandoned for some mysterious reason around the year 1,000.

The name Palenque is not an Indian one, and Carlos Pelissier explained to me that it came from the Spanish word for "palisade."

At first sight Palenque's architecture is rather baroque. Some of the vaults of the buildings are similar to oriental arches shaped like keyholes. The city includes four large, square-based pyramids with small one-room temples on their summits with three square doorways opening onto the majestic staircases that descend the steep faces of the pyramids. Also there are a large palace and various other small buildings built on mounds, giving an over-all impression of a great religious center, and one has difficulty in imagining the city inhabited by anyone but a religious or military elite.

The fronts of the buildings are ornamented with stucco reliefs or stone sculptures, mostly representing men in elaborate costume wearing headdresses of feathers and leopard skins; the headdresses are so large that many are even bigger than the men who wear them.

At first sight the human figures on the stone slabs and plaster reliefs seem to be stylized forms, but Carlos Pelissier pointed out to me that small details in the mouths and noses and teeth tended to show that each carving had been done from authentic models, and that they were portraits of individuals.

This was but one of the many acute observations by Pelissier which made me realize that Palenque was above all the creation of artistic and human individuals; these were no mere silent ruins, but portrait galleries of persons who had held rank and honor in the strange Mayan society of old.

Many theories have been developed to explain the mysterious abandonment of this beautiful and elaborately decorated city— disease, death, sudden decadence—but none seems satisfactory.

Closer observation of the sculptures shows that the Mayas had an acute artistic sense, a notion of stylization often resembling our own. For instance, there is a carving of a dog-like animal whose eye and eyelashes are represented by a neat footprint.

Better prepared and more aware of the great Mayan culture, I bade farewell to Carlos Pelissier and took the Ferrocarriles del Sur Este at midnight, three days after my arrival. I was off on the great adventure Ball and I had imagined when we printed the words "Quintana Roo-Darién."

The first leg of the expedition proper began when late the next afternoon the chugging train entered the province of Campeche and I trod for the first time the soil of the Yucatán peninsula. Little did I know then that I was to be called upon to play a significant if only minor role in elucidating the many mysteries of the ancient Mayas.

II

Mayaluum

To enter the Yucatán peninsula after the ordeal of crossing the jungles of the Isthmus of Tehuantepec at a snail's pace on the Ferrocarriles del Sur Este is like changing worlds.

The Mexican part of the Yucatán peninsula is a geographic freak; its strange physical aspect and characteristics are unique. What at first strikes one is that the country is absolutely flat. Apart from a small, narrow, hilly mound that descends the center of the rectangular Mexican portion of the peninsula, the entire region is a vast limestone plateau barely above sea level.

Another strange feature that does not escape observation, but which is even more evident on a map, is that there is not one river in this whole region. It is, I suppose, in places like northern Yucatán that one fully realizes the importance of water. But Mexican Yucatán, if it has not a single river or lake (apart from salty coastal lagoons), has a considerable amount of invisible water. For the land is of porous limestone, and no sooner do the tropical rains fall than they are absorbed into the ground. The region is but a network of innumerable underground rivers and reservoirs, subterranean lakes and streams. Wells are the only focal points of habitation, the sea having little importance, for there are no large cities by the sea, apart from Campeche, the famed pirate port situated at the border of Yucatán and the Isthmus of Tehuantepec.

The wells are extremely numerous and are of two kinds: man-made wells and *cenotes*. The modern man-made wells are nearly all pumped today by windmills, and so part of Yucatán is a land of a million windmills whose steel frames rise like thousands of marigolds above the roofs of cities such as Mérida. But more intriguing are the *cenotes*, the natural wells formed by the crumbling of the limestone earth crust above underground rivers or lakes. These wells are the only places where water is visible, and vary in size from narrow shafts to gigantic ponds two to three hundred feet wide and often as deep as one hundred feet. For reasons easily understandable, *cenotes* were also the focal point of the ancient Mayan settlements, and every large Mayan city of Mexican Yucatán is built near or around a *cenote*. And where there were no *cenotes* the Mayas made large reservoirs to capture the rainfall, which is quite heavy, varying from 39 inches in the drier parts to 150 inches in the wetter areas; the latter, I was to find out—unfortunately for me—are situated in Quintana Roo.

The limestone rocks that make up the northern Yucatán peninsula seem most infertile, and everywhere are visible as they break through in gray streaks above the thin, patchy, red earth. At first one is amazed that such arid soil can support any vegetation. This surprised the Spaniards too, and Diego de Landa, Yucatán's greatest historian, called it "a land with the least amount of earth" he had ever seen. Coming from a Spaniard who had seen the barrenness of the mountainous regions of Andalusia, this was no empty statement. But probably the first and most striking of the many paradoxes of Yucatán is that it is nevertheless a land of "turkey and deer, of honey and corn," and strangely abundant.

In Campeche I exchanged, with relief, my seat in the train for one in a bus (three times faster than the train and twice as dirty) and made my way to Mérida, the capital of the province of Yucatán, situated in the middle of the peninsula.

I could see for myself that Yucatán was not as arid as might be thought. It is nearly all covered with a low, spiny forest, not of a tropical kind like the surroundings of Palenque, but a shorter and drier sort. As it was the peak of the dry season, most of this bush was brown and had a most desolate look, except for the bright orange outcrop of innumerable flowering trees. These trees, I learned, were typical of Yucatán, and their flower is the flower of the land.

In the course of the one-hundred-fifty-mile run from Campeche to Mérida the bus passed through half a dozen villages. Most of them contained a gigantic old Spanish renaissance church whose austere façade looked down upon the low, one-story stone houses which bordered large, open squares. These houses, with delicately carved windows screened by wrought-iron grilles, were of a dusty brown. But the most striking features of these villages were not the vast plazas of colonial Spanish architecture but the thousands of oval, palm-leaf-covered huts that surrounded the plazas, resembling those I had seen in illustrations of native African dwellings. These huts, set within small square compounds of red earth, made me realize that Yucatán today is still the land of the Mayas. Those thousands of Indians who make up the majority of its inhabitants in many ways have not changed after four hundred years of Spanish and Mexican occupation. Here paradoxically the pre-Columbian elements have not been assimilated by foreign culture, nor have the Mayas even tried to assimilate all that the Europeans brought over.

The neat oval walls of the Mayan houses are made of stakes placed side by side in the ground and support equally neatly trimmed, tall, thatched roofs. The houses have no windows, but one low door. Many of the square courtyards have two or three houses inside them and later I learned that according to tradition most families have a "Sunday" house which is reserved for great occasions, a house serving as an everyday living room, and a smaller hut used, as could be seen from the charred roof and walls, as the kitchen.

It was a shock to realize that there was still a whole region in America where there was yet such a native influence. This was not only visible in the houses but also in both the dress and the language. The Mayan language is still spoken by some 320,000 inhabitants of the Yucatán peninsula, and today it is not very different from that spoken in the days of the great Mayan culture. It is unrelated to the other languages of the American continent, has a particular accent, and the words are more stuttered than spoken.

Mérida is the capital of the province of Yucatán and the largest city of the peninsula. With two hundred thousand inhabitants, it is a large, sprawling city with innumerable parallel streets which were laid out by the Spaniards in the typical style of their early cities.

If there was ever a capital that did not belong to our modern times it is Mérida, for it lacks all common bonds with modern cities. Save for a few up-to-date buildings it is entirely of post-conquest Spanish colonial architecture, its buildings being large, high, one-story rectangular structures enclosing cool courtyards and cloisters. In these courtyards grow tall imperial palm trees beside the inevitable windmills, for every house has its well and windmill. To the road the houses present austere façades of large symmetrical windows and one doorway. Most of the houses are painted in pale shades of blue, yellow, or green.

Since each house is large, the city seems far bigger than it really is. And where the stone Spanish colonial houses end, a large and equally neat peripheral city of Mayan thatched huts begins. Such a proximity of styles that are so different, such a contrast between modern stone, sixteenth-century Spanish buildings, and the traditional ancient Mayan huts is startling and must not fail to amaze all who see it.

I soon realized that if Yucatán belonged to Mexico, if Mérida was a thriving city, both Yucatán and Mérida existed in a world of their own, cut off completely from the general current of modern civilization. They live by their own customs, a strange life, the product of the old Mayan ways and a rather slow nineteenth-century attitude toward our own world.

For the Spanish element of Yucatán is also foreign to modern progress. There are practically no taxis in Mérida and the general means of conveyance is still the horse and buggy. Typical are the *calechas,* horse-drawn carriages that come directly from old prints and by the hundreds still clutter the streets. Since many are brand-new, this is not a historical means of transportation but still the most common method of travel about the city.

The *calechas* are but one of many aspects of life in Mérida which reflect the old-fashioned tempo of Yucatán, one of gentle sophistication. It is a world with lazy schedules adapted to the hot midday sun, a world of good food and leisurely talk, a land of *far niente,* and of quiet exuberance tinged with a certain passive restraint derived from the Mayan character.

If Mexico is a land of fire and death. Yucatán is a land of peace and nostalgia. This radical difference in character between the noisy, bloodthirsty, ebullient Mexico and the calm quiet of the Yucatán peninsula has inspired in Yucatán a great dislike for more powerful central Mexico. The people of Yucatán are above all Yucatecans. They read the poetry of Yucatán, cook according to local recipes, have their own artists and sculptors and universities. Invited to the Rotary Club of Mérida in the large garden of a private house constructed on the model of homes being erected in Paris in 1890, I discovered to my surprise that more of the people in the assemblage had been to Paris or Europe than had been to Mexico City. The Yucatecan, if he needs medical treatment of a sort unavailable on the peninsula, will go more readily to Cuba or the United States than to rowdy, politically hostile, and "savage" Mexico City.

The aristocracy in Yucatán, unfortunately, has been ruined by the edicts of the Mexican Revolution. Large estates were dismembered, and although they were later repurchased by the same wealthy families, the aristocracy remains poor owing to the fall in the price of henequen.

Henequen is the only major source of income of Yucatán. The soil, which is sparse, has, since the time of the ancient Mayas, lost much of its fertility, and as a result, the only crop that could have industrial significance is henequen, or sisal, which above all other plants has the great advantage of having no roots and living on a little water and thin air. It is an ideal plant to grow on barren limestone. In the eighteenth century Yucatán opened itself to sisal planting, and great fortunes were made in the nineteenth century, with the result that the aristocracy could keep up Mérida as a town of pleasant luxury copied from Paris, a city where wealthy Yucatecans lived for part of the year and became known as the Méridians, a fun-loving, rather debauched set. The principal use for sisal was in the manufacture of ropes and cables (of poor quality) and it soon became a dying industry. With the decline of sisal's importance an economic depression fell on Mérida, and the city has since slipped into a peaceful slumber—an impoverished shadow of its former self.

But of the Méridians of Paris and the days of old wealth the Yucatecans have retained many traits, especially those of wanting and attempting to make their town and way of life akin to Europe's. *"Mérida la blanche,"* as its inhabitants call it, likes to consider itself "the Paris of the South."

The city and its hoped-for resemblance to Paris are the pride of every Méridian, regardless of his social position, and a *calecha* driver is proud to explain that the pavements of the streets come from Paris—brought back as ballast in the thousands of trading schooners and square-riggers that used to call at Progreso, the port of Mérida, fifteen miles from the city on the Gulf of Mexico. Furthermore, the horse-and-buggy driver will point out proudly that his carriage is the same as those used in France, and to prove this he shows that the designer was a Frenchman, as indicated by a brass plate nailed to the rear axle.

Little do these fellows realize that on the tarmac streets of Paris today, there are no more *calechas*. Little do they suspect that the Méridian *calechas*, if designed by a French *carrossier*, are of a model so antique that even before the French Revolution they would have appeared outmoded in France. The *calecha*, in fact, consists of a very narrow and very high square cabin, which can be entirely closed by rolled canvas blinds; the driver sits high above the roof. The general impression is one of great antiquarian charm, pleasant to see, but it gives a feeling of total insecurity.

However, the most interesting aspect today of Mérida and of Yucatán in general is the presence of the Mayas. In Yucatán, apart from the old aristocratic families, there is no such deep cleavage between Mexicans and Indians as is found elsewhere in Mexico; both groups mix socially. The Mayan Indians, who outnumber the Mexicans, have been able to imprint their way of life and their mentality on much of the city. They have also retained their costume. A most typical sight in Yucatán is the *huipiles*, a white dress worn by all the Indian women, and even adopted by aristocratic women on great occasions, such as the numerous parties given by prominent families. The *huipiles* is a sack dress made by folding in two a large, narrow piece of white cloth; the two edges are sewn together to form a large pillowcase open at one end. The other end of the rectangular bag is cut to form a square through which the head can pass, and arms are allowed to protrude through slits in the seams of the sack. The square neckline and the hem are then richly embroidered with colorful silk designs of flowers or geometrical patterns. This loose dress of pure white, decorated with brilliant colors, is most becoming. Below the sack dress a small white petticoat skirt is worn and allowed to show below the hemline. On festive occasions a *terno* is worn, a more elaborately embroidered *huipiles* with the petticoat embroidered too.

From this attire the women of Yucatán acquire a Greek classic look, and the *huipiles* can well be compared to a feminine toga.

The sight of thousands of women dressed in such a manner going about the streets of Mérida will remain for me the mark of modern Yucatán.

When I arrived in Mérida I had no idea how to begin preparations for the Quintana Roo-Darién expedition in which I was now so deeply involved.

Bearing a letter for Alberto Ruz l'Huillier, the famous archaeologist who had discovered the tomb of Palenque, I made for the offices of the Mexican National Archaeological Committee. There I found Dr. Ruz, a tall, rather stern man who welcomed me politely and listened attentively to what I had to say. After I had told him of my wish to go down by boat along the coast of Quintana Roo to British Honduras, he told me that it would most likely be very difficult. "The coast, you see," he said, "is entirely uninhabited except for three places—Puerto Morelos to the north, Tankah in the center, and Xcalak at the border of Mexico and British Honduras.

"There are of course, as you know, the great ruins of Tulum isolated on the barren coast. Near there is a coconut plantation belonging to a Señor Pepe Gonzales; he has always been most kind to me when I have gone to Tulum and I can give you a letter for him. At Tankah there is also a small airstrip cleared out of the jungle."

I had of course heard of Tulum and had encountered in Mexico many references to this large city isolated on the barren Quintana Roo coast and accessible only by sea until the construction of the airstrip, which is more often than not closed. Few visitors had been to Tulum, the journey being a long and difficult one.

As for going south of Tulum, Dr. Alberto Ruz seemed rather vague. There were apparently no conventional means of getting there and, as he said, "the local Indians are not interested in the sea and I doubt that you could find boats to take you. But you could always hire a boat from Cozumel Island to take you all the way to British Honduras."

This I decided to do. I planned to set out with Ball to Cozumel Island, a road having just been completed which went from Mérida to the northern tip of Quintana Roo to a spot proudly called Puerto Juarez. At Puerto Juarez one could always find, so I was told, a boat to go to the Isla Mujeres—the "island of women," a small island that marks the bend of the Yucatán coast separating the Gulf of Mexico from the Caribbean—and from there south to Cozumel Island.

I decided that having chartered a boat from Cozumel (if I could find one) we would sail slowly down the Quintana Roo coast, stopping here and there to look at the lay of the land.

I then set about looking for a man who might have been in Quintana Roo and could tell me what I would find there. Results here were unsatisfactory and I could find no one. I learned that the Quintana Roo region, unlike central Yucatán, was covered with a dense jungle, and that no road penetrated that jungle. There were no towns, and, furthermore, I learned that the whole area was infested with bandits—runaway Mexicans, for in Yucatán a bandit is by definition a Mexican. The Mayan Indians themselves are a peaceful, law-abiding people, except for those who live in Quintana Roo, who are known as the *Indios sublevados*, the rebellious Indians. I was soon to realize that in Yucatán, as in Mexico City, Quintana Roo was considered a wild and savage spot about which nobody knew or cared.

I sent a letter to Ball giving him the first results of my investigations, telling him that all seemed well as far as getting a boat was concerned, and that information on Quintana Roo was scarce and I could only gather that the jungle was hostile, barren, and populated by a few rebellious Indians and an equal number of marauding *chicleros*.

From this it seemed that the farther I stayed away from Quintana Roo the better, but I was not discouraged by the information I got. On the contrary, such mystery intrigued me. And I wondered whether it would not prove more exciting and interesting to cross part of Quintana Roo on foot to the sea. When I mentioned this idea to Mr. Pomerat, the director of the Alliance Française in

Mérida, and a man well accustomed to the country and its people, I was given the sharp reply that I was mildly mad. Mr. Pomerat went on to explain that the year before my arrival a young German archaeologist had left Mérida to go through Quintana Roo, planning to travel by land to the ancient coastal city of Tulum. His body was found three weeks later rotting on the edge of a *cenote*; he had been killed by one of his guides. This turned my thoughts back to the more comfortable solution of doing the trip by sea. I decided that our excursions inland from the coast would be limited to a minimum.

I nevertheless attempted to get more precise information on the *Indios sublevados* and the bandits called *chicleros*.

About the rebellious Indians I could at first get very little factual information, except that it was considered most dangerous to go to their districts because the Indians were prone to attack any foreigners, since they themselves had suffered for so long the antagonism of the Mexican state and also the bloody assaults of the marauding *chicleros*.

The word *chiclero*, which I had understood to be synonymous with "bandit," and which was at first always quoted to me in association with crime, was in fact the name given to those who gather chicle. This is the sap of a particular *zapote*, or sapodilla tree, which is used for the sole purpose of making chewing gum. The thousands of hungry jaws in America would alone have been enough to make the chicle business a large industry. Chicle or raw chewing gum is found in only three countries of the world—in the Quintana Roo territory of the Yucatán peninsula, northern Guatemala, and British Honduras. Unlike rubber trees, chicle trees have never been grown in plantations, and the only way to gather the sap is to send men out into the jungles. To gather chicle is a painful and most dangerous operation, the gatherers being exposed to poisonous snakes, polluted water, and, above all, malaria, which is still the plague of Quintana Roo. To perform such an unpleasant task, ex-convicts and criminals are brought into the jungle from

Vera Cruz. The peaceful Yucatecan refuses to go out into the jungle. As a result, the jungles of Quintana Roo are full of bands of marauding *chicleros* battling against the jungle and amongst themselves for the expensive white chicle sap. For years such men have been dumped into Quintana Roo and many live there all year round, preferring to stay on after the six-month chicle season rather than face justice in more civilized areas for the crimes they have committed, before or since their arrival in the jungle.

The strange circumstances that were to befall my expedition were all too soon to familiarize me with the fearful *chicleros,* armed with their shotguns, pistols, and machetes.

Malaria was also a threat on which I had hardly counted. The marshy swamps and damp jungles are one of the worst strongholds of this disease. And in the view of all in Mérida this was sufficient justification to keep as far away from Quintana Roo as I could.

By now I began to wonder whether I had not been a fool to want to go into such a god-forsaken area. Had it not been for the Gothic heading of my writing paper and the fear of making myself look an utter fool if I now abandoned the idea, I might have given up. As it was, I continued gingerly to prepare for the trip. And beyond reason, I was strangely fascinated by the coast that was described to me in such unfavorable terms. It was too late to change our plans anyway. Remembering the long evenings of preparation in Tepoztlán with Ball, I decided to stick to our original route but to make very few visits to the Quintana Roo coast—all this, I imagined, in the company of Alan Ball and the crew of the boat I planned to charter.

I nevertheless attempted to purchase firearms and acquire a guide. Through hearsay I was introduced to a man named Aguilar, who had often served as guide to hunting parties. Game abounds in the dry bush forests that cover central Yucatán, to such an extent that hunting is still practiced for food by nearly all the rural population. Already, on the bus between Campeche and Mérida, I had recognized this for at each stop groups of Indians clambered on with *escopetas* (shotguns) slung on their backs. Black pheasant, wild turkey, and small red deer called *venado* abound. What with wild pigs and occasional *tigres*—wildcats and small jaguars—safaris are not strange to Yucatán. But Aguilar, if he was ready to take me hunting around Mérida and toward Campeche, knew nothing of Quintana Roo and only repeated what others had told me. However, he suggested I get myself a pistol for self-protection and also to complement my meals while on the coast. He introduced me to a dubious-looking friend who sold arms and offered me a small chromium-plated .32-caliber revolver.

I hesitated about purchasing it and sent a wire to Ball for his advice, since he was also to be financing some of the basic expenses of the expedition. Receiving no reply, I began to seek out other equipment that might be necessary.

In Yucatán I found that apart from hotels there are no beds, and Indians and Mexicans alike sleep in hammocks. For me hammocks had always been associated with the danger of falling out of them, their discomfort, and the Navy. I was soon to revise this opinion when I tried out a Mayan hammock, and had to agree with the local legend that the hammock was a present from the gods to mankind. The Yucatán hammock is an honest hammock and does not play dirty tricks in the middle of the night like all the other hammocks of the world. There are two kinds—those made of coarse, henequen string which itches, and the softer, larger, and more aristocratic cotton or silk hammocks. The latter was the kind I chose, and to be on the safe side I bought what is known as a "matrimonial hammock," one so large that it could sleep two people lengthwise or even abreast.

The Mayan hammocks are strange and complicated affairs, with no nasty knots that make other hammocks so uncomfortable. They are made on large wooden rectangular frames; a long strand of string is wound around this frame and then interwoven with a second strand, thus forming a loose mesh that conforms to all the angles of the human body.

The Yucatecans take good advantage of their god-sent gift which goes well with their lazy character, and hammocks are strung up everywhere and the majority of the population sleeps all day and all night. Hammocks are found under railroad cars, between trees, and in all the houses, which have hooks on the walls of every room. This allows the Indians to live in comfort in their small huts, with more living space by day.

Since mosquitoes are the plague of Quintana Roo and I presumed also of the so-called Mosquito Coast, I bought a large, fragile-looking mosquito net, a cocoon affair that could be fastened around my hammock.

As far as clothes were concerned, all I would need, I thought, was a pair of trousers and soft shoes for walking on boat decks; I bought a pair of sandals. As for boots to go in the jungle, I imagined that I could buy those at Valladolid, a largish town shown on my map as the last place between Mérida and Puerto Juarez, where the road ended on the coast of Quintana Roo. This was a fatal mistake, for I found out later that in Valladolid boots came only in sizes to fit the Indians' small feet. At the market in Mérida I purchased two knives twenty inches long, which seemed to me less ridiculous than machetes and yet large enough to serve for cutting vines.

Having acquired this material, I returned to my hotel to find a letter from Ball. It read:

Dear Michel,

I have not been able to obtain the funds that I was expecting; because of the Sterling zone I will only be able to get money in a British colony. I'm sorry, but I will not be able to join you in Yucatán, but will meet you in Belize. I suggest you go down on your own on the first leg of the trip and from Belize we can carry on together as planned.

Yours faithfully,
A.B.

The news was pretty rough, for I felt that it was an excuse by which Ball was withdrawing from our project. I immediately called

Mexico by telephone, and in a jumble of buzzes and parrot noises I gathered that in Mexico things had changed and it was more and more difficult for Ball to break away. I held little hope that I would see him again, even in Belize. And I was right; I was never to see Ball again, but this was not entirely due to his failing to turn up in Belize. I did not go there either until after a considerable length of time.

I was somewhat shattered by the bad news. My youthful enthusiasm had relied a great deal on the companionship and weight that a man like Ball would give to our undertaking. The trip we had planned together was one thing; to go alone was quite another matter. And the night after Ball backed out I had terrible nightmares in which I saw the skeleton of the young German archaeologist.

I began seriously regretting the whole affair, and kicked myself for not realizing from the start that Ball was not the most stable character. And looking at the reflection of my tall thin body in the dirty mirror of my hotel room, I could not manage to see myself as an explorer. I started wondering whether I did not make a good banker after all. No, it seemed stupid to think of going alone, and if I did survive the trip down to Colombia, would I be back in time to start Graduate School at Harvard in August? It was now the end of April, which gave me barely three months to cover the two thousand miles of the proposed trip.

I consulted Mr. Pomerat on my now changed position. He was of little comfort and argued violently that it would be murder to go alone, and "what would happen if you fell ill?"

I agreed with him, but nonetheless decided I would rather die than give up now, and if all went well, the first leg of the trip might not take more than a week. Maybe I could arrange with the police at Mérida to send out a search party if they had not heard from me after a week. To this suggestion Mr. Pomerat burst out laughing, explaining, "Dear fellow, if you think that the police will set foot in

Quintana Roo you are mad. Why, they had so much trouble in the
case of the German archaeologist that if you told them of your
plans they would lock you up and forbid you to go."

The next day, in bed with the local disease, I had ample time to
fret and worry, but between the violent attacks of my stomach
trouble I pored over a map of the coast. The blank smear of Quintana Roo looked more intriguing than ever before, with its long,
straight coastline cut by two deep bays—the Bahía del Ascensión
and the Bahía del Espíritu Santo. How mysterious these names
appeared; was this expedition not a chance in a lifetime? I was now
just twenty-one, and this my first adventure. I decided to carry on
alone.

What worried me most now was malaria, as well as the snakes
and scorpions and tarantulas that I knew could be found even on
boats. I was also worried by the rainy season which was drawing
near—the words "rainy season" conjured up frightening visions of
monsoons, torrential rains, muddy tracks, landslides and devastating floods, about which I had read.

As soon as I was fit to leave the hotel I made my way to Aguilar's
house, and reconsidered buying the pistol. When I had it again
in my hand in the dark back office of Aguilar's friend I suddenly
realized that I had never used a pistol before and wondered what
would happen if I missed my opponents. Finally I decided it would
be no use to me, and partly out of petty heroism, partly for
economy's sake, I did not buy it.

I purchased a large stock of Aralene pills against malaria, and
also enough supplies to equip a very adequate Boy Scout medical
chest; for an expedition, however, this proved rather insufficient.
I had neat little bottles of iodine, bits of bandages, aspirin, and
pills for the disease from which I was already suffering—the inescapable and most common of tropical ailments. Amoebae—the
plague of dirty wells and the water I might have to drink on the
boats—I accounted for by purchasing small chlorine tablets. These
medicines put my mind at rest, leaving only one problem to solve:

snake bites! I consulted everyone I knew and one doctor; the verdict was that antitoxins for snake venom exist but require considerable care in use. One type of venom requires one sort of vaccine; another a quite different one, according to whether the poison is hemotoxic (poisonous to the blood) or hepatoxic (poisonous to the digestive system). In order to be sufficiently secure against any eventual snake bites, one needs to learn the names of all the snakes and their respective venomous characteristics; further, one has to know which one has bitten you and how to use a hypodermic syringe and give an intravenous injection. . . . This competence I had not acquired, nor was I keen on acquiring it. I am one of those people who prefer to die rather than go to the dentist or have an injection. Incapable anyway of taking along such a complete snake kit, I turned to more magical remedies. One which was suggested to me by Señor Alberto Ruz, and which I later found was the snake standby of all Yucatecans, was called Antiviperine and presented itself in a small brown bottle with a wax stopper.

Out of curiosity I read the instructions, and an enlightening piece of literature it was, covering four pages in pale blue ink. One page read like an obituary notice, and a footnote asked politely that the victim fill in the form, which read: when bitten, time and place; what snake bit you; when was Antiviperine taken; date on which patient died, if the case. The last-mentioned was to be filled in, somehow, posthumously. In brief, the remedy was to be drunk after the snake bite and applied to the wound itself. The last paragraph of the instructions read: "If desired, Antiviperine may be taken before each meal as apéritif."

The hammock, mosquito net, Antiviperine, and medical kit, plus twenty rolls of assorted film, cameras and lenses, and a pair of sandals, were all neatly thrown into a large henequen bag. Besides this, I carried a small bluish bag, a cross between a flight bag and a briefcase, for my shaving and toilet articles.

All was now ready, and I decided to spend my last few days

visiting the local attractions—the great ancient ruins of Uxmal and Sayil—at the same time investigating the history of Yucatán. I would then set out for Chichén-Itzá, the famed city with the sacred well from which so many fabulous jewels had been extracted. Chichén-Itzá lay on my route to Puerto Juarez and would be my last stop before setting off definitely.

Fifty miles from Mérida on the road to Campeche stands the ancient city of Uxmal. There, to my amazement, the buildings were of an entirely different architecture from those of Palenque. In fact, they seemed of a different civilization. They date from the year A.D. 900 and are said to be of the New empire, because their culture flourished after the abandonment of Palenque. But beyond the historical facts, Uxmal (pronounced "Ushmal") is probably the most beautiful architectural creation of pre-Columbian America. At Uxmal the buildings have a truly artistic grandeur which makes them among the most glorious structures of the world. Versailles, medieval cathedrals, the tombs of the Moguls in India, the Parthenon itself, have little or no edge on the architectural beauty and majesty of Uxmal. This is true in particular of the palace of the governor, 320 feet long and elevated on a 30-foot rectangular platform perched on a five-acre platform raised 50 feet off the ground. The monumental impression of such terraces, the harmony of the form of the principal building with, for its only decoration, a 320-foot frieze of geometrically carved stone, is a sight of great beauty; this is almost equaled by a beautiful quadrangle enclosing a magnificent paved courtyard, known as the Nunnery quadrangle, despite phallic decorations that ornament the façade of one of the enclosing palaces. Of honey-colored stone assembled with millimetric exactitude, of exquisite proportions and simple lines, Uxmal has never failed to impress all as the most beautiful of pre-Columbian cities. I was very much struck by the paradox that although Uxmal and other Mayan cities were inhabited at the time of the Spanish conquest, we know today so little of the ancient Mayas. After seeing Uxmal I could not help but look upon the

Indians with admiration and attempt to see in their faces what traces could be found of their past glory and civilization. And, as I was soon to find out in Quintana Roo, if the Indians do not remember anything of their past, they nevertheless have retained many of the sophisticated traits that two thousand years of a highly developed culture have left imprinted in their minds and behavior.

Of the temples that made up the old city, only a few have been excavated, and from the summit of the abrupt 150-foot Pyramid of the Dwarfs I could observe, as far as I could see, great mounds of rubble covered with jungle—the remains of hundreds of other buildings that used to make up the city and are still to be excavated.

Near Uxmal are the cities of Kabah and Sayil, the latter having a large palace three stories high whose doorways are supported by great, round columns giving the palace a Greek or, rather, Cretan look. The variety of architectural styles and techniques used and known to the Mayas is astounding. In their structures they incorporated such varied features as round columns, square columns, half columns, keyhole arches, and, of course, the traditional corbelled Mayan arch and vault. This imagination and variety in both architectural techniques and pottery and carving are one of the marvels of the ancient Mayan civilization, and I wondered whether the Indians of today still held the secrets of such versatility.

On the way back to Mérida from Uxmal I passed innumerable henequen fields, with row after row of pale green cactus sisal plants projecting their narrow pointed leaves skyward.

The villages for the most part bore the names of the old henequen estates or of the patron saints of the local churches.

Like all former Spanish colonies, Yucatán had been the scene of great persecutions performed in the name of the Church, and the religious fervor of the Spanish is the main reason why today so little is left of the traditions of the ancient Mayas. Whenever they could, the Spaniards tried to stamp out the pagan Mayan culture, destroying buildings, manuscripts, and even the slightest trace of oral tradition. But at the same time that the Spanish blindly pursued their policy of imposing their culture and religion on the Indians, some of the more enlightened priests, such as Diego de Landa, kept notes on the civilization that his people were destroying. And today De Landa's book, *Relación de las Cosas de Yucatán*, is the main source of written information, dating from the period of the conquest, on pre-Columbian Yucatán. And despite the great number of books written by the Mayas that were destroyed, three have survived until today: the Dresden Codex, discovered in Dresden; the Tro-Cortes, found in Spain; and the Paris or Codex Perez, which turned up in Paris. These three codices contain astrological tables and are primarily concerned with divination. If they have not been deciphered entirely, they have through illustrations and dates allowed some precious information to seep down to us.

With the passage of time not only were the codices lost, three of them to be rediscovered later by accident in Europe, but all Mayan oral tradition became extinct. It is only relatively recently that the Mayas have attracted considerable attention. In particular, the books of Prescott, and the writings of John Lloyd Stephens and drawings of Frederick Catherwood have done much to interest the world in the Mayas.

Through Dr. Alberto Ruz and Carlos Pelissier I was to learn that Mayan archaeology was slowly gaining the place it deserved in the study of ancient civilizations. On the eve of my departure I could hardly have imagined that my rather haphazard expedition was, in a surprising way, going to help to solve some of the riddles of the ancient Mayan empire.

The big day had now come, and I wrote a letter to my parents and paid a last visit to Dr. Alberto Ruz.

In his office near the cathedral, Dr. Ruz explained that the coast along which I was planning to sail had never been thoroughly explored, and he asked me to keep my eyes open for any possible ancient ruins. He then gave me a map that showed most of the few archaeological sites known on the coast. As I left him he recalled me, saying kindly what I knew only too well: "Be careful. You know it's a dangerous and hostile coast."

I then went to see Mr. Pomerat and told him that I was leaving. He asked me to set a time limit for reaching Belize, kindly offering to do his best to arrange for a search party if anything went wrong. Jokingly, although a little unnerved, I said that if he had heard nothing from me within three weeks, he could be sure something was wrong. But I told him confidently, "In a week I'll be in Belize." On this we parted, and lugging with difficulty my henequen bag and my blue flight bag, I made my way through the stifling hot streets of Mérida toward the bus station. Here I was to take a bus to Chichén-Itzá and then on through to Puerto Juarez and the coast.

At last I was off. . . .

III

Ix Chell, Goddess of Love

A bus is rather a pitiful means of transportation in which to start an expedition, and I must say I felt a little foolish when I purchased my ticket. Dragging my bags, I fought for my appointed seat with a crowd of *huipiles*-wearing Indian women, thanking heaven that I had planned to stop for the night at Chichén-Itzá, thus breaking in half the two-hundred-mile drive to Puerto Juarez.

The low stutter of Mayan voices, the proud faces of the Indian women, the harassed look of the men, and the beautiful eyes of the children made me forget the discomfort and the tensions of this departure. What lay ahead I could not tell. Three months of preparation had brought me little in the way of concrete information on the coastal situation. Would I find boats, and where? All I had were a few names scribbled on paper, a map, and a will to go south. My belongings were stacked above my head; my knives seemed perfectly useless at the moment, but little did I then realize how precious they were later to become.

The bus soon left the city limits and I saw my last *calecha* slip by; then the last houses of stone were slowly replaced by thatched Indian huts and henequen fields, followed by the forest, thin, but at the same time mysterious, curling up and drying in the heat. Now and again as the bus rose on a small incline the flat Yucatán bush was visible stretching out for miles, dotted here and there

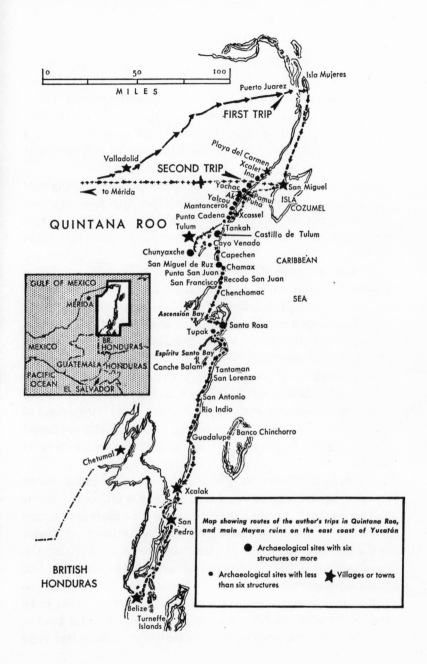

Map showing routes of the author's trips in Quintana Roo, and main Mayan ruins on the east coast of Yucatán

● Archaeological sites with six structures or more

• Archaeological sites with less than six structures

★ Villages or towns

with orange-colored flowers or the occasional yellow blossoms of vanilla plants.

At every stop Indians would get off, the women putting loads on their heads, the men with their *escopetas* slung on their shoulders. Barefooted, in small groups, they would disappear at a hurried pace into tunnel-like footpaths through the bush, off to their distant thatched-roofed houses.

The stone walls that enclosed the henequen fields and the huts of the villages were of loosely piled round boulders forming a precarious barrier through which light could be seen. These walls were invariably painted white, adding to the neatness of the Yucatecan villages and countryside. Already, coming from central Mexico, I had been struck by the clean towns and villages of Yucatán. And I was told, and later could observe, that the Mayas are probably one of the cleanest people on earth. It is a fact that regardless of their social position or the dirt involved in their labor, the women always wear spotless *huipiles*; they achieve this by changing their dress two or even three times a day. When one considers that the poorest women do this, one realizes how dirt-conscious the Mayas are. This was a trait that I felt came from their long past as a cultured people. It is also an interesting proof of the anthropological fact that people who dress in white are almost always clean, whereas peoples with darker clothes tend to be dirty people.

The road to Chichén-Itzá was perfectly straight and of recent creation; before, footpaths had been the only roads, for the Mayas still seem to snub the wheel. And except for the *calechas* of Mérida, in the country one never sees a horse and carriage, although horses and mules are numerous. Because the limestone of Yucatán is rough, the ancient Mayas had built a considerable number of foot roads elevated above the ground. Many of these still remain; one is a road between Uxmal and Khaba. There are also said to be traces of *sak-be* (Mayan roads) all through the Yucatán bush.

It was five in the afternoon when I arrived at Chichén-Itzá. Near the ruins is the luxurious Hotel Maya Land, which caters lavishly to the thousands of tourists who visit the famous ruins every year. Thanks to Dr. Alberto Ruz I was to stay at the *Campamento*, a place better suited for trying out my hammock. I nevertheless went to the hotel for a last civilized meal.

At sunset I wandered around the giant ruins of the city. Chichén-Itzá is the largest Mayan city in Yucatán and stretches over thousands of acres. The city was constructed originally near a small *cenote*, where water was easily accessible, but later spread toward the west where there was an immense circular *cenote* with water sixty-five feet below the ground level. The sides of this *cenote* are vertical and it is a most impressive sight. This is the famous sacred sacrificial well. The Maya dreaded droughts, and in times of drought he paid a special homage to the Chacs, gods of rain. At Chichén-Itzá the Chacs were believed to live at the bottom of this well. Here the high priests performed bloody sacrifices; according to the early accounts of the Spaniards they painted their victims blue and with great ceremony led them to the sacred well. There the victims, mostly virgins, were thrust into the well at dawn; or if they were young men, their hearts would be cut out with a ceremonial flint knife and their bodies, often adorned with gold jewels and jade ornaments, thrown into the *cenote*. Looking into the murky depth of the sacred well today one cannot help but shudder.

Diego de Landa, knowing of the sacrifices performed at Chichén-Itzá, wrote: "If there is gold in Yucatán, it should be in the sacred well of Chichén-Itzá." Surprisingly enough, the gold-seeking Spaniards took no notice of this statement. Three hundred years were to pass before an American, Edward H. Thompson, decided to dredge the sacred well in 1907. At that time the operation was a considerable one; there were no adequate roads to the ruins, and the dredging material was clumsy and difficult to get there. But Thompson's efforts were amply rewarded; he brought up from the well, along with bones of women and men, a considerable number of artifacts that had been worn by the victims of the Chacs. In all, the objects dredged from the mud compose what is known today as the treasure of Chichén-Itzá and include many gold-embossed breastplates, some the size of a saucer, thousands of sculptured jade pendants, and a gold-handled sacrificial flint knife. Innumerable beads and pieces of pottery were also found, and copal, the incense whose black smoke accompanied all Mayan ceremonies. For reasons unknown, since Thompson nobody had thought of dredging the well again, but only a year after my visit a new attempt was made to secure more of the treasures that lay at the bottom.

When night came I turned into the *Campamento*, where I experimented with my hammock by the light of a flickering candle and accompanied by the deafening noise of thousands of frogs in and around the building. Once in the hammock, I dared not move and on the whole that night was rather a poor success. If I did not fall, I could not sleep either. And for the long hours of the night I lay swinging gently, surrounded by the gauze mosquito net. My thoughts flashed back to the ancient Mayan days when the same croaking noise of frogs had stirred the still night after a long hot day of bloody sacrifice at the sacred well, and then to the young German found killed near a *cenote*, and then I sat up with a start, realizing that tomorrow I would be in Quintana Roo, probably also at the mercy of a dishonest guide.

An hour before dawn, considering my hammock a poor invention, I got up and, going outside, clambered up the tallest pyramid—Kukulcan. From its summit I could see to the east the first glow of the rising sun that lit an endless sea of treetops. To the east, I knew, the jungles of Quintana Roo extended, and the strange coast I was soon to see. Below me stood the temple of the "warriors" at the foot of the pyramid, and to the south the strange circular tower of the observatory, and, breaking through the trees, the large buildings of Chichén-Itzá. *Mayaluum,* the land of the Mayas, was at my feet, and I imagined the temples seething with Mayas speaking their strange language and myself the feared high priest.

Slowly the sun rose and soon the high priest started running down the precipitous stone steps of the great pyramid. For it was raining a heavy tropical rain that the earth soaked in with apparent pleasure. As I listened to the clatter of rain upon the tin roof of the *Campamento* my thoughts were very low, and I felt that this rain was a curse from the dreadful Chacs at the bottom of the sacred well.

Had I been an educated Maya I would not have been surprised, for the rain that fell the day after my arrival at Chichén-Itzá fell in accordance with the Mayan calendar, not the old one but a modern transposition of the ancient Mayan weather-forecasting technique which each year is printed in the *Almanac Espinoso*, the great almanac of Yucatán.

I ran over to the ruin keeper's house with the intention of complaining of the weather, but before I could say a word the keeper's wife jubilantly cried out, "*Espinoso* was right again." I cursed *Espinoso*, for I had not even brought a raincoat. I went out and took a last damp look at the ruins, in particular the tall pyramid which is rather strangely built over another pyramid. Inside, a secret passage leads to a small room containing a red spotted jaguar throne. Then the bus came and I sped off to Valladolid.

At Valladolid I had planned to buy some boots. The moment the bus pulled into the town square a thousand children came toward me screaming and laughing; a little later they were joined by some men. Apparently my beard was the cause of this excitement. I must admit it was rather a mess since it was only a few days old. But all the excitement I created did not amuse me a bit; on the contrary, I was rather terrified, and afraid that my bags might be stolen, I ran around attempting to buy boots, dragging the bags with me. But as I have said, my feet are normal size for a white man but definitely outsized for the Mayas, and soon not only my beard but also my feet were a reason for mockery.

I was virtually laughed out of Valladolid, or so I thought, and I must say the impression of my reception there was long to remain an unpleasant memory.

The road was by now only a dirt track. And as we progressed toward Puerto Juarez the bus slowly emptied and the jungle became higher and the villages fewer and farther apart. There were no more churches, only small groups of ill-tended, poor-looking Mayan huts set beside the road in clearings that were half invaded by the jungle. For the first time I discovered that the sun can be as tragic as rain. Here were the sad tropics, damp and humid after the morning rain, burning in the midday sun. Even the trees seemed to offer no shade and all looked like a desolate and putrid mass of green leaves, palms, and vines.

I was now alone with the driver, and for one solid hour we bumped a straight course along the road that seemed like an endless prison caught between two walls of dense foliage.

Suddenly we came into a vast dirt clearing surrounded by tin-roofed sheds and an immense rusty hangar. The transition was so unexpected and the spectacle so appalling and characteristic of makeshift ugly civilization that an air of desolate gloom hung over these buildings. "Leona Vicario," said the driver, addressing me as if guessing my surprise. The bus halted and the driver got out, to be greeted by three men who looked like thugs. A rusty narrow-gauge railroad line crossed the vast clearing, and here and there, strewn upside down, lay minute flat railroad cars.

Leona Vicario, once called Tres Marias, had been the largest *chiclero* station of Yucatán. Situated at the border of Yucatán state and the Territorio Federal, in recent years it had lost a great deal of its importance, and as we were now in April, the chicle season had not yet begun and the station was empty save for a few Mexican watchmen. I did not know then that the rusty sheds of the desolate clearing called Leona Vicario had been and were still the site of the worst murders, brawls, and hair-raising, authentic cases of crime in all of Mexico. Here *chicleros* would congregate by the thousands, and once a week rum would flow as the *chicleros*, rich from their well-paid chicle, would address themselves to the favorite sport of cutting each other up with machetes. They even had balls at Leona Vicario which attracted prostitutes from all over Mexico, keen to rid the devils of their handsome pay. The men would dance with their pistols and shotguns and machetes at their side. On meeting *chicleros* later I was to get a number of gory details about Leona Vicario, where death was as common as drinking and breathing.

The narrow-gauge railway, whose flatcars were known as *plataformas*, was a mule-drawn affair. The rails led in a straight line through the dense jungle to Puerto Morelos, a point on the Quintana Roo coast eighty miles north of Tulum. The line was not now operating, as it was obstructed by dense vegetation waiting to be cleared away for the next chicle season. It takes a day and a half by mule-drawn railway to go from Leona Vicario to the sea, and until the year before my journey this was the only road to the coast of Quintana Roo.

A few miles out of Leona Vicario, as the bus drove on down its solitary route through the jungle, we passed a small cardboard sign and I knew we had entered Quintana Roo. From now on I was in "no man's land"—a land down the coast of which I had planned to sail three hundred miles, and one of the wildest areas of the North American continent.

For another hour and a half the bus droned on in a cloud of dust, shaking all over as we uncomfortably cleared the potholes in the road. On road maps of Mexico that have been sold over the past ten years the road to Puerto Juarez is clearly marked; also on many of these maps one can see the dotted line of the famous Mexico-Cuba ferry. When these maps were printed ten years ago Puerto Juarez did not even exist, much less the road out from Mérida to the coast, and as for the ferry, it never got beyond a political slogan. Such, I learned, are the ways of Mexico. And for over fifty years Quintana Roo has been touted as the land of improvement and change, an El Dorado so unknown that it has been the land of promise for every politician in Mexico, the "new frontier" that was to bring new wealth. Despite maps that lied and speeches that promised great changes in the economy of Mexico thanks to the petroleum, wood, and gold said to exist in far-off Quintana Roo, the federal territory has remained untouched and the fictitious ports of politicians' maps have remained but small black dots on paper. Such names as Puerto Madero, Zazaral, and many others, even Puerto Juarez, are examples of these fictitious towns that were supposed to have been created to open up the wealth of desolate and empty Quintana Roo. The first attempts to do anything with this region were failures, due to the crushing opposition presented by the rebellious Indians. As for the more recent attempts, they too have failed, seeing that the governors of Quintana Roo (appointed by the President instead of being elected by popular vote as in regular Mexican states) have often been known as profit-seeking satraps playing the card of favoritism and growing rich on the territory. At the southwestern tip of Quintana Roo, set deep inland upon the waters of a marshy bay, is Chetumal, the capital of Quintana Roo. Accessible only by boat or by air, it is too cut off from the rest of the *territorio* to have any real significance. It does, on the other hand, have a small commercial importance, being near British Honduras and trading in wood with the British colony. But between Chetumal, with its three thousand inhabitants, and the fictitious Puerto Juarez or any other focal point of the territory, lay two or three hundred miles of jungle virtually without a road. The only other inhabited areas are those bordering Chetumal Bay, the island of Cozumel, and Isla Mujeres to the north of the coast of Quintana Roo, the last island being situated in front of Puerto Juarez.

Unexpectedly the bus came to a halt and to my surprise I could see the sea through the windshield. It was the brightest blue sea I had ever seen, lazily lapping at a yellow sandy beach. I got down and the first thing that struck me was the incongruity of the bus standing there by the water's edge, the jungle looming up behind it, running to the beach. The words "Puerto Juarez" had led me to expect at least a small village, but the beach was empty save for two small palm huts whose doors were closed, and they seemed abandoned. The only thing suggestive of a port was a small rickety wooden dock about ten feet long that extended into the sea.

Here I was on the soil of Quintana Roo; here began my sea route to the Darién coast.

"Wait here," said the driver. "There will certainly be a boat over soon from Isla Mujeres." He pointed to the horizon, where was dimly visible the low, narrow, dark smudge of what I guessed to be an island. The bus driver then proceeded to climb on the roof of his vehicle and unload a dozen brown potato bags which he threw onto the sand.

Brushing his hands, he then came toward me and with a big smile shook my hand and muttered something about getting to Valladolid before night, jumped into the bus, and disappeared in a cloud of dust down the track through the jungle.

I felt rather foolish standing there in the middle of nowhere surrounded by bags and completely alone. In normal circumstances such a beach and such a sea would have called for a swim. But not then; all I could do was sit on one of my bags and wait. I had a few oranges with me and did not fear starving; I had a blind confidence in the word of the bus driver.

He was right and soon I saw a small white dot on the sea—a boat was approaching the coast. It was a small engine-driven cutter with a strange, raised afterdeck that overhung the sea in a galleon-like manner. Its gaff-rigged mast was painted yellow and a dirty mainsail hung loosely from the boom. At its bow stood a man with curly red hair, his trousers rolled up. In Mexico red hair is as rare as green hair in New York, and his weather-beaten face fringed with it struck me forcibly. When the boat was moored to the rickety dock I walked to it, dodging men who took no notice of me as they loaded the bags from the beach. I asked for the captain. An oldish man with a pot belly poked his head out of the cockpit. "*A dónde va?*" he asked. (Where are you going?) "*A Cozumel,*" I answered.

Soon I was clambering aboard, and to the gentle roll of the waves I began my first boat trip from Puerto Juarez to Isla Mujeres. There the captain said I could possibly find a boat for Cozumel.

The blue sea seemed to become even bluer as we advanced over low sand bars toward the small island. The bluest water in the world, I thought. Later I was to learn that I was not far wrong. The strong currents that brush along the Yucatán coast and pass by Isla Mujeres into the Gulf of Mexico are the cause, and nowhere in the Caribbean or the Mediterranean is the water so clear or so blue. A year later at Cozumel tests were made underwater that determined that the water there is the clearest known. One can look down through a hundred feet of it and still see the bottom.

Two hours later we were close to the shore of the "island of women." This island is a narrow sandy strip, at some places no more than five hundred yards wide and in all three miles long; its only vegetation is a few coconut palms.

The island is called Isla Mujeres because in the time of the Spanish conquest erotic statues of women were found in a Mayan temple that still stands at the north end of the island.

Isla Mujeres throughout history has been an island of pirates, and today, as I could see, its inhabitants still have the varied physical characteristics of every race to have sailed the ocean blue—Negroes, redheads, blond children with blue eyes, and dark-skinned Mayas. The population of the island is around five hundred, and the islanders still live on the products of smuggling and a little fishing.

Smuggled goods are taken to secret landing places on the coast from which they are moved inland along little-known jungle paths. Today smuggling is facilitated, for Isla Mujeres, Cozumel, and the entire Quintana Roo coast have been declared a tax-free import zone. This act was passed by the Mexican government since it could not expect to police three hundred miles of barren shore and islands whose inhabitants were so isolated from any central Mexican government office. But the smuggling is now very much reduced, and as an islander told me sadly, "One hardly lives on smuggling today." Occasionally a few small boats dump whisky and perfumes from British Honduras on the islands.

In the old days Isla Mujeres and Cozumel had been thriving pirate stations; here the buccaneers would wait in ambush as slowly the Spanish galleons, weighted down with Peruvian gold, would beat their way up along the coast and through the Yucatán Straits on their way to Cuba and Spain from Panama.

On landing I was informed that the islanders were expecting a boat called *Maria Fidelia* which was due back from Progreso (north of Mérida) where she had unloaded copra, and that most probably the *Maria Fidelia*, after calling, would sail on down to Cozumel. Since there was no telephone or telegraph on the island, all this news was vague, and although I was delighted to hear it, I hardly gave much credence to these rumors.

I left my bags at the house of what seemed to me an honest woman and set out to explore the island—an easy job considering its minute size. Isla Mujeres represented for me exactly what I had dreamed Pacific islands might be. A small sandy island, surrounded by the bluest waters, it was one long sandbank with two slightly rising rocky points at each end; most of the island was not much more than ten feet above sea level.

Coconut trees loomed up everywhere, the plumes of their great fronds shaking in the sky and attached to the thick trunks great clusters of green, unripe coconuts threatening to fall on the heads of everyone on the island. I reflected how fortunate Newton had been to live in an apple-growing country, for here his enlightening accident would have been fatal. The sandy soil of the island was littered with coconut husks and brown, broken-off fronds. The houses were mostly typically Mayan, with stakes planted directly in the sand. There is no soil, and apart from a few cactus plants there is no vegetation worth speaking of.

Luck would have it that upon returning from my inspection of the island I was informed that the *Maria Fidelia* had arrived and was lying alongside the dock. This was a good start, and I set out immediately to locate the captain and find out when he was leaving for Cozumel.

The *Maria Fidelia* was a 45-foot schooner that shuttled between Yucatán, Isla Mujeres, and Cozumel, occasionally going to Chetumal. Her captain, a fat man with greasy hair, was an Arab from Lebanon and commonly known as "El Turco." He greeted me warmly, saying that I could go to Cozumel for twenty pesos if I did not mind sleeping and traveling on deck, as his hold was full. He planned to leave at midnight for Cozumel.

I saw that two pigs were part of the cargo. The captain invited me to bring my things on board and to sleep on the deck, if I chose, before the departure. The trip would take twelve to fifteen hours, according to the sea. I hung my hammock between the masts; night was rapidly falling and a phonograph played in the darkness. I took a long-wanted rest. I was now in a new world, one far from the jungle, a world of peace and quiet water lapping at a gently rolling hull. How far I felt that night from civilization, in that small island, so isolated and so close to the elements.

I was aroused from my reveries by some of the crew playing a guitar and singing *rancheros,* the first of these typically Mexican songs I had heard, simple songs of love and work with one accent in common—melancholy. Mexico is in general a sad country and Yucatán in particular is a land of nostalgia—the nostalgia of its two pasts: the Spaniards and the ancient Mayas.

I was awakened at midnight. All was dark around me and a brilliant moon was being chased and overtaken by fleeting clouds. A stiff breeze was blowing. Apparently this was a bonanza and we were setting sail. All the crew was jumping right and left, lashing objects to the stanchions, readying the sails, and taking in the fenders. There is nothing more mysterious than a departure by sea at night. Noiselessly the schooner slipped away from the creaky wooden dock and out of the lee of the island; here the trade wind caught our sails and with it came the heavy roll of the open sea. The engine was revved up and soon to the chug of the motor the helmsman wheeled the vessel on its course. We advanced steadily, crushing each wave as it rushed madly toward us, and we plowed onward into the night.

Occasionally the monotony of our progress was broken by the crash of an exceptionally large wave whose spray would disturb one of the pigs. There would be a shuffle and then all would return to normal. At times the flicker of a match would remind us that there was a man at the helm. The crew not on watch slept around the deck, each man seeking his own comfort in the form of an old tire for a pillow, or a piece of canvas to lie on. Had I been on a pirate vessel of old the faces would not have been much different from those of the crew of the *Fidelia,* with its Lebanese captain, a bearded bosun, and two mates with a strong strain of Indian blood in their Mexican veins.

Soon the sun started to rise and the tall rain clouds to the east took on a brilliant hue, first of ghostly white, slowly turning to gold and then red: at the peak of this display the whole sky was alight with tall pillars of fire. For some reason both sunrise and sunset are always an extraordinary display in the tropics, so much more violent and sensational than in temperate climates.

As the sun appeared the captain had our course changed and instead of heading south as we had all night, we now surprisingly sailed toward the coast. With a following wind and the engine we advanced at a good speed, the waves rolling in from astern. We were heading back to the mainland of Quintana Roo, to sail on south parallel to the coast behind a reef that would protect us from the big swells of the open sea. We were thus to skirt the coast till we reached a point opposite Cozumel; there we would cut across the straits over to the island.

Soon, before us, we could see the noisy foaming coral reef that formed a neat, straight barrier along the coast about a mile out to sea. The captain took the helm and, scanning the foaming barrier, found the invisible opening he was looking for. We slowly drew nearer and nearer the foaming water. One could see the rocks of the coral reef which all along the coast forms a long wall with only a few rare and narrow openings. Once over the reef, the water was calm and we followed the coast south for most of the morning.

This maneuver saved us the tossing and jolting of the Yucatán Straits, which are known for their rough weather due to the alternation of the strong trade winds and the *norte*, or north wind, which, coupled with the very fast currents, churn up a choppy sea.

For six hours we sailed down the coast of Quintana Roo. And staring out over the blue water, I could take a good look at this coast I had heard so much about. I felt relieved and laughed at all my previous fears. All was going well, and the trip to Belize announced itself to be a picnic. As for the Mosquito Coast, I imagined that all would go well there also.

The coastline, like Yucatán itself, was flat. Beautiful quarter-moon beaches alternated with outcrops of gray-white limestone rock. The jungle could be seen crumbling, as it were, on the edge of the sands: tall chicle trees, *ceiba* trees with their majestic trunks, fan palms, *guano* trees with their date-tree look, a mass of green underbrush—miles and miles of it. On two occasions the coast changed in appearance and coconut palms clustered the beaches. In the midst of these palm groves one could see small fairy-like palm-thatched huts, tropical island dream hideouts sheltered by the coconut trees. These were *cocals*, coconut plantations; for the most part they belonged to squatters who had settled in them recently from Cozumel. After one long grove of palms we came upon a group of four or five huts massed around a wooden jetty and close to a small lighthouse. This was Puerto Morelos, where the *plataforma* railroad from Leona Vicario ended. This had been the main port of all the region until the recent completion of the road to Puerto Juarez.

South of Puerto Morelos the coast was barren except for a few more small *cocals*. Endlessly extended the mysterious jungle —with its *chicleros*, malaria, and, I imagined, snakes and leopards. As we sailed slowly along, suddenly, to my surprise, I spotted a small, square, ancient Mayan temple right on the edge of the sea. It was in such perfect condition that I could not at first believe my eyes. It was a rectangular structure with one large sloping side doorway; built upon a rocky ledge, it had been fortunately erected so close to the sea that the jungle had not been able to destroy it. The temple was a chilling sight as it stood there as if guarding the coast, the lookout of a civilization long past. Farther down the coast we came upon an even more astounding ruin, which loomed high above the skyline—a tall pyramid with the remains of a narrow doorway on its summit. The sight was awesome and appeared to us on the *Maria Fidelia* as it must have appeared to the first Spaniards who ventured up the Yucatán coast almost four hundred and fifty years ago. This last ruin was called Pamul, according to our "Turk" captain, and I took out Dr. Alberto Ruz's map to check. I found it marked on the map and guessed by its location that the first ruin we had seen was the one marked Xcaret. They were ruins which I felt sure must not have been visited more than a dozen times by foreigners.

I could well imagine what must have been the reaction of the first Spaniards when they saw from the sea these menacing buildings. The first Spanish vessels on record to sight the Quintana Roo mainland were those of Juan de Grijalva, who sailed up the coast with four ships in 1518. At that time the cities of Tulum, Pamul, and Xcaret were inhabited, and there must have been more settlements than are known today, for the chaplain of Grijalva's expedition recalled, "We saw three large towns separated from each other by two miles; there were many stone houses and we perceived a town [probably Tulum, although this is not sure] so large that Sevilla would not have seemed larger; there were very large towers and on the shore a great throng of Indians who bore standards and waved them." This sight had so frightened the Spanish that they steered clear of the Quintana Roo coast and sailed around the Yucatán peninsula.

A year later Hernando Cortez had sailed from Cuba to the island of Cozumel, where he landed; then, sailing up the coast, he had been so frightened by the mighty stone cities that he also avoided the fierce Mayas and led his conquering expedition on to less dangerous-looking central Mexico. He also sailed cautiously around Yucatán and landed at the present Vera Cruz, where he started his extraordinary conquest of the Aztecs. So that, as one can see, Quintana Roo has never inspired confidence, even in the past.

I could not help thinking how ironical it was that the first part of the ancient Mayan world to be sighted by the Spanish should remain four hundred and fifty years later still an incompletely explored territory, one of the least-known areas of the North American continent. The frightening aspect of the Quintana Roo coast had defended it from the early assaults of Cortez, and today the jungle keeps men away. The principal reason for Quintana Roo's remaining a little-visited, unexplored land, however, is not so much the jungle as the presence in Quintana Roo of what could be called the last defenders of the Mayan people, the feared *Indios sublevados*—the true rulers of Quintana Roo. There is also the dangerous coral reef protecting the coast, and as the *Maria Fidelia* pursued its course south, the rumbling of the great foaming barrier that closed us off from the open sea was a menace at the same time as a shelter.

At about eleven o'clock the captain of the *Fidelia* took the helm and, scanning the reefs, found the narrow opening that was to let us out. Soon we were rolling madly in the open sea, heading for Cozumel.

This island is some fifteen miles from the coast. Twenty-four miles long and seven miles wide, it is the largest island belonging to Mexico. It has only one village, San Miguel, situated on the side facing the Quintana Roo coast. In the time of the Mayas it was densely populated, but today it has only three thousand inhabitants.

The presence on the island of seven ancient Mayan ruins and the testimonials of the early Spanish *conquistadores* prove that Cozumel was a sacred island. It was the Mayan shrine to the goddess Ix Chell, goddess of fertility, childbirth, and basket weaving.

The Mayas are known to have been navigators as well as traders. Christopher Columbus, when he set out on his third voyage, stopped at one of the Bay Islands, Guanaja, situated on the coast of Honduras. There he was greeted by Indians of the southern Maya group. They came in large dugout canoes with high bow and stern, some of the canoes forty-five feet long and seating up to fifty people. It was from this first encounter with these canoes that the Mayas got their modern name. When asked from whence they came the Indians answered, "Maiam," the name of their small local province. This was then erroneously extended to all the people of the civilization. An even stranger mistake brought about the name "Yucatán." When Grijalva sailed along the coast of Quintana Roo he landed at Cape Catoche, the northeast corner of the Yucatán peninsula. Some of his men having gone aground on what is now the northernmost tip of Quintana Roo, somewhere northwest of Isla Mujeres, one man asked, "Who built the buildings on the coast?" The Indians answered, "*Ci u than*," which meant, "We do not understand you," but the Spanish understood this to be the name of the people and "*Ci u than*" became "Yucatán."

Dugouts of the same type as those seen by Columbus at the Bay Islands would bring pilgrims to Cozumel, to the shrine of the goddess Ix Chell. Most were women coming to pray for fertility or because, being expectant mothers, they wanted a special blessing from the goddess of childbirth.

Judging from the rough weather that is characteristic of the straits between Cozumel and the coast, the dugout canoes of the

Mayas must have been seaworthy craft and the oarsmen good sailors.

From the summit of the waves I could catch a glimpse of the island which now appeared as a low gray streak on the horizon.

As we drew near I shared the crew's simple meal, prepared over a charcoal fire lit inside a tin on deck. My first crude experience with native food was not a great success, although I was unable to tell how much of my stomach ache was due to the cooking and how much attributable to the sea.

At three o'clock we were up against the flat coastline of Cozumel and the small village of San Miguel came into sight. I was quite disappointed, for the village looked ugly, composed of an odd assortment of stone, cement, and wooden houses of various styles that were stretched along the waterfront. There were practically no early Spanish buildings on the island, and although Cozumel is reputed to have been the first part of Mexico visited by Cortez and it was here that the conquistador in 1519 had the first Mass said on Mexican territory, the church is most disappointing—an ugly modern cement structure.

When the *Maria Fidelia* pulled alongside the large stone and cement wharf, many of the villagers were there to greet it. All around the dock, moored on the crystal-clear blue water, were dozens of sailing boats, all much smaller than the *Fidelia*. To me this was a good sign, for certainly, I thought, I could find someone to take me south, possibly all the way down to British Honduras.

Although for the most part of Indian stock, the islanders were much less typical than those of central Yucatán, and I could not find one woman with a *huipiles*. As on Isla Mujeres, many of the inhabitants of Cozumel were the offspring of pirates of old. Now they were for the most part engaged in fishing, some working the land as keepers or owners of coconut plantations around the island, or living in huts looking after small *cocals* on the Quintana Roo coast.

When I arrived at Cozumel I did not yet speak Spanish fluently and had trouble making myself understood. Before tackling the problem of going farther south I stored my bags with a uniformed guard in a small shed at the end of the dock. Then, taking my leave of the captain of the *Maria Fidelia*, I made my way to the village square, a vast, desolate cemented plaza with a few scraggy bushes, a bust of a one-time governor of Quintana Roo, and a few lampposts.

But if the exterior aspects of Cozumel and its inhabitants are on the whole depressing, I soon found out that the island is rich in other things.

The first thing that struck me was the charm and politeness of everybody. In the same manner that the captain and the crew of the *Fidelia* had been so amiable, everyone I met on the island was more than charming. This is the main characteristic of Cozumeleños. Cozumel, a lazy island in the sun isolated from the rest of the world, has over the centuries developed a character of its own, something that could be called an amiable family attitude. In Cozumel one can forget that one is in Mexico or Quintana Roo territory, one can forget the Mayas and the Spanish, for here one is in a world apart that oscillates between the sky and the sea, coconut groves and the *monte*, as the jungle is called.

The Cozumeleño is a modern man insofar as his contacts with the outside world through his boats have given him a polish that the farmers of Yucatán have not. He has traveled, and I was reassured to learn that usually he had been at least once in his life to British Honduras. The British influence in Cozumel is not great, but nevertheless the British products that make their way to the three stores of the town of San Miguel have added an element of sophistication to the island.

Gentle people, the Cozumeleños like to be liked. And no sooner had I set foot in the square than a man stepped forward and bade me have a drink with him at the counter of a small wooden soft-drink stand.

My host was Professor Perez, a self-appointed teacher at the local school. On learning that I was French, he rapidly passed in review the odds and ends he had learned about my country and its rather inextricable political complex. Having given me a Pepsi-Cola he then proceeded to look upon me as a representative of civilization to instruct his few drinking companions about France. After his rather summary description of France as a country near England with a great general called De Gaulle, he then proceeded to explain with great enthusiasm that when two parallels were cut by a straight line the alternate angles were equal. It was evident that his audience had never heard of geometry, but Professor Perez in his enthusiastic and original way of teaching managed to make this dry problem one of such fascination that his audience swallowed every word he said as children gape at the words of a fairy tale.

He was probably the most ignorant professor I had ever met, but he certainly was also the most brilliant and the best, for he not only knew how to interest his audience but also how to make even trivial things sound vital to a group of men the youngest of whom was at least forty.

He told me that Cozumel was the most delightful island in the world and its people the most civilized, and then he told his son, who was my age, that I would sleep the night in their house. Turning to me, he said and meant what so many Mexicans say but do not even dream of, *"Mi casa es su casa"* (My house is yours).

This welcome put my spirits into good shape. And I took the opportunity of my acquaintance with Professor Perez to ask if I could find a boat to take me along the coast down toward Belize.

Rubbing his plump hands and taking on a look of importance, he licked his lips and, as if beginning a sermon, said ceremoniously, "Well, you want a boat to go on the Quintana Roo coast. Yes, you can get one here to go to the ruins of Tulum, but not other parts of the coast. It is very dangerous, all *monte,* no good, and do you not like Cozumel?"

I had difficulty explaining that if I wanted to go to the Quintana

Roo coast and then on to Belize it was not because I did not like Cozumel. But this Professor Perez did not seem to want to understand. "Stay for the night," he said confidently. "Tomorrow you will not want to leave. Anyway there is here a *paisano suo* [one of your countrymen] Señor Chamberlain. You should go and see him. There used to be three Frenchmen here also; they came from Isla del Diabolo [Devil's Island]. They escaped on a small boat and drifted to Cozumel from Jamaica. They were good men. One built a nice house here; his name was Louis. Another went into the chicle business. Now they have all left." I was grateful that the three escaped French convicts had left the island, not knowing very well what I could have said to them. As for Señor Chamberlain, his name sounded rather too British to be French.

I thanked Professor Perez and followed his son down one of the streets of the village which soon became a grassy, rocky path bordered by thatched-roofed houses. At one of these Miguel Perez stopped and after untying a string opened a wooden door into a vast, dirty room with no ceiling other than the high roof woven of fan palm fronds neatly tucked under one another.

Here I could "set up my hammock," as the expression is. Taking a rusty steel bucket, Miguel Perez opened a back door and went to a well in the courtyard, bringing back some water for me to wash. Having refreshed myself and after much difficulty set up my hammock and mosquito net, I went out again into the square. I decided to go and see the certain Señor Chamberlain.

Inquiring where I could find him, a man directed me to a small pink house by the water. I gathered this was a restaurant or some kind of bar. To my surprise, when I entered I found myself in what would have been a smart night club in any country of the world. The floors were of beautifully designed ceramic; as for the walls, they bore a color reproduction of the ancient Mayan frescoes found in 1946 at Bonampak in Chiapas. These frescoes, the best-preserved of Mayan mural paintings, represent richly adorned nobles in a procession with musicians playing on Mayan drums draped with leopard skins or blowing at clay pipes. A more modern rhythm coming from the courtyard brought me out onto a tiled terrace overlooking a garden of palms bordered by rows of banana trees. Five men were seated informally about the patio, all playing with great gusto on drums, tom-toms, and guitars to the tempo of a fashionable South American dance. I could not believe my eyes. And for a moment I wondered whether I was really in Cozumel. When I asked for Mr. Chamberlain, a gentleman in his late forties came up to me, drum in hand.

Having settled that he was not French but spoke French fluently, he offered me a drink, and over a dry martini, to the rhythm of his friends' continued playing, he explained what he was doing in Cozumel and told me something of the house we were in.

I gathered he had been a great musician, some sort of child prodigy at the violin, and that after various careers and much traveling had chosen to settle in Cozumel, which he said was the happiest island in the world. His interest in music had brought him to teach some of the islanders how to sing and play the guitar. He had consequently opened a restaurant-night club which for the moment served the sole purpose of entertaining his guests on the island, but which he hoped would soon be the heart of a new Cozumel Island development for tourists. If I shuddered at the idea of tourists at Cozumel, I must say I could not congratulate him enough on the extraordinary and delightful atmosphere of his club.

Conversation then proceeded onto a whole succession of unusual subjects, and what with the martinis, the fatigue of the day, and the strangeness of the whole situation, I can remember little more of that evening than that until very late Ilya Chamberlain entertained me on the beauties of the Hermitage Museum in Leningrad while I yawned with fatigue and disbelief.

I was long to remember that evening with Ilya Chamberlain; all too soon it was to be for me the last memory of civilization. His martinis were a send-off to adventure, not the one I had come for but the adventure that events forced upon me.

The next morning, after a terrible night in the course of which I ripped my mosquito net wide open, I staggered to the village square and met Professor Perez, still engaged in enlightening conversations about equal triangles with a group of ragged, dirty-looking men.

Seeing me, he stiffened and ceremoniously greeted me: *"Mi amigo,* if you still want to leave, go to the dock; you may find a boat of someone who lives on the coast. They could take you over and possibly sail you down as far as the ruins of Tulum. There, who knows, you might find a boat south, although I doubt it. Anyway, after seeing the ruins you could always come back here to Cozumel later with another boat." I did not like the idea, all too vague, but I thought it was worth considering and headed for the dock.

Although it was around nine in the morning the heat was appalling. I could see a few men working about the dock and I asked a fisherman if he knew of a boat going south and whether I could find one to go along the coast and eventually to Belize.

"Oh no, there is only the *Fidelia* which came in yesterday; once or twice a year it goes to Belize. There used to be the *Claudio Canto,* but it sank a year ago in the hurricane in Chetumal bay. A bad hurricane that was—called Janet. Many a man it killed in Chetumal, and broke up all the coast. Yes, a bad hurricane that was."

This was the first mention I had heard of hurricanes; till then I had had no idea that the Quintana Roo coast was one of the most frequently devastated coasts in the Caribbean. Each year, apparently, the hurricanes never fail to strike Quintana Roo on their way up to the Gulf of Mexico or the Florida coast. Quintana Roo being so isolated and sparsely populated, the damages caused by the hurricanes never reach the front pages of the newspapers. They nevertheless are considerable. "Janet," I learned, obliterated the small town of Chetumal. An idea of the force of these hurricanes and their effect on Quintana Roo is given by the terrible toll they claim when they pass a little to the south over British Honduras. In thirty years, Belize has been twice obliterated and rebuilt. I was to learn all too soon about the damage done by hurricanes in Quintana Roo.

Looking about the dock for a likely person to inform me on the boat situation, I came across an Indian stripped to the waist. A fine-looking young man he was, as far as Indians go, short, with a large barrel chest, beautiful eyes, and a strange, typical triangular head with the long hooked Mayan nose so like those of the statues of Palenque. He was busy folding bags and coiling ropes on the edge of the wharf when I approached him. In my best Spanish I explained my case. He understood me probably because he himself spoke very scanty and poor Spanish. From our conversation I gathered that he lived on the coast and had a boat. He was planning to leave by midday and would take me over for twenty pesos to where he lived. Further, if I would wait at his father's house on the coast for three days, he could take me down to Tankah, the coconut plantation belonging to Señor Gonzales situated a few miles from the ruins of Tulum. Dr. Alberto Ruz had spoken in Mérida of the Gonzales plantation and confident that at least I could stay there to await a boat or further developments, I decided to accept the young Indian's proposition.

In my mind I made a rather hurried plan. I could go first to the coast with the young Indian; I was delighted at the thought of staying for a few days in what must be his simple home. Then he could take me to Tankah, and from there I would certainly manage to find a boat to go south to a port called Vigía Chico, which on the map was situated halfway between Tulum and the village of Xcalak that marked the border with British Honduras. If there were no boats south I thought I could always come back to Cozumel, since Professor Perez had guaranteed that at Tankah there were often boats.

My mind made up, I hurried to purchase a few cans of food—tinned beef—and two pounds of crackers. The young Indian said I could eat at his house on the coast but might not like their *khana* (Mayan for "food"). Having got these provisions, I hurried back to the dock with my bags. There I found the Indian with another young man, his brother, aged around sixteen. They did not look much of a crew, but I was confident and ready for everything.

I nevertheless got quite a shock when I asked the boys where their boat was and they pointed to the horizon. I could see nothing there. Then I realized that by leaning over the side of the dock I could see the boat: it was not a foot over eleven feet long. At first I thought it was a joke. Crossing the Yucatán Straits in the *Maria Fidelia* was bad enough; I had much respect for the ancient Mayas who crossed the same straits in open thirty-foot canoes with forty paddlers. But definitely my admiration for ancient Mayan seamanship was not great enough to envisage calmly crossing the same straits in an open eleven-foot "sailboat"—so-called because it had a bamboo mast and a rag dangling from it.

I did not have time to change my mind, for the two young men were loading my bags. Thinking that death at sea was perhaps not such a bad death, I jumped onto the boat. As I sat inspecting the homemade craft I noticed that not a piece of metal was used in her construction—everything was of wood. Looking up from my low position I had still a further shock, for there now stood on the dock three ragged-looking men with machetes preparing to board my boat. One by one they lowered themselves into the half-sinking craft and were joined by the two young Indians, and all together they raised the water line to within a few inches of the rail. This was sure suicide. But already the rough and rugged look of the three passengers started to worry me more than the chances of sinking. Were they bandits? Was this a trick to rob and kill me? Here I was sitting like a fool in a near-sinking boat with five foreigners, three of them armed, and setting out for somewhere on the coast. I had been foolish to be so confident; what if they were *chicleros?* Already we were drifting from the dock and the strong current was running us rapidly past the shabby waterfront of San Miguel.

Six in such a small boat was not comfortable. The younger Indian straddled the bow, hanging onto the mast with one hand and holding the jib in the other; the elder of the crew was squatting in the stern negligently holding the tiller with his left foot. As for myself and the three other passengers, when the mainsail was set we lay in a tight embrace on our noses so as to clear the boom. I envied a sardine in his tin—at least he has no head! As for *my* head, caught between a machete and the thigh of its owner, it buzzed with thoughts as to how long it would be on my shoulders.

To heighten my fears, not a word was spoken by the five men. They seemed to keep on looking at me, as I from my cramped position made attempts unobtrusively to study them and decide whether or not they were about to kill me. The two young Indians seemed all right; I had confidence in them because they were Indian, and in my childish way, for some reason, I sincerely believed all true Indians to be good. But regarding the other three men, it was a different matter. Their unshaven faces and hard looks all pointed to their being *chicleros,* and as far as I was concerned no *chiclero* could be anything but a crook.

Rocking madly, we made out for the Quintana Roo coast, and for the first time I regretted the comfort of the back seat of a small gray car, and wished I were still in Tepoztlán. . . .

I V

Stranded on an
Unexplored Coast

In dead silence the little boat sailed on. From her bow I had read
that she was called the *Lydia*. No matter how stiff were the waves
she always managed to stay afloat, while I held my breath at each
pitch. The *Lydia* was so small that each time we were in the hollow
of a sea we would lose all our wind and come to a halt, which
caused the boat to righten up, thus adding to the rocking and
making every moment a nightmare. We soon lost sight of Cozumel
and rolled slowly on with the elder boy still at the helm and the
young one still at the bow. Of course there was no compass on
board, and it was with a sigh of relief after two hours that I sighted
the dim outline of the coast of Quintana Roo. In my heart I felt like
congratulating the helmsman and I began to believe I would not
be murdered at sea after all. However, I kept a close eye on
everyone on board. I ventured a smile to the helmsman. "You not
seasick," was his startling reply, and I answered, with a confidence
engendered by fear, "No." My breaking the silence brought three
glares from the other passengers and consequently I spoke no
more, attempting hard to kill time by alternately dragging my
hand in the water or feeling under me, through my henequen bag,
the hard sheaths of my two baby machetes. They had a com-

fortable feel about them, and I imagined that I could use them to good purpose against any foe.

Toward five o'clock the wind slackened and we made no progress at all for a few hours, the coast seeming as remote as ever. The trip was to last eight hours altogether. At around six the coast that had for the last few hours filled all the horizon and seemed at a standstill suddenly loomed up close ahead. And before I knew what was happening we were being knocked about by the eddy caused by the high waves breaking against the reefs through which we were now steering by a narrow passage. The noise was tremendous as wave after wave came running with a great crash onto the jagged yellow and brown rocks. I thanked heaven when finally we were navigating inside the calm protected waters behind the reef. We began sailing south close to the shore, which sometimes came within feet of us. It seemed that we were sailing down a giant causeway bordered on one side by the tall, noisy barrier of the foaming reef and on the other by a dense, high hedge, the sprawling jungle.

For some reason the coast seemed different from the day before when I had looked at it from the comfort of the *Maria Fidelia*. I could now distinguish clearly every detail of every variety of tree and plant that formed the great hedge. Here and there fan palms would protrude above the skyline, waving their graceful leaves to the evening breeze. I could also notice the shiny trunks of the ceiba trees, red against the general green background. The rocks of the coast, which alternated with sand beaches, were a bone white with dapples of gray and occasionally green moss. The rocks in contact with the water were bright yellow or brown. As for the beaches, they had a wild deserted look about them which I found fascinating. They were perfectly clean save for small stacks of red seaweed neatly lined up by the last waves that gently fell upon the sand. Here and there a dead tree would cut out its dark black silhouette against the sand, half submerged in the milky whiteness of the flat smooth surface of the beach.

The continual line of the jungle, the repeated mass of trees all different but yet all so alike, a vast waste of foliage, gave an impression of mystery I had never felt before. Despite the limited view I had of the jungle, I knew and felt that it was endless, one great sprawling mass cut suddenly by the water, like a sentence that has been interrupted. One felt that there should be more to come, that the sea had no relationship with the jungle, that the jungle would have swallowed the sea if it could.

Now and again the beaches would form a deep crescent and taking a straight course we would draw farther from the coast until we suddenly came upon the scraggy rocks that closed the ends of the crescent; then land would be only feet away and the weather-beaten faces of the rocks would be visible with their pimpled skin of barnacles and their hair of seaweed. I could not help but feel amazed that here nature was so beautiful, yet the place was so abandoned and desolate that there would be few humans to admire it. Here were landscapes that would perhaps be looked at only once.

I began to feel that this was my coast and my jungle, and to consider the jungle as my own property with mixed sentiments of awe, amazement, and affection.

The sun began to set and we were still parading along the coastline. Where we were going I had no idea. I tried to imagine the house of the two young Indians.

Slowly the sun set and soon the jungle was nothing but a spiny black outline looming above us and echoing the roar of the reef which with the darkness had become an incredible display of fireworks as the phosphorescent waves blew up against the rocks. The *Lydia's* wake in the same way was alight. Occasionally, arising from the jungle, came the strange cry of a startled bird, ringing out above the din of the reef.

In the *Lydia* all were silent. The elder Indian was now standing, and like his brother he scanned the dim coastline, steering a good course through the rocks with his foot.

Suddenly in the silence there came a familiar sound, the barking of a dog, which followed us along the beach for some distance. Together the two brothers let out a mingled howl and guttural noise which sounded like "U-ugh." This call is used in Yucatán by men in the jungle to attract attention or to indicate that one is present. The deep "U-ugh" from the *Lydia* was answered by an equally deep voice coming from somewhere in the dense foliage of the coast. Who lived there I could not tell, and soon we had sailed on, leaving the lonely voice behind. No doubt we had passed a *cocal* inhabited by some Indian or poor man from Cozumel.

The night was very dark and to my eyes the jungle was but a blurred mass. I wondered how we could ever find a particular point on the coast, although I now had confidence in the helmsman whose superb handling of the *Lydia* proved that he knew what he was doing.

An hour or so later the two boys began howling again; at first there was no reply but an echo from the jungle. They shouted again and again, and soon I could faintly distinguish an answer slightly weaker and slightly deeper than the echo. As these strange noises darted over the water in the darkness, there came a sudden flash and a small yellow light moved down across a beach. We had arrived.

The boy on the bow dropped anchor and the *Lydia* swung round, its stern slowly drifting toward the beach. The mainsail was flapping as we came to a stop.

All was dark around us save the little glare of the lamp that shed an eerie light upon the loose sail. I could now see that the lamp was held up high by a woman. Within the narrow circle of light at her feet I could see the outline of three small children clustered against her. A deep male voice attracted my attention to a man who was slowly advancing toward us in the water. His elbows raised above his head, he was chest deep when he reached our side. Two knotty hands grasped the side of the boat and the head of an old Indian peered up at us. The man then exchanged a few words in

Mayan with the elder of the two boys. The other three passengers started rolling up their trousers, and one by one jumped over the side, wading ashore with their machetes and small bags over their heads. The old man then made signs that I should climb on his back to get ashore, but not wanting any special treatment I refused and jumped into the water, giving my bags to the old man.

I staggered up onto the beach soaked to the waist. The woman came up to me and, putting the kerosene lamp into my face, pronounced one word, *"Joven,"* and then bade me and the three men follow her. She led us under a palm grove whose gray trunks and long palms shimmered in the light of the lamp. We came upon a small thatched hut set in the sand. It was so low that I had to bend in two to enter. A fire of coconut husks was flickering on a hearth set upon a sort of table. Here, the woman said in Spanish, we could set up our hammocks. I was about to do so and was opening my bag when she changed her mind and, taking me by the arm and calling me *"Mistre,"* led me to a yet smaller hut, the size of a hen house. Here slept her children and here she bade me hang my hammock for the night. In the incredibly narrow and low palm hut, with soft sand as floor, there were already three hammocks, and with the help of the woman I slung mine so that it dangled underneath the other three.

Placing my bags in one corner of the hut, I clambered into my hammock for the night. Soon I was joined in the hut by the elder of the two boys who had taken me across and two of his small brothers, who clambered like monkeys into their respective hammocks and then stared down at me with their large brown eyes.

I slept very little that night, what with the excitement of the events of the day, the roar of the reef, and thousands of mosquitoes that kept on pestering me since my mosquito net was torn. Lying on my back and swinging gently, I reviewed the events that had brought me all the way from New York to this distant palm-thatched hut lost somewhere on the wild coast of Quintana Roo. . . .

When I awoke it was broad daylight and from my hammock,

looking through the narrow opening of the hut, I could see row upon row of small coconut trees and, beyond the forest of gray trunks, the pale blue of the sea.

Rising, I surveyed the place where I had been landed. To all appearances I was in a coconut plantation, although the term plantation is a little too impressive to describe what the Yucatecans call a *cocal*. An immaculately white beach formed a large crescent some two miles long. The upper part of the beach that lined the dark marshy jungle had been planted with coconut trees whose long palms dragged in the soft sand. In the center of the crescent there were three huts, one a largish, typical Mayan circular hut made of stakes planted in the sand side by side and covered by a very slanted roof of overlapping fan palms. Next to this hut stood a smaller one that I guessed was the kitchen, and to which I had been taken at first the night before. The third hut was the one I had spent the night in; its walls were made of odd pieces of timber that had been apparently gathered on the beach. The three little huts there on the sand nestled among the neat palm trees made a most beautiful sight, which lived up to all the dreams I had had of a paradise retreat. The *cocal* was called Puha, which in Mayan means "bad water," a name that probably came from the fact that the beach was wedged between the sea and a smelly marsh in whose dirty water were growing dense bushes of mangrove and various slimy tropical trees.

Puha was the first *cocal* that I was to see, and like all the *cocals* of the Quintana Roo coast it was above all an isolated island in a sea of jungle.

Puha was an island in more ways than one. By land the nearest civilized spot lay one hundred miles away beyond endless impenetrable jungle; its only means of contact with the outside world was by boat. *Cocals* are practically self-contained small universes inhabited usually by no more than one family. At Puha this was the case. My host, Señor Mesos, had come from Cozumel and had settled on the coast with his wife, who spoke good Spanish and had

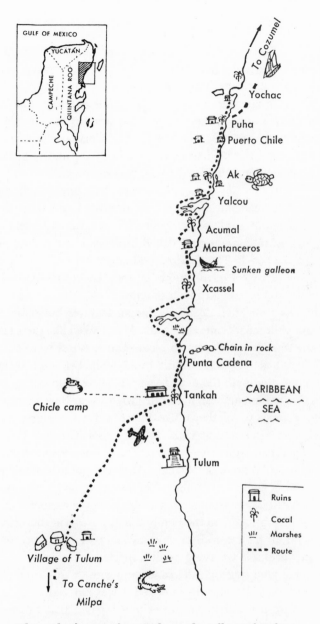

GULF OF MEXICO
YUCATÁN
CAMPECHE
QUINTANA ROO

To Cozumel

Yochac
Puha
Puerto Chile

Ak
Yalcou

Acumal
Mantanceros
Sunken galleon
Xcassel

Chain in rock
Punta Cadena

Chicle camp
Tankah

CARIBBEAN
SEA

Tulum

Village of Tulum

To Canche's
Milpa

Ruins
Cocal
Marshes
Route

The author's route from Puha to the village of Tulum

less Indian blood than he. Of their six sons, the eldest were Samuel and Jorge, who had sailed me over, while the four youngest ranged from twelve down to three years old. Of a poor family, they had come here as squatters as soon as the *Indios sublevados* had toler-ated intrusion by Cozumeleños on their territory, which I learned had only been since 1935. Before then no Cozumeleño dared ven-ture onto the coast for fear of being killed. Apparently in the last twenty years the *Indios sublevados* had signed a peace and their acts were less hostile to the inhabitants of Cozumel, in particular to those like Señor Mesos who spoke mostly Mayan. The younger sons of Señor Mesos lived in what could be a child's dream, spend-ing the day running around naked fishing and swimming on the edge of the beach. The children had never left the coast and did not know of cars or civilization. All they knew they had learned watching and listening to their parents.

The elder sons had decidedly Indian features but some of the younger children, despite their dark skins, looked like their mother, with more rounded European faces. The Mesoses were still very poor and had themselves built the *Lydia*—their only means of communication with the outside world. Their main occupation at Puha was to hunt and fish for food. Twice a year they collected the fallen coconuts which they broke open to extract the meat (copra), which they later sold at Cozumel. Robinson Crusoe lived in no more simple and primitive a fashion, and I was soon to realize that life on a *cocal* is probably the closest one can get to absolute primi-tivism, for a completely isolated family living on its own is never encountered in any communal society, however remote and back-ward it may be. Around the family the Mesoses had therefore con-centrated all their world, beyond any social interference whatso-ever, a world self-satisfying in all respects.

A small well dug into the sand only three yards from the sea yielded the fresh water they needed. I was amazed at such prox-imity of fresh water to sea water and learned that this was not uncommon on the coasts of Yucatán, and that there are even sand banks off the coast from which, if one digs, one can get fresh water. Going to the kitchen, I noticed that the three men who had come over with us had gone. When I asked who they were Señora Mesos replied that they were *chicleros;* the thought made me shudder but I was relieved that they had done nothing that I had expected *chicleros* to do. These thoughts, I was later to discover, were premature, for I had not seen the last of the three men, whom I later found out were nothing less than a trio of robbers.

Toward eleven o'clock Samuel went out to the *Lydia* and asked if I cared to accompany him and his brother up the coast to a creek where they were going to tie up their boat. I readily accepted, and soon we were out on the crystal blue water sailing up the coast. Seen from the sea Puha appeared as one great crescent of pale green palms set before the dark outline of the jungle; below the palm trees one could barely distinguish the three small brown huts. How many people, I thought, would envy the peace of life on a *cocal*.

Soon Puha slipped out of sight, and for an hour we cruised up against a rocky part of the coast where the jungle died but a few feet from the water's edge. Suddenly the straight line of the rocky coast was broken, Samuel steered the *Lydia* through a narrow river-like opening no more than ten feet wide, and to my surprise we were soon floating in the calm blue waters of a sheltered lagoon that cut its way through the dense vegetation. The water was so clear that bright tropical fish were visible as they swam around the boat. The lagoon seemed quite large and wound its way farther inland. Coming around a bend of the lagoon, which was bordered with rock like a swimming pool, I saw a sight that astonished me. There on the edge of the blue lagoon, reflected peacefully in the crystal waters, was a perfectly preserved ancient Mayan temple.

The small structure was rectangular in shape and no more than three yards tall. It had but one small narrow opening—a doorway with slanted sides and a recess above it forming a lintel. Above the doorway a double-barrel stone projection formed a simple frieze. Its proportions were perfect and, apart from one small cactus plant on the roof, it looked as if it were new and still inhabited.

I could not contain my enthusiasm and could hardly wait for the *Lydia* to come to rest alongside the natural dock formed by the edge of the lagoon, to go ashore and inspect the structure.

It was little wonder to me that the ancient Mayas had chosen the sheltered lagoon as a port. And later I was to learn that the *caleta* or lagoon of Yochac, as it is called, is one of only three such *caletas* which offer the only shelter for boats along the northern part of the Quintana Roo coast. Here I could imagine the canoes had set out bearing the pilgrims to Cozumel Island. Nothing, it seemed to me, had changed since the time of the ancient Mayas. And in my mind the *Lydia* was but a continuation of the long list of boats that for more than a thousand years had crowded the natural port of Yochac. Inquiring as to the meaning of the Mayan word "Yochac," I was told that it meant "above the color." No more appropriate name could have described the site, with the small gray temple literally sitting above the deep and clear shades of blue of the lagoon.

Crawling, I entered the small temple, and there on the walls were still traces of mural paintings. On one wall the head of a dragon was clearly visible; another bore the head of a snake with a long, spotted body. Close inspection revealed that the walls had been painted and replastered on several occasions, and here and there, where the plaster had peeled off, one could see traces of the earlier paintings and different layers of plaster. I counted eight in all.

I was to learn that the temple had been visited by other white men before me, but at that time I hoped that I was the first to have seen it.

Samuel and his brother did not share my interest in the building. And when I inquired about it later they simply said that there were many more like that in the *monte* behind the lagoon. The casualness of such a statement put me into a frenzy and immediately I asked to be taken to the other ruins. But neither Samuel nor his brother seemed delighted at the idea of going there, and they promptly stated that the other temples were very far off, that they did not know exactly where, and that anyhow they were broken up—"just piles of stones."

Having walked back to Puha, I decided to take my cameras and return that same afternoon to the lagoon; the walk, like the one in the morning, was long and painful, alternately in soft spongy sand and on rough, razor-sharp gray coral rocks. The sun was unbearably hot and mosquitoes by the thousands swarmed down on me.

Alone, I could contemplate the small building in peace. The single narrow room had a typical Mayan vault with slanting sides, made by the successive overlapping of great slabs of stone. Being less than a yard from the water's edge, the temple had not been cracked or broken by vegetation.

That evening I tried to get more information about the temple of Yochac. But all I could get was a strange story. Señora Mesos, who spoke the best Spanish of the family, explained to me that the small house had been built by dwarfs, and that when the moon was full nobody dared pass or walk by the *caleta*, for men had seen the great, dark sails of a ship moving into and out of the sheltered lagoon.

Despite my efforts to explain that the temple had probably been built by ancient Mayas, she insisted that it was the work of the dwarfs.

In the evening there was a short rainstorm which I weathered inside the small hut in my hammock, listening to one of the younger boys, called Rosalio, play the guitar, using a homemade instrument. After the rain there rose from the marsh a strong putrid smell, and soon with the dampness came thousands of mosquitoes. In desperation I tried to repair my mosquito net, which I had ripped at

Cozumel. And contemplating my poor handiwork, I mused that if the hammock was a gift to the Mayas from the gods, the mosquito net was no less divine a thing.

The next morning I was awakened by my two young roommates, Rosalio and his small brother. They asked me if I wanted to accompany them turtle hunting. Taking me down the beach, they pointed out two or three places where giant turtles had come up during the night to spawn. The sand was marked with what seemed like great caterpillar tracks. Creeping along in the hope of surprising a giant turtle, we walked all the length of the beach. We saw none. Rosalio then proceeded to approach a spot where fresh gigantic tracks led up from the sea to about five yards inland. Kneeling down where the tracks ended, he began to dig, and soon from a depth of about twelve inches he withdrew a white round egg, then another, and in no time there were more than seventy eggs lying on the sand. I had never seen a turtle egg before, and must admit that I was surprised to see that they were the shape and size of ping-pong balls, with in many ways the same texture, the eggs being half soft, so that if one pressed lightly on them they would dent. Rosalio broke one open for me and I could see that they were quite like chicken eggs, with large yolks. Then, to my disgust Rosalio and his brother gobbled some raw, and with a grin of relish bade me to do the same. I refused; a raw egg is bad enough when it is a chicken egg, but the egg of a reptile— at that moment I would have preferred to die.

When we returned from our egg expedition, to my surprise Samuel and his brother were gone. When I asked where to, I was told that they had gone with the *Lydia* up the coast but would soon be back. How long would they be, I asked. "Quite long," came the noncommittal reply. Protesting that they had promised to take me to Tankah, I was told that I could stay until they returned. This put me at ease and I settled down for what was to prove a long and fruitless wait.

I had nearly run out of provisions and approached Señora Mesos to see if she could feed me. She willingly proposed that I share the family's meals. To my horror, I discovered that the main element of the diet was turtle eggs, eaten raw. I limited myself to eating tortillas, the flat corn cakes that Señora Mesos incessantly shaped with her hands, squatting before the fire. Because these tortillas are to be eaten warm and because everyone in Mexico, among the poorer people, eats as many as twenty at a meal, meals are taken in a family one person at a time, each eating alone and in turn.

In the afternoon, seeing that Señor Mesos was getting ready to go hunting, I asked to join him. He rather reluctantly accepted and soon, in my sandals, I was off, hard on his heels.

Just behind the kitchen a path had been cut through the mangroves and tree trunks had been laid out on rocks to form a pontoon over the marsh. After three hundred yards this catwalk ended and we were on firm soil in the jungle. I was not to go farther, for to my amazement where we entered the jungle stood three badly damaged but nevertheless unmistakable Mayan pyramid-like structures. The sight was so unexpected that I did not know what to say. Calling Señor Mesos, I told him that there were too many mosquitoes and I would stay here looking at the buildings. He readily agreed, probably pleased to get rid of my noisy presence, which would certainly have frightened away any game.

I had not yet overcome my excitement at the discovery of the small temple of Yochac, and the idea that at Puha there were three ancient Mayan ruins within a few hundred yards of where I had slept the night before seemed to me incredible. Although the buildings were badly damaged, one pyramid some twenty feet high still had standing on its summit the small slanted doorway and two walls of what had apparently been a small oratory or a sort of tabernacle. Another was so destroyed that there remained only a pile of white-faced stones. The third structure, which I had taken for a small pyramid, was in fact a broken-down, square temple like that of Yochac. There were still very faint traces of paintings on the walls. This last building had been erected on the edge of a small *cenote*, a natural well whose narrow entrance opened at the base of the structure. Immediately my mind flashed to the *cenote* of Chichén-Itzá, and I wondered whether this *cenote* contained any artifacts.

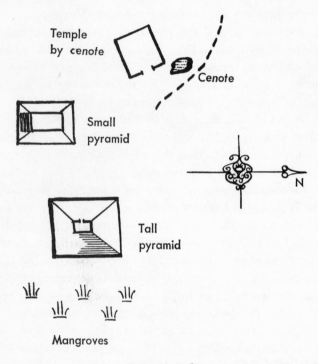

Ruins at Puha

The mosquitoes now buzzed around me mercilessly and managed to dampen my spirits. I decided that before I started digging and turning over stones I had better get my camera and take photographs and ask more information from Señora Mesos about the ruins, which I felt certain—and I was right—I was the first foreigner to see.

On my way back to the *cocal* I saw that the catwalk was resting

Beside this lagoon stands the Mayan temple of Yochac, seen in the background

(Above) Señor Mesos before his hut at Puha, ready to go hunting
(Below) The top of the pyramid at Puha

(*Above*) The author rests by the temple of Yochac
(*Below*) The small oratory at Matanceros

(*Above*) The author at Matanceros. Taken by Benanzio
(*Below*) Pablo Canche

(*Left*) A house in the Indian village of Tulum (*Right*) The stone head
that protects the corn at Pablo Canche's *milpa*
(*Below*) A family of the village

The main pyramid at Chunyaxche, 62 feet in height
(Photograph taken on second trip)

(*Above*) Palace entrance at Chunyaxche. Note the remains of the ancient wooden lintel (*Below*) The tall pyramid at San Miguel de Ruz

(Above) The palace at Chamax—on it the three smugglers
(Below) Red hand prints on the interior wall of the palace at Chamax

upon faced stones which beyond doubt had been taken from the Mayan buildings.

Señora Mesos had some interesting information. She treated the ruins lightly, again as houses of the dwarfs, and explained that they must have been built by dwarfs, for the door of the oratory on top of the pyramid was so small that no man of reasonable size could have walked through it. This legend of dwarfs I was to hear repeated many times, and I found it to be the general belief amongst most of the Indians and Mexicans who had encountered Mayan ruins.

But Señora Mesos added information that made me jump when I asked her if they had found any pottery (the Spanish word for which I did not know, so that it took me hours to explain). She said no, but they had found a stone pig by the *cenote*, and a foot made of clay. When I asked her where they were she nonchalantly said that the children had thrown them away on her orders. Not wanting to accept defeat, I pressed her with questions, and had one of her children come with me to the ruins to show me where he had thrown the *cochino* and the *pie*. He rummaged for some time near the *cenote* and then, leaning down, picked up what seemed at first a shapeless rock. Turning it around, he jubilantly showed me the *cochino*, adding that it did not look very much like a pig after all.

He was right, for what he showed me certainly was not a pig, but rather some strange combination of a pig's head with a duck's bill and front paws like a squirrel's. I took a few photographs and then pressed the child on to find the foot. This he had no trouble doing, since he had neatly put it aside at the top of the largest pyramid. It was a neat clay foot with delicately embossed straps of an ancient Mayan sandal. I at once thought that if there was one foot, certainly there should be another, and possibly an entire idol, somewhere amongst the rubble. The child then showed me the exact place where he had found the foot and I began frantically searching. There were on the ground at the spot he had indicated numerous pieces of the same kind of pottery, but none of them had any particular shape, and the fragments were so small that they gave no clue as to where they fitted in. Searching with one hand, I attempted with the other to repel the mosquitoes that swarmed about me, and so spent an hour without success. As it was getting late and my face was but one great itch, I finally gave up for the day and made my way back to the beach. Entering the *cocal* after the stuffy dampness of the jungle was like arriving in paradise, and I immediately stripped to the waist for a swim. I decided that the next day would be one of hard work at the ruins.

That evening I ventured to taste a turtle egg, and seeing that my small supplies were exhausted, I stuffed myself with tortillas. Señor Mesos came back at dusk. Slung to his waist were two bloody, slimy iguanas, the giant carnivorous lizards that abound in Quintana Roo. Iguanas are the living descendants of dinosaurs and are most ugly things to look at, yet are good to eat, especially the way Señora Mesos prepared them. But that evening, although I had been told that they tasted like chicken, I could not, after my turtle-egg efforts, steel myself to eat any of the iguana.

That night I fell asleep to dreams of finding jade treasures, and already, for my two small archaeological finds, saw myself as a great hero. Life at the *cocal* seemed so pleasant that I was in no hurry to leave. I decided that if I was to make any good of these finds I should concentrate on taking measurements and precise notes on all that I came across. In my diary I proudly wrote "Puha: discovered two pyramids." And I added two dots to Dr. Ruz's chart.

I spent most of the next morning back at the site, but regardless of how much I gazed and scratched, I could find nothing among the rubble that resembled an idol or even a sculptured stone. I therefore contented myself with making a detailed plan of the three structures. At noon when I returned there was no sign of the *Lydia*, for which we were all waiting. And in the heat of the afternoon I fell asleep in my hammock after a swim. I would have had less pleasure swimming had I been aware that the waters were infested with barracuda.

That afternoon, accompanied by Rosalio, I walked four miles south down the coast, following the beach and then cutting my way along the rocky shore. As we stepped over crevasses in the limestone rocks that descended to the sea, Rosalio casually pointed out to me a stone house hidden in the palms of the jungle a few feet from the water's edge. And there again stood a small temple, of the same shape as that of Yochac but slightly smaller. It was not too badly damaged and, despite great cracks here and there, was probably little different from what it must have been years before. There were two doorways, one facing the sea and the other looking to the jungle. Imprudently I crawled in, immediately to be greeted by the buzzing of thousands of wasps. Two stings on the face made me retreat and I contented myself with examining the exterior of the building. This was truly a dwarf's structure, some sort of miniature sentinel's house before the sea. Possibly it could have been some kind of lighthouse or lookout. And certainly it must have been sighted by Grijalva when he first sailed along the Quintana Roo coast some four hundred and fifty years ago. To my surprise and delight, like the structures at Yochac and Puha this other temple was not on my map.

Back at Puha I asked whether there were more temples in the area. Señor Mesos at first said no, then went on to add that farther back in the *monte,* behind the temple I had found that afternoon, there were more structures; he could not remember exactly where since he had encountered them two years ago while hunting. At my insistence he agreed to accompany me the next day and try to find them again. That evening, having had my fill of tortillas, I was about to retire when Rosalio asked me if I would accompany him turtle hunting. With two of his brothers we crept down the beach, Rosalio shielding with his hand the vivid glare of the lamp, and he explained to me as best he could what I was supposed to do if we saw a turtle. We were in the *temporada,* the season during which the giant turtles called *cawamos*, or big-headed turtles, come up on the beaches to lay their eggs. They lay as many as 100 to 180 eggs at a time, and the same turtle lays batches of eggs every two weeks. The purpose of our hunt was to surprise a turtle as it came up on the sand to lay its eggs. The turtles being of considerable size and Rosalio being a small child, I had been elected to perform the uncomfortable, and possibly dangerous task of grabbing the turtle by the shell at its tail end and overturning it—a rather frightening assignment. As I was reflecting on my probable inability to perform it, Rosalio waved his hand as signal that he had spotted a turtle.

All I could see was the darkness of the beach and the phosphorescent glow of the reef. Rosalio crept on forward, bidding me to follow. Soon I could see on the sand the large tracks of a giant turtle; the fins had cut two parallel furrows and the turtle must have been gigantic, for they were more than three feet apart. I understood why I had been unable to see the huge animal, for where the track ended it had already started burying itself into the sand and only its head and a large domed bump on the top of its shell showed. The head was the size of a human head and the reptile must have been close to four feet long. Wasting no time, I got behind the turtle, which by now had spotted us and was hissing and shaking its head in a menacing way. A bite from the jaws of the turtle would have meant losing part of a leg. Turtles, I knew, have such powerful jaws that they can bite right through human bone with no effort. Having been warned about this and that their hind flippers are used in defense for throwing sand to blind their opponents, I rapidly grabbed the rear of the shell before the turtle could completely free its rear flippers. To my horror, with all my strength I could lift the animal no more than a few inches. Rosalio rapidly came to my rescue and all four of us raised the rear end of the turtle, which fell on its neck, its hind flippers now free, beating madly against us as, close together, in one great thrust we overthrew the turtle and rolled it on its back. Tragically, it began beating the air with its flippers, hissing and rubbing its neck in the sand in violent efforts to right itself. But the weight of its own body was too great and the turtle was doomed to die. I never quite understood how we had managed to overturn it, for it was of tremendous size and must have weighed close to two hundred pounds. Leaving the turtle on its back, the three children rushed back to the huts to announce their catch. My part in the hunt was looked upon favorably and Señora Mesos congratulated me by giving me a coconut to drink.

Since I had arrived at Puha I had thrived on coconut water, fearing amoebae. Till then I had never realized what a good drink it was. Each coconut would contain close to a pint of liquid. The choice of a coconut to drink was no little matter, for, as I was to find out, every tree has a different taste according to its proximity to the sea, and on each tree every nut is different according to its age. Fallen brown nuts are very salty, small young green nuts sickening and jelly-like; the best are the large green coconuts that are beginning to turn brown and ripen. In two strokes of a machete the ends of the nuts are cut off and a small hole is chopped into the hard shell for drinking.

We left until the next morning the job of killing and dissecting the turtle. The next day at dawn it was still alive, flapping on its back; it had not moved an inch and all its efforts had only resulted in imbedding it a little deeper in the sand. Above the turtle in the sky loomed the frightening shadow of deadly *zopilotes*, the scavenger birds of Mexico. They also knew that the turtle would die, and attracted as if by magic, they had come over Puha by the dozens and swirled in wide circles, waiting.

With his machete Señor Mesos cut the soft under-shell of the turtle, raising this as a lid while it was still alive; then he cut into the body of the turtle, dealing it a mortal blow. The dead turtle on its back with its stomach open was now only a slimy mess of blood and a yellowish pink oil or liquid fat that floated all over in the dish formed by the turtle's shell. The smell was appalling and the *zopilotes,* knowing their victim was dead, started landing on the beach and made, on foot, tentative approaches toward it. The children threw sand at them to keep them away as Señor Mesos prodded elbow-deep in blood inside the turtle. He was looking for the ovary bag, and soon began to extract one by one the 130 eggs that the unfortunate thing had not had time to lay. Having withdrawn the last of the eggs, he then proceeded to draw out the ovary skin which, to my surprise, contained no less than a hundred more eggs, those of the next lay which had no skins and were but yellow pellets the size of large marbles. These Señor Mesos took out enveloped in the intestine tissues, and promptly carried them home where he hung them up to dry in the sun. The unlaid, partly formed eggs of a turtle are a rare delicacy, and when dried they keep forever and are eaten raw. Later I tried some and found them quite good; they taste a little like hard-boiled egg yolks. There were many strings of these premature eggs already hanging from the roof of the Mesoses' kitchen, held together inside the dried, parchment-like ovary intestine.

After extracting the fresh (extra fresh) eggs and the yet unformed ones, Señor Mesos filled six one-liter bottles with the orangy fat of the turtle. The meat later was cut into strips and hung to dry in the sun. The shell and the skull were left to the *zopilotes.* The shell of the *cawamo* is of no use as opposed to the rare and expensive shells of the smaller-headed turtles, which one rarely encounters in Quintana Roo, although these turtles are numerous in the Gulf of Mexico around Campeche.

The putrid, orangy turtle fat is greatly prized in Yucatán; the Indians believe that it is a good remedy against colds and also consider it an effective general medicine.

Around eleven, in the heat of the day, I set off with Señor Mesos to search for the buildings he had told me about. We marched down the coast for a few miles, then at a given point Señor Mesos made for the jungle, cutting with great, regular blows the dense foliage that obstructed our passage. The march was most painful, especially for me; having only sandals, my feet were soon bleeding and bruised as I stumbled on through the dense foliage, trying hard to keep close behind Señor Mesos for fear of getting lost. I could not help shuddering when I thought of snakes. With no shoes I felt most vulnerable and had but two consolations, the fact that Señor Mesos was barefooted also, and the knowledge that at Puha I had my famous bottle of Antiviperine. This was the first time I had ever penetrated a jungle on foot off a beaten track, and I could only admire the agility with which Señor Mesos proceeded. How he found his way in the endless unchanging green tunnel he cut through the foliage I do not know. Occasionally he would stop, look around as if searching for something, then either breaking a branch or making a mark in the bark of a tree, he would suddenly start off again as if knowing exactly where he was.

An hour or so later I was exhausted, covered with perspiration, and itching all over from mosquito bites. Señor Mesos fortunately stopped and asked me to stay and wait while he rummaged around in a circle, soon letting out a shout. "*Aya*" (There), he said pointing to what appeared to me to be more jungle. Approaching, I could finally distinguish the grayish shape of a wall. This was the wall of a small temple entirely covered with vegetation and choked with vines and roots of trees. Next to it stood the remains of a smaller structure reduced now to nothing more than a pile of stones.

The larger of the two buildings was still in good condition, despite the tree growing on its summit. Reluctantly, at my request, Señor Mesos started to clear the ruin of vines and vegetation. In so doing he unveiled from the leaves a grinning statuary face that stuck out from an ornamental stone projection that circled the summit of the building. I could not contain my delight and urged Señor Mesos on. Soon the whole temple stood clear of minor vegetation. Making my way around it I came on another decoration, a dragon-like affair projecting from the same ledge; in place of an eye it had a large hole like some kind of ornamental ring. The interior of the small structure was full of rubble and showed no signs of paintings on the crumbling stucco that still remained in patches on the walls. The doorway was similar to that at Yochac, with slanted sides and above it a lintel stone set back into the wall,

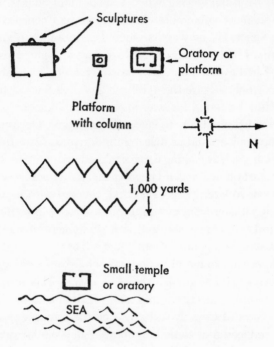

Ruins at Puerto Chile

forming the cross bar of a T above the door. These recessed lintels are characteristic of Mayan coastal architecture and I had also seen some at Chichén-Itzá. Having taken photographs and had a good look around for any objects, I was obliged to leave, regretfully, for Señor Mesos seemed impatient and in no manner shared my enthusiasm. I determined that I would come back, for certainly there were bound to be more buildings around, despite the denial of this by Señor Mesos.

Returning to the coast, I realized that that temple and its

neighboring ruin must have been no more than a few miles inland, for we rapidly covered the distance that had taken us so long on the way in when we had to cut a path. I must say that had Señor Mesos wanted to he could have lost me by simply letting me out of his sight, for although we had cut our way to come in, it took a well-practiced eye to find the broken branches and other signs of our earlier passage. Dead tired but contented, I reached Puha in time for a refreshing swim before the sun set. Samuel and his brother had not yet returned and I began to have some anxiety as to when they would be back.

That evening, after tasting turtle meat, which was excellent although a little fatty, and having an after taste of turtle eggs, I retired to my hammock with an oil lamp to look at the map that I had been given of the ruins of the coast. There was no sign of a ruin that could have corresponded to the ones I had seen that day, and I proudly marked a third dot. The place on the coast being known as Puerto Chile, I used that name for the three ruins, the one on the coast and the two inland.

Possibly the structures I had found were remains of some of the towns spoken of by Grijalva's chaplain and since forgotten. Perhaps also, I thought, my finds were part of the enigmatic domain of the ancient ruler Xamanzana, the Mayan chief who had purchased as slaves the two unfortunate Spaniards who survived a shipwreck in 1511 and were the first Spaniards to come to Yucatán.

Twenty survivors of the wreck had drifted in a small boat all the way from Jamaica to Cozumel, after their vessel sailing back up from Panama had foundered in Jamaican shallows. Like the three modern French escapees from Devil's Island, the shipwrecked mariners had been carried by the strong currents of the Caribbean to Cozumel. There the Indians killed all the survivors save two, a priest, Geronimo Aguilar, and Gonzalo, later known as Gonzalo Guerrero. These two men were sold as slaves to a certain Lord Xamanzana who lived somewhere on the Quintana Roo coast. There for eight years they remained slaves of the Mayas—eight years before other Spaniards even knew of the existence of Yucatán.

Aguilar kept his faith and suffered a great deal in so doing. As for Guerrero, he adopted the customs of the country, filing his teeth, piercing his ears, and taking many women. When Cortez landed in Cozumel in 1519, eight years after the shipwreck, the Mayan chief allowed Aguilar to go to Cozumel and join Cortez. Guerrero, satisfied with his new life, refused to go and returned to the Quintana Roo coast where he eventually organized great resistance to the Spanish conquest and died leading Mayan soldiers in 1537.

Aguilar was a great help to Cortez since he spoke Mayan. Nobody knows much of the life that these two men led on the coast, and as for the realm of Xamanzana, I liked to think that I would finally discover its true extent. Possibly Guerrero had lived at Puha, and most certainly he must have been through the lost villages that I had now found.

On my map, somewhere south of where I expected Puha to be, and before Tulum, was a small triangle indicating ruins that were marked under the Mayan name *Ak*, which I knew meant turtle. I decided that if the *Lydia* had not returned by tomorrow morning I would attempt to go there and see the ruins which could not—I imagined rightly—have been visited by many foreigners.

By ten there was still no sign of the *Lydia*, and I asked where Ak was. Señora Mesos said that it was the name of a *cocal* eight miles down the coast, and that there was a small dwarf's house on the coast there. When I told her of my wish to go there she seemed surprised—so far just for a small building. "There is no path; you will have to walk by the sea and it is all rough stone." Having nothing to do, and strengthened by my previous day's experience, I decided to set out alone for Ak. There, Señor Mesos told me, lived a young *soltero* (bachelor) called Miguel who looked after the *cocal* that belonged to a man who lived on Cozumel. He could show me the ruins.

I walked for three hours along the coast with occasional peli-

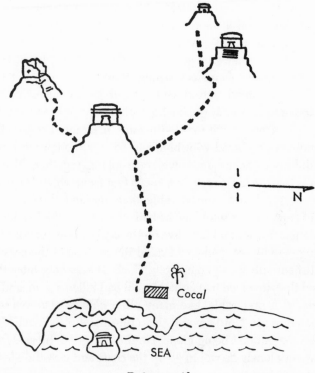

Cocal

SEA

Ruins at Ak

cans, which in formations of three hovered above the coastline in search of fish, as my only companions. After two hours I thought that I must be lost. Clear beaches alternated with difficult rocky passages all bordered by jungle, and it seemed impossible to me that I had not yet covered the eight miles to Ak. It was only an hour later that I finally arrived exhausted at a large bay on whose beach were planted row upon row of the now familiar coconut trees. This, I thought, must be Ak, and walking under the shade of the groves I searched for a small hut where I might find the man called Miguel. I did not have to search for long; right in the middle of the beach rose a large rock projecting out into the sea and separated from land by a narrow channel. There on the large, flat isolated rock stood a minute Mayan temple, and back from the temple in the sand was a hut.

My approach somewhat startled a young Indian who had been lazily sleeping in a hammock strung between two coconut trees. Miguel, I presumed, introducing myself as having come from Puha to see the ruins. Miguel, who could not have been more than thirty, was a handsome man with most pleasant features. I immediately sympathized with him, and soon, although we were of such different backgrounds, we were joking together. The first joke was that we had the same name, a fact from which Miguel did not recover till after considerable laughter and showing many signs of friendship. He told me he had once been a *chiclero* but had abandoned that rough life to live on the coast. I was surprised that a young man like Miguel could stand the solitude of the coast and be satisfied with living completely alone. It was only later that I learned that, involved in a fight, Miguel had killed a man, and now considered it preferable, like many other *chicleros,* to live in unpopulated areas. Not knowing this (fortunately), I asked Miguel whether he minded being alone. He did not mind, he said; when he was very lonely he would go up the coast and visit the Mesoses. I much admired the way the *cocaleros* accepted solitude and with what ease they did away with companionship. On Miguel this had had the effect of making him a bit of a philosopher; he spoke little but well, and I was surprised by the extent of his knowledge and the sharpness of his mind.

He was the first *chiclero* I was to meet, and also the least fearful. But like all *chicleros,* and one could say nearly all people who live a dangerous and independent life, he was highly intelligent, with a perceptiveness and quickness of mind that surpassed any that one would expect to encounter in such people as peasants or even bank clerks, people whose set pattern of life requires no violent intellectual effort for survival.

Miguel took me into the *monte* to look at some ruins that were

two miles from the coast. Here some American archaeologists had
come from Cozumel by boat. Had they walked up the coast they
would no doubt have found Puerto Chile and Puha. But, strange as
it may seem, no foreigner—at least on record or in the living memory of the *cocaleros*—had come down the coast at all. The ruins
known on the three hundred miles of Quintana Roo coast, I later
found out, have always been approached from the sea, and were
discovered that way, since they were clearly visible from offshore.

It was nearly dark by the time I returned to Puha, and there was
as yet no sign of the arrival of the *Lydia*. I now began to worry. I
had spent five days at the small *cocal*, and despite the exciting
finds and interesting happenings I had no desire to stay forever,
what with no more provisions and a deadline for reaching British
Honduras.

If I had no intention of staying forever at Puha, I learned with
surprise that Señor Mesos shared my point of view. The following
morning when I got up he came over to me and rather roughly
informed me that I could not stay. "There is little food here, and the
Lydia not come. You must go on foot." I could not believe my
ears and protested violently. It was ridiculous, I explained; Señor
Mesos himself had told me that there were no paths to Tulum.
There were more than thirty-five miles to go, and I would certainly
get lost. The idea was unthinkable. "At least, then," I suggested,
"you must send one of your sons with me." Señor Mesos flatly
refused. I could not think what had overcome the man and for a
moment felt quite panicky. Seeking explanation, I approached
Señora Mesos, but from her I could get no more information than
that since the boat was not back and there was little food at Puha,
I had to go on foot. When I protested that I had paid my fare, she
replied that I had been fed. She suggested that perhaps Miguel at
Ak could help me, as he knew the coast better than they.

Nothing seemed to change their minds, and I returned dispirited
to the hut where my hammock was strung to consider what lay
ahead. At first it seemed folly; with only my sandals I could never

make it. My short experience on the coast had already shown me that walking was most difficult and painful; furthermore, where could I find water for such a journey, which would take at least three days? My only hope lay, I felt, in Miguel's being willing to come with me. Although I hardly knew him I felt confident that he could help. What worried me more than water was the question of snakes and finding my way, for often along the coast I had noticed marshes thick with impenetrable mangroves that came right up to the sea, and if I was to skirt them inland through the jungle I would certainly get lost. As for my big henequen bag and small flight bag, I would not be able to lug them thirty-five miles in the heat of the tropics. And as to encountering marauding *chicleros,* I preferred not to think what would be my fate.

I decided that, despite Señor Mesos's insistence, I would stay a day more and see what would happen—at least it would give me time to rest.

When I awoke next morning I saw two men whom I had never seen before talking to Señor Mesos. Where they had come from, and why, I could not tell. Everything seemed most suspicious and for a moment I wondered whether I had not better leave right away and run before anything unpleasant cooked up.

It turned out that one of these men was the brother of Señor Mesos and had come down from his small *cocal* called Chunyuyun, situated five miles north of the lagoon of Yochac up the coast. He was accompanied by a worker who lived with him at the *cocal.* They had, it seemed, come to pay an informal visit to their isolated neighbor. I felt more confident when, on approaching the men, I found that one of them spoke fluent Spanish. They asked what I had come to do at Puha and on the coast. I quickly explained that I was on my way to Belize and that I had been set off at Puha, waiting to go with the *Lydia* to Tankah, from where I planned to sail south to Belize.

From their looks I gathered that they did not believe a word I said. And for the first time it dawned on me that perhaps I seemed more suspicious to the Mesoses than they did to me; after all, living in an isolated world backed against a jungle known to be the hideout of marauding bandits, they had every reason for doubt as to my true purpose. Had I not also come with no food, like a *chiclero*, with only a pair of sandals, and had I not snooped about and shown an uncommon interest in the sacred houses of the dwarfs? Also, with my scraggy beard and by now rather dirty clothes, I felt that I could not myself have been such a confidence-inspiring person.

Sensing all this, I launched myself into a long and involved explanation that I was not a *chiclero* or a *bandito* but just traveling down the coast to take photographs, and that I was interested in the ruins because they were very important to certain people back in Mexico City. I soon realized that my audience knew nothing about photography and as for the importance to Mexico City of the crumbled houses of the little men, this seemed to make me look more suspicious to them than ever.

I was in some manner saved by a man whom we spotted coming up the beach from the south. To my relief it proved to be Miguel, and I realized that today must have been some sort of prearranged visiting day. Miguel greeted me with great enthusiasm and was evidently as pleased to see me again as I was to see him. I immediately told him that I had to leave Puha and go on foot to Tulum and that I needed his help. Could he, I asked, take me down and help to carry my bags? Miguel hesitated and the idea did not seem to thrill him at all; on the contrary, he began to formulate some kind of excuse which I cut short by suggesting that I would pay for his services. This rather mercenary attitude of mine had no effect on him whatsoever. "It is very bad to walk," he said, "*pura piedra* [all stone] and there is the *caleta* of Yalcou, and one has to go deep into the *monte*."

But Miguel finally agreed to go. "I can take you part of the way to a *cocal* called Akumal," he said. "There you will have to find someone to go farther south." We therefore agreed that Miguel would, on his return that night to Ak, take my large henequen bag, and that the next morning, with my other bag, I would join him at Ak and he would take me down the coast through the jungle and around the lagoon to the next *cocal*. From there on I felt I would have to rely on luck.

Among the four men at Puha conversation was very active as they exchanged news in Mayan. The Mayan language, with which I was already familiar, is nearly always spoken softly and well reflects the reserve of the Mayan Indians. It is furthermore spoken with an abundance of hand gestures but these are unlike the dramatic gestures of Italians (or most Europeans), for the Mayans use small, restrained movements, the most common being to move the hands gently before one's neck, palms facing outward. It was quite a sight to see these men speak and hear their strange language, the only direct legacy from those who had once been the mighty rulers of Quintana Roo. How much modern Yucatán could envy the ancient Mayas. What had once been a thriving coast, with innumerable ports such as Yochac, Puha, Puerto Chile, and Ak, was now nothing more than jungle and occasional isolated palm huts.

Being curious about the lives of *chicleros*, I got Miguel to talk to me about his experiences.

The subject was apparently a good one, for soon Señor Mesos, Miguel, and the other men began telling of the deeds of *chicleros* and of their own experiences, of murders committed by their colleagues, and of the bloody orgies at the great chicle camps such as Leona Vicario (the god-forsaken corrugated-iron inferno I had passed through on my way by bus to Puerto Juarez).

To my horror I was soon to realize that the worst tales told about the *chicleros* were true.

Apparently the chicle areas of Quintana Roo, which are situated behind the coast from Tulum up to Cape Catoche, are exploited by several companies, but for the *chicleros* the two most important companies are two clans of *chicleros* who are constantly at war with each other. For the first time I heard mentioned the name of the famed El Cawamo, the former leader of one of these gangs (*cawamo* being the big-headed turtle); the other leader, and Cawamo's deadly opponent, was called ironically "La Tortuga" (the tortoise). Listening to the conversation, I learned that El Cawamo had finally come to his death three years ago. This man, whose life was spent in searching out isolated *chicleros* of the rival gang and killing them to steal their chicle, had finally been caught up with at Ak. There the men of La Tortuga pounced on him, and sticking a dagger through his jaw, had dragged him all the way up to the *caleta* of Yochac, more than twelve miles, and had thrown him into a boat that had taken him off to Cozumel. He was murdered the following day in prison. Listening to the conversation, I soon began to realize that in the *monte* there were *chicleros* who would make any Chicago gangster seem like a timid child. The law among *chicleros* is to shoot upon the slightest provocation and to finish off one's enemy with machete blows.

When I ventured to ask whether such violence was now disappearing, I received the disturbing information that it still went on. Apparently in January, three months before I had come to Puha, Señor Mesos had found on the beach the body of a *chiclero* with thirty dagger thrusts in it, and to quote the calm account of Señora Mesos, "the poor man took eight hours to die; each time he breathed a great squirt of blood would rise in the air." All this seemed quite normal, for apparently he had offended someone, a few years before, and his murderer had sworn to get his life.

I was to hear many more blood-curdling stories of attacks and murderous brawls—especially those of Leona Vicario, where the *chicleros* would get drunk on Saturday evenings after getting paid toward the end of the chicle season. Following these bloody nights of drinking and dancing there would invariably be two or three cadavers lined up outside of the central hut of Leona Vicario. Apparently now there was less chicle business and murders, while frequent, would not exceed one a week at the chicle camps; as for the settlement of personal quarrels in the jungle, nobody could give any figures as to how many died while on the search for chicle. I was to have all these stories confirmed later on by the man who had headed the camp at Leona Vicario.

It was impossible for me at Puha to believe all I heard about the *chicleros'* deeds. Had not the men there been *chicleros* themselves, I would have laughed off all their stories as tall tales. For in fact to believe the deeds of the *chicleros,* one had to understand their morality and code—their world in which death is always present and survival is only possible at the cost of someone else's life. To the *chiclero,* death is but sport, and commonplace. A word, a foul expression, anything, in their eyes is enough justification to take a human life. If these men are violent, they nevertheless are in many ways good men. Such was the case of Miguel, of Señor Mesos's brother's helper, and many more *chicleros* I was to meet, men who for the most part had the deaths of two or three men on their hands, but never on their consciences. Listening to the men as they spoke at Puha, I recalled the wild brawls at Tepoztlán when the Indians had drawn knives at the first provocation. The *chicleros* were but the worst of many, a school of cutthroats hardened by the fight for survival in the jungle, where their foes were not only nature but every man who could not be counted a sure friend.

However fascinating the conversation was that afternoon, I nevertheless came out of it wiser as to the stuff that made *chicleros,* and also most of the *cocaleros.* And I learned my first lesson, which was in the near future to save my life: never speak loudly in front of a *chiclero* and never, when speaking, touch a gun or a machete.

That evening I saw with mixed sentiments my henequen bag disappear down the beach on the back of Miguel, my friend and a murderer. Tomorrow I planned to leave at dawn. . . .

V

Cocals and *Chicleros*

When I got up the following day to leave for the journey south the sun had not yet risen. Señora Mesos was awake and kindly gave me for the trip two dozen tortillas which she had prepared and a cluster of premature turtle eggs. A stiff breeze blew from the east over the sea and the rustling of the palm trees mingled with the rumbling of the reef. In the grim light that preceded the rising of the sun I picked my way along the beach. The sand where it was dry was so soft that each step became quite difficult. I therefore chose to walk along the shiny border of the beach wet by the sea. In the eerie light I came upon the ghastly remains of the turtle we had killed three days before; the *zopilotes* had already picked it clean and the skull was but one shiny mass with two dark holes for eyes. At the end of the beach I penetrated the edge of the jungle, following the sea a few yards inland, thus avoiding both the pointed and treacherous rocks of the coast and the denser vegetation that grew farther back in from the sea. As I walked on I could see through the leaves the hot tropical sun slowly emerging above the horizon. I hurried on, knowing that in a few hours it would be unbearable.

That morning I felt exceedingly lonely walking along a strange coast in the midst of nowhere. How remote I felt from the throb of civilization, from the masses who rise to the sound of alarm clocks

to be swallowed by the crowds in public transportation and carried
away to a day's work in an office. A world far away, and yet one
with which I still felt faintly akin.

To my right, from the blackness of the undergrowth, came
strange noises, each one startling me as I walked on, my sandals
crunching on the rocks and stones of the ground. Every now and
again I would startle a large spider-like land crab that would dart
away in a flash, frightened and leaving me even more frightened.
As I concentrated on where to put my feet I became more and
more afraid of snakes. Could I see them? What were my chances
of stepping on one? I had heard so much of the deadly *barba
amarilla* (the yellow beard), a small coral snake only fifteen inches
long whose venom gives its victim less than fifteen minutes to die
in terrible agony. The name alone brought to my mind frightening
visions. There was also the *quatro narices* (the four-nostril snake),
equally terrible. But I soon became tired of worrying about snakes
and started taking a more reasonable and philosophical attitude
toward them.

A particular phenomenon about walking that has always struck
me is that it makes one's mind work madly, and that morning every
step became a thought, a hope, an observation, a quandary, a question. Would I find Miguel? What if he had decided to steal my bag?
What if he did not like me after all? I was at his mercy; no one
would ever bother to look for me here. But fortunately, that early
morning on my way to Ak, I did not yet know what lay before me.
For that morning was to be the first of the forty days' walking that
was going to take me slowly south all the way to British Honduras
by foot through the endless jungle, marshes, lagoons, and beaches
that form the strangest coast in Central America, the one whose
name Ball by accident had had printed in blue ink and Gothic
lettering to bolster my enthusiasm. I had been innocent to trust
Ball, but not half as innocent as I had been to believe that I could
reach Belize in a week. Belize was to be the elusive goal; between
Puha and Belize stretched more than a month of unknown adven-

ture and fear, a world from which I was to emerge another self.

The sun was already high when, exhausted, I reached the end of the beach of Ak. From where I had emerged from the jungle I could see the seemingly endless rows of coconut trees forming a dark outline on the beach, and in the center of the beach the curious natural jetty, the great rock with its small temple. Would an ancient Maya greet me? I felt somewhat as the first Spanish *conquistadores* must have felt, treading a strange soil, a land so different from all they had known, with a new vegetation, a new climate, and strange people with a culture so elusive, so beyond the occidental register of values. It is quite comprehensible that the Spaniards looked upon the civilization of the New World as the work of the devil. Were not these civilizations so remote from, so foreign to all the standards of the Christian world as to appear demoniac?

It took many years before the Spanish were even ready to admit that the Indians had souls. But it certainly took them less time to discover that they had bodies, and the flag bearers of Christianity were also the messengers of syphilis and of moral corruption that exceeded the worst that had ever existed among the pre-Columbian Indians.

When I arrived at Miguel's hut he was cooking for himself, in clumsy bachelor fashion, a morning meal of some rather revolting fish stew; he had also made some stupid-looking tortillas the size of a phonograph record and about half an inch thick. His warm smile put me at ease, and seeing my perspiration, he went to cut down a coconut and opened it for me. Side by side we sat drinking and eating facing the sea. I took this opportunity to look Miguel over. He was a tall man, as Indians go; it was only much later that I realized from a photograph that he was so very much smaller than I. His body was one bundle of iron-hard muscle, his chest a barrel of strength. Also, looking at a photograph of him later, I saw that he had a face so frightening in its Indian beauty, in its piercing eyes, that I would have shuddered had I met such a man in an alley of some civilized town. But at Ak on the sand of the beach, with his back to the jungle and his eyes on the sea, he seemed most handsome with his copper features, his eyelids hewn as if by the chisel of a sculptor, his high cheekbones cut out as if by brute force, and his long elegant nose rising without indentation up his slanted forehead. Being young, he intrigued me, so that I tried to imagine his thoughts and how he reacted to the things that we both saw.

But I was not able to understand the mind of a Maya, the mind of the people whom I came to think of as the silent people. For I learned rapidly that the Mayas are a silent folk; they maintain a silence that is often unbearable to us loquacious foreigners, to extrovert Latins, to voluble Saxons, a silence that in the Mayas is not only oral but sentimental and philosophical, a silence full of much thought and to me of much mystery. Later, in the Far East, I was to become familiar with the silence of the Orient, the negative silence of the Chinese, of one who does not talk because he does not want to speak. And if it may sound trite to want to define silence, I nevertheless can state that that of the Maya is distinct, a silence that I hoped I would soon be able to understand. An economy of words also characterized Miguel, and like most Indians he did not feel the European necessity to comment on his actions. He omitted such phrases as "Let's go here," "Have a drink," "Come along," "Wait a minute," and all those other remarks that we perpetually make, expecting no answer, but speaking as if to clarify our actions, to consolidate orally decisions of our minds. Miguel, for one, just acted; when he spoke his sentences were precise, acute, and always meaningful.

Soon he finished eating and when he rose his only word was "Kohosh," the first word of the Mayan language that I was to learn. "Kohosh" simply meant "come"; how many times I heard it repeated I do not know, but those strange syllables soon became familiar, only too familiar, and meant in my mind that the path had not ended, that we had still farther to go. In silence Miguel went to pick up my henequen bag, and attaching a rough henequen strap around it he thrust it on his shoulders, passing the strap over his forehead. Seeing that I was clumsily lugging my flight bag, he stopped and helped me with the aid of a piece of rag to tie it so that I too could carry its weight on my forehead. To my surprise this method of carrying took all the weight from the load and enabled me to advance with my hands free to keep my balance, and in greater comfort.

Two miles farther south we left the *cocal* of Ak and made our way along the rocky coast. The water from the sea had so eaten away the gray coral stones that they were one rough spiny surface riddled with holes like a cheese. To fall meant to tear one's skin on the jagged edges of the rock. Occasionally erosion had drilled deep holes; one had to take great care to avoid stepping in them, for their sharp edges would have snapped a leg in a second. How far and where exactly we were going I could not tell, and to my inquiries I got as answer only the number of *leguas* (leagues)— three *leguas*. Someone has told me that a league was two and a half miles, but soon I had to revise this definition, a *legua* in Quintana Roo being a very variable unit of length, for it is taken for the distance that can be walked in an hour and varies according to the terrain and the speed at which one walks. Three *leguas* seemed interminable. And in fact it took us four and a half hours to walk to Akumal.

After one hour of walking we reached the edge of a lagoon that through the rocks made its way inland among high mangroves. This was the *caleta* of Yalcou. We could no longer proceed along the coast, and Miguel, taking out his machete, started hacking out a path into the dense mangroves. Progress was very slow and the march made more difficult by the fact that we walked ankle-deep in a warm, slimy, hot mud. We had gone around three hundred yards in this fashion when Miguel, climbing halfway up a fallen tree, pointed out to me the four walls of a crumbling ruin sticking up above the mangroves—another small testimonial of the ancient Mayas. For the first time it struck me that after all the Spanish *conquistadores* had not had such a hard time.

Was not the land then a large thriving community? At least they had the ancient Mayan trails to walk on, and what was now but barren expanses of jungle was then a succession of towns and villages where water and probably food and shelter were available. As for us, we had only the machete with which to advance. I admired the regularity of stroke with which Miguel wielded his machete, root after root, palm after palm, endlessly falling before it as we made our way slowly to the noise of the blows and the rustle of the falling branches.

An hour or so later, after much hacking and little progress, we came out again onto the edge of the lagoon; like a turquoise river, it made its way ever deeper inland. Soon we were walking on a barren, pitted rock surface. To my surprise we were on a natural bridge, walking on a thin crust of limestone riddled by the sea. On all sides stood clear pools of brilliant blue water where the limestone crust had crumbled. All these pools connected with each other underground in a network of small sea-water *cenotes*. This I learned was the kingdom of the manatee, the strange tropical seal-like animal that has often been considered an ugly ancestor of the mermaid. The manatee, the size of a large walrus, is hunted still today by the Indians for food; its flesh is said to be better than pork; its hard and thick skin is used for making whips and leather cords. A legend goes that a man never recovers from a blow given with a manatee-leather whip. But no matter how hard I looked into the clear blue pools that seethed with bright fish, I could not see the famed manatee.

The sun was by now coming down with full force upon our backs as we made our way over the rocks among the pools of the *caleta*.

It was with delight that we entered after a while the cool shadow of the jungle, again cutting a path through the vines and palms, our feet bathing in putrid mud and our heads pestered by swarms

of mosquitoes that took advantage of the immobility of our faces
to sting us. For if we had our hands free, we could not move our
necks, the straps of our loads keeping our heads pinned down.
Miguel did not seem to be excessively bothered by the mosquitoes,
but at each step I rubbed my hand over my face in an attempt to
scare away the insects.

Toward one or two o'clock we at last reached the open sea again
and plodded on along a sandy beach, coming up to familiar coconut groves. We had arrived at Akumal. We eventually came upon
three palm huts set on the beach and enclosed by a wooden
stockade. Making the characteristic "U-ugh," Miguel got a reply
from within the stockade. and a half-caste Indian of small size
came forward and opened the gate. Exhausted, having walked
eight hours since dawn, I sat down to rest, asking Miguel for a
coconut. This refreshed me and I set about seeing whether I could
stay at Akumal for the night. But Miguel had other plans, and
chatting away in Mayan, he arranged for someone to accompany
me farther down the coast. After having refused any form of
gratuity, Miguel left, hurrying up the beach on his way back to
Ak. I thus found myself alone with the man of Akumal. Offering
me no food, he made me wait while his tiny, beautiful Indian wife,
dressed in a *huipiles*, prepared him some tortillas. Rising at last,
the man, who was called Rufino, explained that he was going to
take me to the southern end of his *cocal*. There, some two miles
away, lived four workers whom he employed gathering copra.
One of these he thought might be able to accompany me farther
down the coast.

Carrying all my bags with great difficulty, I followed Rufino
down the beach that bordered his *cocal*, under the shade of the
coconut groves.

As we were proceeding in silence we suddenly heard a distant
noise that soon became louder. Rufino stopped and we listened;
the noise was now quite audible, the voice of someone shouting.
It became louder and louder till somebody running came into view

from the far end of the *cocal*. As he drew nearer, still shouting madly, I could see it was an Indian.

Panting and covered with perspiration, the Indian muttered something in Mayan to Rufino, and before I could realize what was happening Rufino turned around and ran off up the coast, leaving me stranded with the exhausted and apparently angry Indian.

I immediately realized that something was wrong, and for a moment I wondered whether I had not better leave my bags and run after Rufino.

I was even more frightened when a few minutes later Rufino returned, running madly, with a shotgun in his hand. Without a word of explanation he shot straight down past us and disappeared among the coconut trees.

Turning toward the Indian for an explanation, I realized that he hardly spoke Spanish, and at first I could make no sense of what he was trying to tell me, beyond the fact that he was called Benanzio and was, as he repeated proudly, from Chan Santa Cruz.

I had heard enough of the *Indios sublevados* to be wary of my unexpected companion. To my pleasure though, I noted that he was unarmed, not even having a machete.

He had now stopped panting and I began to understand what was going on. Apparently three of the workers who had recently been hired by Rufino, along with Benanzio, had been robbers and had just stolen from Benanzio not only his shotgun but, worst of all, his machete. Rufino had just begun a manhunt and had set off down the coast in an attempt to catch the fleeing robbers and give the alarm to the *cocal* farther down the coast.

I soon gathered that the three robbers were none other than the men who had crossed over from Cozumel on the *Lydia* with me. They had asked for work at Akumal and apparently wasted no time in making off with all they could lay their hands on. I had not been wrong in thinking the three passengers of the *Lydia* were blackguards. And I thanked heaven that I had not spent the night with them in the kitchen at Puha; they had left at dawn and would probably have stolen my things if I had slept near them.

Benanzio picked up my two bags and, swearing gently at the men who had taken his machete, made his way along with me down the beach.

Walking before me, bent in two under my load, he trudged ahead through the soft sand and then along the rocky coast. Two hours later we arrived at another *cocal.* There we found the man of Akumal with his shotgun, speaking to another man. Apparently the three robbers had been seen passing through two hours ahead of us, and the manhunt, I thought, was abandoned. The man of Akumal decided to return to his *cocal,* leaving me with Benanzio. We were at a *cocal* called Matanceros, and upon inquiring about ruins I was told that there was none but that there was at the *cocal* a *tesoro* (treasure) and a house that had belonged to pirates.

Intrigued by this, I asked to be led to the pirate house and soon was contemplating yet another small square Mayan oratory set back ten yards from the sea. It was still in good condition. I immediately thought that as at Puerto Chile and the other points I had seen, if there was a structure on the beach there would certainly be some more in the *monte* a few miles inland. But when I asked if that was so, I could get only a negative answer and a repeated statement that the Mayan hut on the beach was a pirate hideout. As if to prove this, the man from Matanceros waded into the water, joined by Benanzio. For a moment, knee-deep in the sea, the two men bent over as if groping for something. Soon, after considerable tugging and hauling, a black mass started to show above the water. Little by little a long object looking like a log appeared, alternately covered and uncovered by the light swell that ran up onto the rocks of the cove in which stood the small Mayan ruin. Wading into the water, to my amazement I realized that the long thinnish object was nothing less than an old cannon. In a last effort the two men managed to slide it onto a rock, where it rested, its muzzle sticking out of the sea and occasionally spouting water. It was an amazing sight and at first I could not believe my eyes, as I stared at the watery cannon insolently pointing toward the shore.

About four feet long, the barrel was covered with seaweed and a rusty green color. Judging from the size of the bore compared to the diameter of the barrel, the cannon must have been very old. When I hopefully asked if there were more such cannon, I was told that nine others could be seen on the bottom of the sea in calm weather just a few yards from the shore. The existence of the cannon explained the story of the treasure and the belief that the Mayan structure had once been the refuge of pirates.

For an instant I imagined myself discovering some long-lost treasure, as I hopefully thought that the galleon that had wrecked upon the barren coast of Quintana Roo many hundreds of years ago had been carrying gold from Peru to Spain.

The *cocalero* of Matanceros, when I questioned him about the treasure, went on to say that he had searched the area without success, although he believed that someone in Cozumel had a map that showed its location. He also told me that three pirate treasures had already been found either in Cozumel or on the Quintana Roo coast. He went so far as to swear to me that a Captain Canto, the owner of a boat that had sunk in Chetumal bay, had many years earlier discovered a chest full of diamonds, and that to this day Captain Canto wore on his finger a diamond ring from that treasure chest.

Alone, there was unfortunately little that I could do but take photographs of the cannon and the temple. After I passed through Matanceros an expedition was set up to dive to the wreck, which after considerable difficulty was identified as a Spanish trading ship that had foundered on the coast in the late eighteenth century. The ship had been partly salvaged the year after it sank, but the expedition was able to find some remains of the cargo, among which were numerous brass crosses. The ship had been called *Nuestra Señora de Matanceros*, the last part of its name having remained to designate the spot on the coast where it had sunk.

The location of the wreck, I found out later, had in fact been determined through research by the brilliant young American diver Bob Marx, who during my trip down the coast was actually in Cozumel, preparing the expedition to the wreck.

After drinking another coconut I started off again with Benanzio down the coast. Toward five o'clock my guide stopped and informed me that he was going back, and that I could proceed alone. He told me that less than a *legua* down the coast I would find a *cocal* called Xcassel and could sleep there, as he wanted to return to Akumal before nightfall. Frightened at the idea of going alone, I nevertheless had little choice. Before Benanzio left, having learned that I was going to Tankah, he urged me to visit his village in the jungle. He assured me that I would be most welcome and asked me to go there and see his brother, Pablo Canche, to whom he would like me to give a message saying that he would soon be coming to the village. Having no intention of going inland any distance, I said anyway that I would try my best to give this message. Little did I realize that Benanzio had given me an introduction to one of the remotest villages of Quintana Roo, one of the last strongholds of the *Indios sublevados,* the feared and renowned *Indios de Chan Santa Cruz.*

It was close to six o'clock when I stumbled along the wide beach of the *cocal* of Xcassel. There were three huts, one completely demolished and two in fair condition. There I found two men who lived with three women; of pure Indian stock, none of them to my dismay spoke Spanish, and judging from their expressions on seeing me they must have considered me a man from Mars. After a small pantomime I managed to explain I was dead thirsty and wanted to spend the night at their *cocal.*

An old woman speaking Mayan and attempting to tell me something finally gave me, in a calabash bowl, some rather grim-looking water. I hesitated to drink it, fearing amoebae, but on the other hand, it being obvious that I was drinking from the communal bowl, I dared not put into the water any of my disinfectant pills.

Being exhausted from about twelve hours' walking I just could not bother, but drank the water, and set about hanging my hammock and mosquito net in the old rundown hut on the beach. By the light of a small candle that I had with me I wrote my entries for the day in my diary. I must have walked close to twenty-five miles, I guessed. All was silent around me save the occasional voices of my hosts chatting in Mayan. That night I wondered whether I would not be attacked and imagined my hosts pouncing on me to rid me of my bags. I did not yet know that, because of the immutable rules of hospitality, when I was in someone's house no harm whatsoever could happen to me.

I dozed off to the idea of being murdered in my sleep. Toward midnight I fell right out of the hammock in fright. All was dark around me and a hand was pulling at my hammock. I at once felt for my knife, when a voice in Spanish coming from the dark repeated, *"Levanta te, vamos a Tankah"* (Get up, we're going to Tankah). Half asleep, I could not understand what was happening and for a moment I thought I must be dreaming or dead. Then a light came near and I saw that the person who had awakened me was the man from Akumal. What did he want, I wondered. Awake, I understood. Rufino had gone back to get a mule and was now continuing his hunt for the robbers whom he had chased in vain that morning. He had traveled by night from Akumal and on arriving at Xcassel had heard I was sleeping there and now offered to take me down to Tankah.

Still only half awake, I packed my bags which were fastened onto a small white mule. Then to my disappointment the man from Akumal, Rufino, climbed on the mule and, giving me his kerosene lantern, asked me to take the bridle and made me lead the way. Thus like Sancho Panza in the middle of the night, carrying a lantern, I advanced leading Don Quixote, although there seemed to me something drastically wrong; during the five long and painful hours of the forced march that night I could not help feeling that with my being six feet tall and having a scraggy beard I should have been on the mule, while the chubby Señor Rufino would certainly have made a perfect Sancho.

I soon discovered that if it is one thing to walk along the coast and in the jungle by day it is an entirely different thing to do the same by night. The kerosene lamp barely lit the ground, and although there was now a narrow path down the coast that followed the beaches or cut the rocky points through the jungle, I nonetheless stumbled at each step. The eerie light of the lamp made the shadows of the palms dance about before me and I imagined a thousand wild beasts and snakes ready to pounce on me. Having already walked for twelve hours the day before and only slept a few hours at Xcassel, I was so weary that I must have fallen half asleep during that long walk. For I remember little more than the moving shadows, the endless green tunnel lit by the lamp and the darkness beyond the circle of light, darkness from which occasionally emerged the head of a mule that on more occasions than one had to nudge me on. What I do remember is that five hours later, having made not a single stop, and dying with thirst, I emerged into a *cocal* as the sun was beginning to rise in a flamboyant display of colors over the sea. It must have been five in the morning. We had at last arrived at Tankah. In twenty-four hours I had walked forty miles and done in one full day what should have taken three.

I now felt relieved; from here, I thought, I could pursue my journey by boat and would soon be in Belize, after the short intermezzo of eight days living the life of a *cocalero* and finding ancient Mayan temples. Already I dreamed of hot coffee, ice-cold drinks, and all the other small amenities that are what civilization really boils down to. I was soon to be disappointed.

After the barrenness of the coast I had seen and the primitive simplicity of Puha, Tankah with its stone house, two tin-roofed sheds, and four palm huts certainly seemed already like civilization.

Everyone was asleep when we arrived, but the mad barking of a watchdog soon attracted attention, and after a short while, half asleep and half dressed, a man emerged from the square flat-roofed stone house. It was Señor Jorge Gonzales, better known as Don Jorge.

In a few words Rufino explained why he had come. And Don Jorge said that he had in fact seen the three bandits the preceding evening and that they had asked for work on the *cocal*, but he had refused and sent them away. The criminal matter being more or less settled and the robbers left alone to pursue their route of pillage, Don Jorge turned to me in surprise, asking me what on earth I was doing along the coast. He had seen many foreigners at Tankah who had come by boat from Cozumel, but he had never seen a man arrive by land. And he seemed rather suspicious of me until I could tell him what had been my plans and why I had come this way.

Don Jorge, after listening, heartily welcomed me to his house, offering me some hot coffee to drink. A tall, slim, and rather elegant man, Don Jorge was one of four Gonzales brothers—another was Pepe, to whom Alberto Ruz l'Huillier had given me a letter—who owned the *cocal* of Tankah. Each brother would in turn come and spend three months a year at the *rancho* with his family to look after the coconut plantation and the *chiclero* station that they ran during the chicle season.

Don Jorge had some bad news in store for me; there would not be another boat in at Tankah for at least a month, one having just arrived a few days before with a group of *chicleros* and stores. Furthermore, the boat that would come in a month or so would be going to Cozumel. "There are never boats to Belize that stop here and the only thing you could possibly do is stay here and wait to return to Cozumel." That idea suited me even less than it did Don Jorge.

But that morning I was too tired to think of what my next move would be, and with the permission of Don Jorge I hung my hammock up in one of his storerooms and fell asleep.

When I awoke it was close to midday, and outside the dark shed the sun shone with all its force on Tankah. Getting up, to my horror I noticed that my feet had swollen to the size of small canoes. And it was with great pain that I shuffled over to the main stone house where Don Jorge and his family lived. Seeing my feet, Señora Gonzales gave me some ointment which soon reduced their size to normal, although they remained cut and scratched and badly infected where the thick leather strands of my sandals had rubbed them.

After having a simple lunch which seemed like a banquet after my diet of turtle eggs, I set about trying to solve my predicament with Don Jorge. As he had mentioned before, there was no hope of a boat calling before one month. Further, the rainy season having begun, the small airstrip at Tankah was closed, and no planes could be expected to land. Don Jorge then suggested that he could call Mérida by radio and have them notify Cozumel from where a boat could be sent, but he warned me that this would be not only expensive but not likely to be successful, since the bad weather that was due with the beginning of the rainy season could well stop all boats from crossing the one narrow entrance in the reef that gave access to Tankah. He encouragingly told me that sometimes the *brecha*, as it is called, was closed for months on end.

There was virtually no solution, unless I was prepared to wait and providing Don Jorge was ready to extend me hospitality for a month or more. And even though a boat should come to bring me to Cozumel I would still have to go to Belize or admit defeat and make my way back to Mérida.

That evening in my hammock I reviewed the events of the preceding days and the general outlook for the future. Not wanting to accept defeat, I decided to get to Belize at any cost. I made up my mind. I would go on foot.

The next morning when I revealed my plan to Don Jorge he simply stated that I was mad.

"Do you realize," he said, "that it is more than two hundred miles down to Belize? There are no paths whatsoever, and no inhabitants."

"But what about Vigía Chico?" I said, pointing to a small port marked on my map as being at the bottom of Ascensión bay. From Don Jorge I learned that Vigía Chico had been completely destroyed by hurricane Janet, along with the few *cocals* that lay to the south of Tankah. Anyway, as Don Jorge remarked, Vigía Chico had only been an abandoned depot with three thatched huts. As for the small mule-drawn *plataforma* railroad that led from Vigía Chico inland to Chan Santa Cruz, it had also disappeared many years ago. I then discovered that my map was not only wrong but also fifty years old. Such places as Puerto Madero had never existed; furthermore, since the publication of my map the *Indios sublevados* had destroyed—in 1915—the town of Chan Santa Cruz.

Don Jorge then went on to tell me some of the facts about the much-feared *Indios sublevados* and their amazing history.

In 1847, in the Yucatán peninsula, the war known as the War of the Castes had broken out. This was a rebellion of the Mayas against the Mexicans. To the cry of "Perish the whites," the Indians, no longer able to stand the infamous treatment they had been subjected to, rose against their masters.

The revolt began in what is now Quintana Roo and rapidly spread through the entire peninsula. In those times Quintana Roo was relatively well populated, there being a fair number of small villages and large haciendas in the now barren Territorio Federal.

In ever-increasing numbers, the Indians marched north, killing all the Mexicans they met. They successfully attacked the town of Peto, situated on the border of Yucatán state and Quintana Roo. Strengthened by this victory, the Indians carried farther north their frightening crusade of vengeance, and as they progressed all the natives abandoned the haciendas and joined the rebellion. The Indians attacked Valladolid, then one of the most important towns of the Yucatán peninsula. After a short but bloody siege, they stormed the city, killing the Mexicans mercilessly. The *Indios sublevados* now marched on Mérida, inflicting defeat after defeat on the Mexicans in their way. It seemed that nothing could stop them and that a terrible massacre would wipe the Mexican intruders from the face of the Yucatán peninsula. The descendants of the ancient Mayas were about to reconquer their land. Yucatán would be the first American territory to return to its rightful owners. Siege was laid by the Indians on Mérida; the Mexicans' position was desperate.

When all was apparently lost a strange thing happened. As Mérida was about to give in, the Mexicans saw, before their eyes, the Indians leaving; on the verge of victory they were slowly retreating.

The sudden withdrawal of the Mayas was no god-sent miracle to save the ruthless Mexicans, but the result of the irresistible call that the Indians felt at the approach of the planting season. As had been traditional with the ancient Mayas, the Indians disbanded, for as all of them knew, "There is a time for war and a time to battle for food." The rebellious Indians still respected this tradition, even when at the point of being victorious at last over their invaders. The fact that the Mayas respected a strict law regarding warfare which the Mexicans ignored was the reason why the Spaniards had been able to conquer them in the first place. (Yet the Spanish conquest of the Mayas took nearly two hundred years, the last of the ancient Mayas surrendering in Guatemala only in 1696, after having fought the Spaniards since 1519.) Now again the Indian custom was to be the salvation of the Mexican Yucatecans, for after the sudden and unexpected withdrawal of the rebel Indian forces, the Mexicans slowly regained control over what is now Yucatán state.

The rebellious Indians still controlled Quintana Roo and in no way gave up their claim to independence. Three years after their strange retreat the first of the Indian talking crosses appeared. In a clearing in the jungle a cross carved in the trunk of a mahogany tree began miraculously to speak. It urged the Indians to take up arms again against the Mexicans.

The speaking cross was to have a strange and long-lasting influence. It stood in a spot known as Chan, which later became the site of the village of Chan Santa Cruz, the town that was, until quite recently, the capital of the rebellious Indians.

Before the arrival of Cortez the ancient Mayas had had a considerable number of "speaking idols," which like the oracle of Delphi counseled all those who came to ask advice of them. This explains the considerable success of the speaking cross of Chan, and why the Indians—who became known as the Chan Santa Cruz Indians—readily responded to its exhortations to war.

The original speaking cross was soon replaced by three crosses, which became the objects of a special religious cult. Placed in a sort of temple, the crosses had their guardians and military chiefs. The talking crosses were masterminded and operated by a revolutionary half-caste Indian called José Maria Barrera, who used an Indian called Manuel Nahuat (a ventriloquist) to speak for him. These crosses spoke in Mayan, and even sent messages to the British government ordering it to furnish the Indians with arms to fight the Mexicans. Thus for fifty years the Chan Santa Cruz Indians reigned as masters over the whole of Quintana Roo, signing treaties with British Honduras and governing their small domain. Toward 1895 they requested that Quintana Roo be annexed to British Honduras, and the British took this request up with the Mexican government. The Mexicans curtly refused, and immediately decided to send an expeditionary corps to reconquer Quintana Roo.

Thus began the second sequence of the incredible history of the rebellious Mayas, the feared *Indios sublevados* who today still consider themselves as the sole rulers of Quintana Roo.

In 1899, under President Porfirio Díaz, the Mexican government named General Ignacio A. Bravo to go and conquer the Chan Santa Cruz Indians, who were a blot on Mexico's pride and unity.

General Bravo was a hotheaded Mexican and a character worthy of an operetta. Arrayed in a gold-trimmed uniform, he heroically set out to conquer the last rebellious Mayas.

Heading south with a small army, he left Mérida for Quintana Roo. But what must have appeared to General Bravo as a simple military excursion against a band of primitive Indians turned out to be an entirely different matter, for his soldiers had to battle their way not so much against the rebellious Indians as against the thick malaria-infested jungles.

For three years the Mexican force, led by their operatic leader in his now not so gilded uniform, pushed slowly forward into the jungle inferno of Quintana Roo, harassed incessantly by the well-armed and elusive soldiers of Chan Santa Cruz.

Exhausted, the Mexican troops finally entered the abandoned town of Chan Santa Cruz. In appearance General Bravo was victorious, and the Mexican flag for a short while flew above the ruins of the town, which was modestly renamed Santa Cruz de Bravo. But renaming Chan Santa Cruz was not a sure sign of victory, and to his horror General Bravo realized that he now stood encircled by the rebellious Indians and isolated from central Mexico by impenetrable jungle. He and his soldiers could only lick their wounds and care for their thousands of malaria cases, while the hostile Indians waited all around them.

General Bravo was not defeated, but now he was a prisoner within the capital of the rebellious Indians.

The Indians were led by a man later known as General Mayo. The powerful commander of the Mayan forces, General Mayo was chief in the true ancient Mayan tradition. Feared and respected by his men, he knew his superiority over General Bravo. And in no way did he hurry into a head-on battle, but simply looked on as every day General Bravo's position became more and more intolerable.

While the Indians surrounded General Bravo, he set about fortifying and rebuilding Santa Cruz. His first concern was to open a road to the outside world in order to get provisions. This he managed to do by forcing a passage through the jungle to the sea at the bottom of Ascensión bay. Thus was founded Vigía Chico.

With communication to the sea, it looked as if General Bravo's position was on the mend and that after all he might prove to be the conquistador he had imagined himself to be. But soon he was to learn differently. To begin with, his troops were perpetually attacked, and more often than not his road to the coast was cut by the Indians.

It also appears that General Bravo was mildly mad; within his "prison city" he had his malaria-stricken troops parade every day to the music of an old band. One day General Bravo's son, having ordered the band to play without his father's permission, was killed on the spot by the General. It is not surprising that many of the General's troops deserted him, fleeing into the jungle, where most of them were immediately killed by the Chan Santa Cruz Indians. The only reinforcements General Bravo could get were criminals, and Santa Cruz de Bravo became a penal colony.

In 1911 President Porfirio Díaz resigned, and with the Mexican revolution, General Bravo was relieved of his command. His successor, faced with an uncontrollable situation, having to command a territory run by hostile, rebellious Indians and infested by ruthless criminals, finally had to give Santa Cruz de Bravo back to the Indians.

In 1915 the Chan Santa Cruz Indians entered their capital again, dynamiting the buildings that the Mexicans had constructed there. Once more the Mayas held Quintana Roo. And General Mayo was recognized officially as the leader of the rebellious Indians.

The Indians carried on as an independent state, dealing occasionally with British Honduras. They even went so far as to negotiate wood concessions to British firms in their territory. And if the British are known as shrewd businessmen, so were the Santa Cruz Indians. On one particular occasion they authorized a British company to cut mahogany trees in their territory, asking as payment a levy of one peso per tree cut. The British firm proceeded to build a small-gauge railroad to haul out the logs they intended to cut. When the railroad was finished the Chan Santa Cruz Indians pointed out there was no provision in the contract for the felling of trees to make the railroad ties. They therefore claimed breach of contract, asking a one-peso fee for each railroad tie cut. There being many hundreds of thousands of these ties, the company had to withdraw.

Years went by and the Chan Santa Cruz Indians were still masters of Quintana Roo. All foreigners would, if they penetrated the territory, be shot or have to pass before a council headed by General Mayo. When by accident Cozumeleños got shipwrecked or for some other reason landed on the coast, they were automatically killed. This was the case when a boat from Cozumel containing six men and a young boy was wrecked on the coast. The Chan Santa Cruz Indians killed all the men, but one of the Indians, seeing that the child had in his hands various books, spared his life, asking him to stay to teach them how to read and write. They consequently took him to Chan Santa Cruz, their capital. The child, now an old man, is still alive and even today remains a "hostage," although a willing one, of the Indians.

The history of the Chan Santa Cruz Indians does not end with their acquiring their capital again. From 1915 to our day the Indians have virtually run the interior of Quintana Roo. A peace treaty was later signed between Mexico and the famous General Mayo. His soldiers were acknowledged as official troops, and the administrative setup of the Chan Santa Cruz Indians was approved and endorsed by the Mexicans. The Indians remained hostile, although their hostility was greatly weakened by the great chicle boom that hit this area. For a short while this boom changed the character of Quintana Roo. General Mayo profited personally from the chicle boom, since it was he who gave the permissions to companies to exploit the precious latex. In 1935 chicle prices fell and since then the chicle business has much decreased; and Quintana Roo has steadily declined in population.

In the same year (1935) a new effort was made on the part of the Mexican government to settle Quintana Roo, and the authority of General Mayo's associates, the head men of various villages, was officially recognized by the government, who even went so far as to take General Mayo to Mexico City. But poor General Mayo was so dazzled by the modern city, and his primitive innocence was so exploited by the Mexicans, that he had to be literally dragged back to Quintana Roo, where he died in 1952.

With the signing of the peace in 1935, the Mexicans rapidly took advantage of the situation, settling men in Santa Cruz, which was now rebaptized with the less Christian name of Felipe Carrillo Puerto.

The long years of lonely struggle of the Chan Santa Cruz Indians, who, cut off from all civilization, had fought for ninety years to keep their independence, had not been without a heavy toll on their numbers, and famine had caused many to abandon Quintana Roo to seek employment in Mexican Yucatán. As for the remaining Indians, many had died of malaria and other contagious diseases. In 1935, after their final victory, they were not more than ten thousand.

Don Jorge Gonzales went on to explain that when his father had first come to Quintana Roo and started the *cocal* of Tankah he had had to deal all the time with the Chan Santa Cruz Indians, who levied taxes and considered the land their own.

The incredible story of the Chan Santa Cruz Indians, instead of making me change my plans as Don Jorge had intended, made me all the more eager to continue southward. Don Jorge then went on to tell me how since the peace treaty of 1935 the Indians had pursued their independent way of life. With time their numbers had shrunk even further, the true Chan Santa Cruz villages now numbering no more than half a dozen. Closest of these was the village of Tulum, situated some fourteen miles inland from the famous ruins on the coast.

Remembering that Benanzio, the Indian of Akumal, had given me a message for his brother Canche, I told Don Jorge that I would go there, the message seeming a good excuse and introduction. But Don Jorge warned me that I should be most careful, for over the past years the *chicleros* had made the Indians wary of foreigners. At the thought of seeing the last of the *Indios sublevados*, and on hearing that some of the officers of General Mayo still lived in the villages of the coastal area, I was now absolutely determined to go on south by foot.

After my encounters with *chicleros* I felt that the Indians could cause me little or no trouble. My worst problem was how to cross the two swampy bays, Espíritu Santo and Ascensión. In this matter Don Jorge was not able to help me; he had never himself left Tankah and all he knew was that there were, north of Ascensión bay, two *cocals*, and that on the stretch of coast between Ascensión bay and Espíritu Santo bay there was another *cocal*. As to a route farther south, he knew nothing. There had, he said, been a few *cocals* below the Espíritu Santo bay, but these had been completely wiped out by recent hurricanes.

"I doubt," he said, "that you will ever get farther than Ascensión bay. You could of course, providing you find someone to guide you, go inland until you come to Felipe Carrillo Puerto, the one-time Chan Santa Cruz, and from there you would find mule paths that go down to Chetumal. They are now in the process of opening a road from Felipe Carrillo Puerto to Chetumal, a road that eventually should link Chetumal by land with Mérida." But the idea did not appeal to me. For I felt that if I was going to get to Belize on foot I had better go directly instead of making a detour inland.

I now felt sufficiently confident in my walking capacity and in my short experience of the coast to think that if worst came to worst I could always attempt to follow the shoreline, although I then secretly hoped that I could find some Chan Santa Cruz Indians who would be willing to come with me.

Seen from a distance, my decision to push through on foot to Belize was pure folly, and many were those who told me so afterward. But in my mind I felt that if everything did go completely wrong I could always backtrack to Tankah. In a straight line two hundred miles now separated me from Belize, two hundred miles of virgin unexplored territory. I could not help but want to go ahead, for, I thought, if I had already found on the coast four ancient Mayan sites yet unrecorded, how many more could I now discover!

I now also felt that after turtle eggs I could eat anything, and the Indians were sure to have game, which would certainly be better than what I had eaten at the *cocals*.

The following morning, after having purchased from Don Jorge some much-needed mosquito repellent, a few pounds of biscuits, and two dozen packs of cigarettes, I set off in his jeep to the ruins of Tulum. There was a rough but passable road running the length of Don Jorge's *cocal*, and it was in the process of being extended down the coast to another distant coconut plantation of the Gonzaleses. Five miles from Tankah we came upon the edge of the landing strip that had been cut in the jungle behind a bluff that rose above the sea. It was strange to think that this clearing was sufficient to put me in contact with civilization within a few hours, while by land I was cut off by one hundred impenetrable miles of jungle. I felt secretly glad that the rainy season had closed the airstrip, for I would have hated to meet some airlifted tourist when I had paid so dearly to arrive at the ruins of Tulum by foot.

Our modern world is full of such contrasts and it is more than common that primitive and isolated tribes ride in a plane before they even see a bicycle. Virtually nowhere today is one farther than six hours' flight from a large capital, and every day planes fly over deserts in Persia, above the heads of men dying of thirst. In its strange way, Tulum is therefore a most isolated spot, yet close to civilization if one has the means to use the airplane.

Passing the airstrip, Don Jorge told me how Lindbergh had come to Tankah when making an aerial survey of the Quintana Roo coast nearly thirty years ago. He had then landed on the beach in front of Tankah.

It was with mixed sentiments that I said good-by to Don Jorge Gonzales before he drove off, leaving me alone at the foot of the great wall that encircles the city of Tulum. I had been told that at the ruins lived an Indian who had taken shelter in an abandoned lighthouse just beyond the ancient city limits. There I planned to stay the night.

Of all the larger Mayan cities known, Tulum is certainly the strangest and the most awe-inspiring. When the first Spaniards sailed up the coast they compared Tulum with Seville. A frightening sight the city must have been to the Spaniards. For Tulum was the first sign, with the other cities of the coast, that there was anything like a powerful culture on the American continent. Columbus on his voyages had seen only primitive Indians living in huts, and neither Peru nor Aztec Mexico were known when suddenly the Spaniards had spotted the first city of the New World, the city of Tulum, which rises up on the summit of the only cliff on the Quintana Roo coast.

The first city to be seen by the Spaniards was also the last city to belong to their descendants, if one can say that Tulum belongs to the Mexicans even today. For had not Tulum been the last stronghold of the Chan Santa Cruz Indians? Thus for over three hundred years of Spanish and Mexican rule Tulum has stood out as an independent and proud Mayan city. And one can rightly say that Tulum has never been conquered but was ceded by the Mayas in 1935 to the Mexican Government through General Mayo, who died only in 1952.

The archaeological history of Tulum is also a strange one. Tulum was in a fashion rediscovered in March 1842 by Stephens and Catherwood, the two famous founders of Mayan archaeology.

They came to the town by sea five years before the revolt of the Chan Santa Cruz Indians. Then followed a long period of seventy-nine years during which the ruins were visited by no foreigners, being a stronghold of the Chan Santa Cruz Indians. The Indians' hostility prevented the Allison V. Armour Expedition from landing there in 1895, though two sketches were made from its yacht off-shore. The explorers Howe and Parmelee were forced by the Indians to leave after a two-day stay in 1911. Dr. S. G. Morley, with different associates, made daring visits to Tulum in 1913, 1916, and 1918. Accompanied by Dr. Samuel K. Lothrop, Morley again came to Tulum, from Cozumel, in 1922. This was still during the reign of the *Indios sublevados.*

On landing, Dr. Morley and Dr. Lothrop were greeted by a delegation of fierce-looking, well-armed rebel Indians. They asked whether the two archaeologists had the written permission of Queen Victoria. Despite the ridiculousness of this demand they showed all signs of hostility, and no doubt the archaeologists would have been killed at once had they not been able to explain the situation with a long story about the death of the Queen and the existence of the heir to the throne.

Then Dr. Morley with a stroke of genius saved the day and his life by producing a phonograph which astounded the Indians so much that they allowed the archaeologists to pursue their explora-tory survey in peace.

As a ghostly reminder of the Indians' hostility there lies still today at the foot of the principal building in Tulum a skeleton imbedded in stucco that is said to have been that of an archaeolo-gist killed by the Chan Santa Cruz Indians and placed in a prominent position as a warning to intruders.

Tulum is one of various Mayan cities to be surrounded by a wall. At Tulum the wall forms a three-sided enclosure, the fourth side of the rectangle being the sea. At each corner of this wall stand square blockhouses of somewhat the same style as the small temples I had seen up the coast. There are three narrow openings that cut through the wall. These openings, only three feet wide, were easy to defend and Tulum was practically impregnable.

Cliffs some fifty feet high protect the town along the sea, though there is one gap where the cliffs tumble down to a small narrow sandy beach. Wedged between the rocks and dominated by the Castillo, this beach must have been the base of Tulum's fleet of large canoes.

The Castillo itself is a mighty building that soars high above the edge of the cliff, turning its back on the sea and presenting to mariners the large blank wall of a mighty tower, a citadel so impressive that even today it is awe-inspiring, which explains the Spaniards' reluctance to land in Quintana Roo.

The entrance of the Castillo is gained by a monumental staircase whose ramp at its base is flanked by two large dragon heads, a motif which also protrudes from the base of the two columns that support the entrance to the temple on the summit of the castle. From this temple one can behold a most impressive panorama. Never, until I reached the summit of the Castillo, had I fathomed what could be called the immensity of the jungle. From the top, one can see the horizon all around, flat, infinite, and mysterious; to the west stretches the limitless sea of the Quintana Roo jungle, flowing treetop after treetop over half of the panorama. The other half of the horizon is the open sea, crystal clear and with vivid shades of blue becoming gray to the east. Both jungle and sea meet at Tulum in their common vastness, separated by the endless streak of coastal beaches and rock, a vertical line running north to south separating the world into its elements of land and sea.

The shoreline also, as it were, cuts the sky in two. To the west over the jungle the sky was pale blue and clear, but to the east half a dozen menacing squalls rose like great mushrooms over the water. The air was electric and heavy; it was about to rain. From my position I could see in one glance all the ancient city. Tulum had been, it is assumed, a large religious center and within its wall had lived only the high priests caring for the shrines and temples which now lay partly ruined at my feet, half covered with a net of vines. Like all Mayan archaeological sites, Tulum's size must not be judged from the number of structures, for although these are indicative, they represent only religious and official edifices, as if all that remained of a European town were its churches. Thus when I had found three small pyramids, this could have meant a town with over two thousand inhabitants. Tulum, with its forty-odd structures, could have encompassed many more or perhaps less, according to whether it was a place of religious pilgrimage or a true city. For the Mayas lived in the old days in much the same huts as they do today, and of these nothing remains except for an occasional "house mound," the stone basement of what was once a wooden hut.

How mysterious seemed the deserted city, and what secrets, I wondered, lay hidden beneath the endless treetops. I considered with excitement and also with fear that I would now be setting out into the unknown jungle, hoping to tear away some of the many secrets hidden there. As I descended from the high Castillo I had the impression of diving into a deep, dark sea. I was slowly slipping into a world submerged. There under the green foliage lay a world about to sink into oblivion; there lived the few remaining Chan Santa Cruz Indians, the last heirs to ancient Mayan tradition, the descendants of those who had erected the mighty castle upon which I had stood.

In deciding to carry on south alone I fully realized that I was placing my life in the hands of fate, depending entirely upon the reception the Indians would give me, and on their generosity and kindness, for survival. I was blindly counting on their support, without which I knew I could not survive.

I was so inexperienced and so ignorant of the obstacles that I would have to overcome that I did not then realize the foolishness of my decision. Had I been wiser I would have decided to stay at Tankah and await the next boat for Cozumel. My ignorance was thus to serve me by leading me to undertake a journey that no one

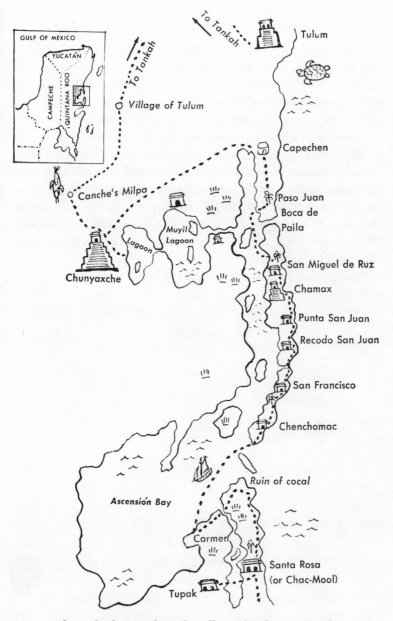

The author's route from the village of Tulum to Tupak

had yet dared to perform. In more ways than one my ignorance was going to prove an asset, especially in securing the cooperation of all the people I was to meet, in whom I placed such naïve and disarming confidence that even the worst of crooks dared not fail me. Thus I obtained assistance that no one else would have dreamed of soliciting or could have hoped to receive.

After rummaging around the ruins, where can still be seen some elegant frescoes of warriors and high priests, as well as a most intriguing statue of a diving goddess very similar to those found on palaces in India, I made my way out of the city walls toward the small crumbling tower of what had once been a lighthouse. The sun was setting and in its last rays it lit up the ghostly forms of the ancient Mayan city.

"Larger than Seville . . . ," I reflected.

VI

The Last Defenders of the Ancient Mayas

As planned, I spent the night in the abandoned lighthouse that stands a few hundred yards from the narrow southern gate of the city of Tulum. There lived an Indian by the name of Xool. He lived entirely isolated and was neither a *chiclero* nor a Chan Santa Cruz Indian. He spoke a bit of Spanish and said that he was originally from Yucatán. He had been given the care of the ruins by chance when the previous Indian in charge had gone mad, confirming what I learned later was an Indian legend: that all those who spend a night at Tulum are bound to lose their heads. The previous guard had been an Indian of the Chan Santa Cruz group. He had lived in a small ramshackle hut at the foot of the Castillo, his task being to see that nobody came and stole objects or damaged the statues. The mysterious Xool, who camped in a small, round, broken-down structure called the *faro,* had been asked by Señor Gonzales to keep an eye on the ruins in the absence of the keeper. I was his first visitor since he had taken office.

No matter how hard I tried I could not find out exactly why Xool had come to the coast, but most likely he had been seeking work in the *cocal* of Tankah.

When I told Xool of my plans, he was little help; he did not know the coast. As for the interior, he seemed to fear the Chan Santa Cruz Indians more than I did myself. As I did not feel physically prepared to go immediately on my trip south, I stayed for an extra day at Tulum, taking ample time to look over each ruin again. Most of those within the wall had been cleared of the jungle and some had been rather roughly restored.

While bathing on the narrow beach between the two towering cliffs I noticed that in a small grotto halfway up the cliff on which stood the Castillo there was a small shrine with some wooden crosses. I asked Xool about them; he suspected that this was the shrine erected by the previous guardian.

I thought no more of the shrine, and at the end of the day, returning to the lighthouse, I shared Xool's evening meal. Again I was struck by how lightly the Mayas seem to take to solitude. For here, like Miguel of Ak, was Xool living entirely alone and not minding it at all, a trait rare in our gregarious Western civilizations, where those who live isolated and alone are looked upon either as sacred men, hermits, or terrible cases of misanthropy. What, I wondered, went on in the minds of these lonely inhabitants of the coast? I could not yet tell.

The following morning I told Xool of my intention to go to the nearest Indian village and asked him to accompany me to carry my bags. He politely refused, and no offer of money would make him change his mind. "I can show you where the path begins," was his only suggestion. Seeing that it was no use, and rather frightened at his categorical refusal to accompany me, I set out alone. Walking slowly, I would, I thought, get to the village of Benanzio's brother before dusk.

Xool tied my bags together, making one large bundle, and arranged for a stronger strap than the one I had to go about my head. He then led me back to the airstrip and down all its length to its western extremity; there he showed me, breaking through the edge of the jungle, a small narrow path. "Follow this and you will reach the village; it is but four *leguas* away." That was roughly fifteen miles.

Having said good-by to Xool, I started off. At first all went well; the path, some three feet wide, was clearly marked and I had no trouble following it. It twisted its way through the vegetation, around large trees, and skirted occasional pools of muddy water with clusters of palms. The jungle was fairly thick and no direct sunlight penetrated the foliage. I was in what seemed like a narrow, dark tunnel lit by a strange green glare. After about half an hour, I started feeling the strain on my neck from my heavy load, and stopped for a short rest. This was the wrong thing to do, for no sooner had I stopped than thousands of mosquitoes swarmed down on me and I had to continue walking as fast as I could to drive them away. They had no respect for repellent!

The muddy pools became more and more numerous and soon I was slodging through them, my feet bathing in putrid warm water. The path would narrow and disappear in the shallow pools, leaving me ankle deep in water and guessing where the path carried on through the fence of vegetation that bordered these pools. Twice I had to backtrack, having taken for the path what was nothing more than a small gap between some trees.

After a short while I arrived at a fork. This I had not expected; both branches of the fork were of equal size. After much reflection and worry I took the path that turned to the left, only to discover that I could have spared myself the worrying, since the two paths soon merged again. They were only alternate routes.

Walking along alone, I had the leisure to examine closely the vegetation that bordered the path and listen attentively to all the noises of the jungle. Predominant was the strange croaking of thousands of frogs like those I had heard at Chichén-Itzá, endlessly belching at each other. Now and again there would be a fierce, almost human call, that of the chachalaka, a bird whose cry is well illustrated by its Maya name. These birds, the size of a large partridge, are very much sought after by the Indians for food. They are quite tame and their loud cry is a great aid in hunting them. Now and again I would catch the vivid blue glitter of a Yucatecan jay, a bird whose bright plumage had made it greatly prized by the ancient Mayas, who used its feathers extensively in the making of their complicated and enormous feather headdresses. The feathers were also used to make feather mosaics, an art unique to the New World and one in which the Mayas excelled. They would weave thousands of feathers into the warp of a cotton quilt. These robes must have had a sheen and brilliance that no silk could equal; unfortunately this art is today totally lost.

No matter how much I stared at the ground, I saw no snakes, which comforted me. After about three hours' walking the path had become so narrow that it was necessary to part fallen branches to make a passage through the vegetation. I then came upon another fork and then a narrow crossroads, one more perplexing than the other. I chose the paths that seemed the widest, and did not have to regret it. I was just beginning to think that I might be lost when, coming from somewhere ahead of me, I heard a cock crow. Advancing a little farther, I finally caught sight of the village.

It stood in a clearing and was composed of ten small oval huts, their backs to the jungle and doors opening on the village square, within which there stood two larger huts, one of them oval, with its walls painted white, the other a large, rectangular, communal structure. In the center of the village was a small well.

I burst from the dark tunnel of the jungle path right into the clearing. Seeing me, a couple of Indian women wearing *huipiles* immediately fled to their houses, taking with them their children, and soon I stood alone in the village square. Not a soul was in sight, although I knew and could almost feel that from within each hut curious eyes were watching all my movements through the cracks in the staked walls.

At first I did not know what to do, and putting down my load I walked rather casually around the clearing, hoping that someone might pop out. But no one did, so I approached one of the huts. A few yards away I ventured a timid "Canche"—the name of the only person who I felt could help me. There was no reply, and I tried approaching a second hut, this time getting near enough to see through the walls someone moving inside. Upon my repeated calling of "Canche," a sturdy, bare arm shot out of the dark doorway, pointing across the clearing to one of three huts within a small, rickety, stone enclosure. I walked up to one of these huts and, not waiting to be asked in, I lowered my head and entered. It was nearly dark inside, and when I straightened up I found myself nose to nose with two rather unpleasant-looking Indians, bare-chested and with long black hair falling onto their square shoulders. I was quite frightened and could only repeat "Canche," wondering by now if I was being understood and whether Canche really existed. As their only reply the two men's arms pointed toward a narrow door in the back of the hut. Without another word I silently crept out feeling a little guilty and quite embarrassed. Outside I found another hut, apparently new. The stakes of its walls were yellow and the palms of its roof had not yet acquired the usual old rusty-gray patina.

A young and most handsome Indian with long hair, and stripped to the waist, came forward. With a big smile, to my relief, he said, "Canche," and shook my extended hand.

I had found the man I was looking for and thanked my luck that he was in the village. I explained that I had met his brother and that he had told me to come here and tell Canche that he was coming down from the coast soon. All these explanations were of little use, for having finished, I realized that Canche spoke practically no Spanish. I explained my message again, with gestures, and to my delight this time Canche understood.

His smiling face lit up and he beckoned me to enter his hut. Like all the others of the village, it had no doors, which I later learned was the case in the times of the ancient Mayas. They, like the Indians of Chan Santa Cruz today, had severe punishments for theft, and it was therefore considered unnecessary to have doors. Only a small knee-high barrier closed the entrance of the huts, a barrier made of interwoven sticks to keep the pigs and chickens from wandering inside.

Canche proudly introduced me to his wife, a pretty, frail woman who was nursing a small child. Canche had two more children, a small girl only three, neatly dressed in a miniature *huipiles*, and a small boy about four who was running around naked on the earthen floor of the hut. Neither his wife nor, as I found out, any of the villagers spoke Spanish. Mrs. Canche slipped out and came quickly back with a small calabash full of water. Having taken a long-needed drink, I lay down at Canche's invitation on a coarse henequen hammock that had been lowered for me, and Pablo Canche and I were soon swinging on our backs as we exchanged a few words. Canche told me that I could live in his house for the time I wanted, and that I had been lucky to find him, for he was about to set out to his *milpa* to get some corn. (A *milpa* is a spot in the jungle where the Indians grow corn.) My arrival made him change his mind and he sent his wife with a large calabash to fetch some corn from the house just to the side of his.

Pablo Canche's house had indeed been recently built, for he had only just been married four years, and according to ancient Mayan custom had lived the first four years of his marriage in the house of his father-in-law, the large house beside his where his wife had gone to get the corn. His house had been erected through the joint work of the villagers. Not a nail had gone into its construction, and its high sloping roof had been assembled by clever inter-notching of long forked stakes whose intricate crisscross made up a delicate pattern beneath the rows and rows of neatly tucked-under fan-palm fronds. The thatching of the roofs of Mayan huts always astounds foreigners. Many thousands of fan-palm fronds are used to make one roof. They are first dried, and the stem is cut just below the spread of the leaf, which is then slit in two places, the fan thus being divided into three tufts. Next, the leaf is closed like an ordinary fan, making three tassels attached to the small cut end of the stem. The center part of this fan is then slipped over thin ribs of wood that are tied along the frames of the roof like laths laid out to support tiles. The two other ends of the split palm are tucked underneath the ribs; thus the complete roof is covered with the leaves, which cannot fall, being held by the overlapping tassels. The leaves are packed against one another so tightly and in rows so narrow that the roof is exceedingly thick, there being often as many as seven or eight gathered palms overlapping each other. From inside all that is visible are neat rows of the short cut stems of the fan palms. All the frames that are not held together by natural forks in the wood are bound with vines. The Mayas today still have a very good knowledge of the different kinds of vines. Many of these they soak in water before binding anything with them; the vines then soften up, setting when dry with a powerful grip. These bindings are so strong that they never break, and a Mayan house may lean over on its side or even blow upside down, yet the walls and the frame will never part.

Inside the hut, hung from two transverse poles, were all the hammocks of the family, which during the daytime and until my arrival had been gathered up and tied with a string so as to hang overhead. In one corner of the hut, on the ground, was a small fire made between three rocks covered with limestone stucco. Various strings dangled down from the roof, attached to circular wicker baskets in which were kept odds and ends of food. There was also furniture in the hut, if one can so describe little logs that had been cut on one side and hollowed to make tiny seats. An Indian never fails to offer a seat to his guests, although to us whites such a low, hard piece of wood can hardly be considered a comfortable chair.

Despite there being no openings save one small door, the Mayan huts of the village were all very light inside, seeing that the walls were made of thin stakes of wood planted in the ground and set half an inch apart, thus allowing light and air to enter. This also enabled the women to observe, without being seen, all the happenings in the village, and to keep an eye on their children as they played around the huts.

Pablo Canche and his wife made a most handsome couple. In general it is hard for foreigners to find the Mayas beautiful or handsome, for they have very marked physical traits which give them a rather strange appearance. But Pablo bore the traits of the Mayas with great elegance, having a long aristocratic eagle-beak nose, a narrow chin, and a slanting jaw with practically no bend in it, which rose straight up from his chin to his ears. His forehead was slanted but tall and his long black hair made him look a bit like a dandy. Canche had swan-like eyes set slightly slanting, facing, as it were, outward. His skin was of a light sun-burn brown, and like all pure-blooded Indians he had no beard. His wife's features were most delicate; she had thin ankles and wrists and an elegant torso, her long dark hair black but not a coal black, rather of the deepest brown, gathered into a chignon with a large red ribbon in the fashion of a panache. In her ears she wore little rings from which dangled small round gold balls, a type of earring that I had noticed on nearly all the Mayan women of Yucatán.

Her spotless *huipiles* was a rather poor one, like those of all her neighbors. The little material that ever reaches the villages is brought in by *chicleros*, or by purchase through Don Jorge Gonzales at Tankah. But strangely, the Indians of Tulum rarely go to Tankah, and all their families, rather than work chicle, live on the corn they plant and the game they shoot.

I was to spend three days with Canche at the village of Tulum—three days of festivity and most welcome hospitality.

After my arrival, when I had refreshed myself and eaten a few tortillas, Canche proudly showed me off to all the villagers. Taking me by the arm, he led me on a grand tour of the families, visiting one hut after the other.

To my surprise most of the Mayan women had never seen a foreigner before and touched my beard in amazement, laughing a little nervously. I quickly became the great attraction. Pablo Canche chatted away in great excitement as he repeatedly explained my presence to every family of the village. Fortunately there were in all only ten families. There were hardly any men in the village since, as Canche explained, most of them had gone to their *milpas*.

The Mayas' method of planting corn has not changed over the centuries. They set out into the jungle and erect a small hut where they live while they clear a section of jungle, felling the small bushes and medium-sized trees. They cut the trees at about five feet off the ground. When the trees have been felled the Indians then set fire to the slash from the cutting; this is done toward the end of the hot season, just before the rains. The burning of the slash is the reason why *milpas* cannot be made too close to the villages, and in fact they are often very distant, as was the case with most of the *milpas* of the village of Tulum—some were as far as a day's walk away. When the slash has been burned the Indians plant their corn among the remaining charred tree stumps. The land being very rocky, one has to search for small pockets of earth in which to plant. Despite the poor appearance of the soil, it yields good crops, and it was the excess of these crops which allowed the Mayas of old to take so much time out to build their many cities and the temples and shrines that covered their land.

When the men go to their *milpas* they stay overnight, and most often for ten days during the planting and cutting season. This was why I had seen so few men on my arrival in the village, as we were at the beginning of the rainy season.

Each year the Indians cut a different part of the jungle so as to give the soil a rest, thus allowing the vegetation to return; in general a cycle of twenty years is allowed to pass before the same area of jungle is used. Having no set fields requires a communal organization and a strict policing of the zones where each year corn is to be sown. It so happened that at Tulum the man who had the job of assigning the *milpas* to the other villagers was the father-in-law of Pablo Canche, headman of the village and second in rank after the high priest.

The village of Tulum has retained a communal organization most similar to that of the ancient Mayas. It and three other villages of the Chan Santa Cruz Indians are the only ones to have escaped so far—and not for long—the influences of modern civilization. Here at Tulum the Santa Cruz Indians continue to live independently. When I questioned Canche about the Chan Santa Cruz Indians, he proudly said that all the village was of Santa Cruz and that they had defeated the Mexicans and were now in a period of long peace. To further this statement he took me to see an old man whom he introduced to me as the priest of the village.

When we entered the hut, the priest was sitting in one corner dabbling with a long thick stick into a large earthen pot. He was in the process of making sacred candles of scented beeswax for the temple which was the structure in the center of the village clearing, the small hut whose walls were painted white. There was to be a ceremony there the following day, and for this he was preparing the candles. The priest was highly regarded by all the villagers, and Canche explained to me respectfully that he alone was allowed to wear short hair. Patiently I sat for two hours in the high priest's hut while Pablo translated into poor Spanish all that the old priest said in Mayan. I gathered that the supreme priest of Chan Santa Cruz lived in Chumpom, one of the three other independent villages of Quintana Roo. There also lived General Vega, who was none other than the "hostage" taken by the Chan Santa Cruz Indians to teach them how to read. As a child he had not been able to do this, but he was now held in high esteem by the ignorant Santa Cruz Indians and was so well off that he never attempted to return to Cozumel after the peace treaty of 1935. He was headman of Chumpom, having been made cacique after the death of General Mayo.

I was surprised to learn that the Chan Santa Cruz Indians have a religion of their own, their priest and their beliefs honoring the three memorable crosses of Chan, the ones that had played such an important role in the War of the Castes. The high priest was therefore the servant of the revolutionary crosses and the religion itself a strange mixture of Christianity and ancient Mayan paganism. Like the ancient Mayas, each family in Tulum had a household god, these being represented by crosses, and Pablo Canche pointed out to me that at the four entrances of the village, where the various trails to the *milpas* of Tulum start, there stood four sanctuaries, set back from the path, where each family was to place its cross so as to ward off evil spirits. And Canche told me sincerely that I could not have been an evil man since the gods would otherwise have given me fever and stopped me from reaching the village.

It is customary for the villagers of Tulum to carry their personal crosses with them everywhere. These crosses they call their "house saints," and they carry them around to their *milpas* or in their baggage when traveling to other villages.

The crosses of the Chan Santa Cruz Indians are the usual shape except that the top of the cross fans out to form a large, wide triangle. The ones I saw were nearly all veiled, as usual in Mexico. Although the Chan Santa Cruz Indians used the cross as a religious symbol, this was the only analogy between their religion and Christianity. In every basic respect their religion was pagan.

Once a year the few remaining Chan Santa Cruz Indians hold a mass gathering. The ceremony lasts a week and consists of the carrying of the original three crosses of Chan from the village of Chumpom, where they are now kept, to the village of Tulum. The distance separating these two villages being considerable, the sacred procession stops at a small settlement halfway between the two villages. On arrival at Tulum, a great feast is held and for a whole week a pig is slaughtered every morning by the high priests of both Chumpom and Tulum. In the course of the eight-day stay of the revolutionary crosses in Tulum the villagers go to the ancient ruins of the old Mayan city where they hold a short ceremony, apparently in homage to the crosses which are set into the cliff at the foot of the Castillo.

Most of the rest of the population of the Chan Santa Cruz Indians come to the village of Tulum for the festive week, and they all sleep in the large open-sided communal hut standing in the square. Armed guards protect the pilgrims and the sacred crosses, which are brought over with what I understood to be a "treasure" —no doubt some valuable religious ornaments.

In a way, the religion of the Santa Cruz Indians is quite political and helps to keep up the independent spirit of the *Indios suble-vados.*

I had considerable trouble obtaining from the high priest of Tulum, through Canche, any very elaborate explanations of the strange religion of which he was minister. The priest kept telling Canche to tell me that "now the Chan Santa Cruz Indians were in a time of great peace, and that foreigners could come without being killed," explaining that before they had won the war against Mexico they had had to kill all foreigners like myself. "But now that they had conquered Mexico, of course everyone was friends." I had never heard such a strange and touching declaration, so incredible in the twentieth century. The high priest had probably been among those who had greeted Morley at Tulum in 1922, and there was no telling how many shipwrecked mariners or stray explorers he could have killed. The high priest recalled battles he had fought with General Mayo, and I could not help but admire these courageous Indians who had battled so long for their independence.

Unlike most of the Mayas of Yucatán, those of Chan Santa Cruz no longer have any complex against foreigners and were most proud to show off their noble origin and repeat to all who would listen that they had defeated the Mexicans and had signed the peace of their own free will.

Unfortunately the Chan Santa Cruz Indians are dwindling away, and already the village of Tulum showed signs of the migration and abandonment of the Chan Santa Cruz villages; about six huts were closed and uninhabited, their owners having died or gone to the outside world never to come back. In general, if the Chan Santa Cruz Indians had once been powerful, they were now reduced to what would be called a miserable lot, and it was evident that in intelligence the men of Tulum were well above their poor economic standards. Their gentle hospitality, their exquisite politeness, and their pride clashed with their surroundings. They had kept many of their ancient Mayan traits, not having had to suffer Mexican rule. The most striking of these traits was their calm. During all my stay I never heard a voice raised, and shouting or screaming seems unknown to the Mayas. In the same calm fashion they bring up their children, who rarely cry and seldom scream or shout. The Mayan language itself has quiet tones.

Their restraint is also striking in the field of affection: greetings are calm, and expressions of affection in a family are reduced to a mere soft word. One feels a great restraint in the Mayan attitude. The calmness of their behavior is not the result of apathy, as might at first be thought, for on the contrary the Mayas are very alert and have most inquisitive minds. This I found out while attempting to answer all the questions of Pablo Canche, who wanted to know every detail about the country I came from: whether corn grew well there, what fruits were to be found, whether the jungle in France was damp or dry, whether there was much game to hunt—questions often difficult to answer, but all motivated by a sincere and keen desire for knowledge. One can judge the intelligence of a person by the kind of questions he asks, and whereas I had found the peasants of central Mexico asking such stupid questions as how many days' walk it was to France, I found that the Mayas had no trouble in understanding distances and the possibility of a world existing that was entirely unrelated to theirs. And when I had explained to Pablo Canche that our jungles had been cleared to leave place for fields and large towns, it was easy to see by his questions that he fully grasped what I said and that his imagination had little trouble in stretching over to the strange world of Europe.

My camera quickly became an attraction in the village and having a reflex lens it gave much enjoyment to everyone who came in his turn to look through it. One woman was rather horrified, observing that it made the world tiny. I had some trouble explaining what was to become of the photos; having no prints with me, I tried hard to tell Canche what the exact mechanism was, but he seemed satisfied that I wanted to take pictures and kindly explained to everyone I intended to photograph to stand still and not be shy.

I lost no time in making good friends with Pablo Canche; it was easy for us to have long and interesting conversations. I soon had to admit that my concerns of the moment were not much different from his, and we talked a lot about the jungle trails, hunting, and especially eating. Since my arrival on the coast eating had been my main concern. It did not take me long to understand that it was also that of the Indians, who would seem to many people like greedy gourmets from the passionate way they talked about food. One must remember, of course, that all their lives are oriented toward the quest for food, by either hunting or planting. There were in the village of Tulum a surprising number of fruit trees that had been purposely planted: orange and lemon trees, guavas and sapotes, and a variety of the chicle tree bearing large, pink, fleshy fruits. It dawned on me that perhaps the ancient Mayas had been great fruit eaters, a supposition that seems confirmed by the early Spanish chronicles.

Among the various fruit trees that surrounded the huts were innumerable calabash trees, whose fruits, coming in a great pod narrowed in the center somewhat like a peanut, are used for making bowls and jars. The interior is not eaten, but grains that look like giant watermelon seeds are kept and dried. Their kernels, which have a delicate flavor somewhat like a pistachio or almond, are eaten as a rare delicacy.

The only manufactured objects found in the village were the cloth of the men's large, baggy, white trousers and the women's *huipiles*, and of course the machetes and shotguns, these last being mostly very ancient and used with homemade cartridges made from powder bartered at the *chiclero* camps. Some of the villagers would also set out on the twenty-day trip through the jungle to Yucatán to buy powder with the proceeds from the sale of chickens, although such trips to the borders of civilization were rare. The greater part of the manufactured objects were inherited and most likely came from the spoils of the military campaigns of the Chan Santa Cruz Indians.

The men of the village went around stripped to the waist, wearing typical white Mayan trousers that stopped short above the ankle. After work in the evenings some would don a characteristic Mayan shirt which is almost never worn in central Yucatán. Very short, with bouffant sleeves, it reaches only to the waist, is never tucked into the trousers, and, being pleated, flares out above the waist. I was struck by the clean clothes worn by everyone; even if some were patched and ragged and of very poor material, they were spotless. While living with Pablo Canche, I could count how many times a day his wife changed her *huipiles*. At the end of the day, Pablo would always take a full bath, hidden behind a curtain that was hung up for the purpose in a corner of the hut. Upon entering a house when paying a visit, and before and after each meal, the Indians would wash their hands and faces. The children are washed every night and generally kept clean, although this is a difficult job with children all over the world.

Every day is washing day for the Mayan woman, unlike European women, who wash on Mondays. The washing is done in miniature dugout canoes, rectangular basins carved out of large logs.

Another daily occupation of the women was the grinding of the corn to make tortillas. This is done by crushing the grains over a large, flattish, gently curved stone with a stone roller. The corn is previously soaked in water containing lime which takes off the outer skin of the kernels and gives the tortillas a particular chalky taste. The lime in the tortillas also accounts for the Indians' spotless white teeth. The lime is made in outside furnaces, wood being piled to a depth of one yard in a square hole and the limestone placed on top. This same lime was used to make cement and stucco with which the ancient Mayas covered their buildings. The white lime also serves as paint, and at Tulum had been used to whitewash the wooden wall of the little temple hut in the center of the square.

When night fell upon the village of Tulum mosquitoes swarmed in from the dense jungle and bothered us all. To my surprise I noticed that Pablo Canche's smallest child was not stung by the mosquitoes, though being an infant not more than three months old it was laid naked in its mother's hammock. This, I was told, was the case with all small Mayan babies, who for some reason medically unknown are unaffected by mosquitoes when very young.

After sunset Mrs. Canche prepared another meal composed of tortillas and a highly spiced stew, artificially colored a bright red with little red seeds. The stew contained chopped-up chachalaka meat from a bird Pablo had shot a few days before my arrival. In many ways I thought the fare of the Indians was abundant compared to that of the isolated and lonely inhabitants of the coast, who had neither fruit trees nor the abundance of corn that the Indians had. Honey was also abundant, and the inhabitants of Tulum village keep hives made of hollowed logs blocked at each end by round rocks. Mayan bees are stingless!

The Indians of Chan Santa Cruz live in a very similar manner to what must have been the way of life of the poorer class of ancient Mayas. Their food is the same; the houses, clothing, many customs such as those of marriage and childbearing, and even traces of their original moral outlook remain little changed. One

Finding this oval Mayan temple at Recodo San Juan gave the author fresh energy on his waterless trek from San Miguel de Ruz to the *cocal* of San Francisco

In search of the temple of Tupak
(Above) Chuc hewing a way through tangled vegetation
(Below) Wading through a swampy lagoon

(Above) The temple of Tupak *(Below)* Entrance to the temple

(*Above*) Carved stone dragon's head, Rio Indio (*Below*) The author photographed in San Pedro, British Honduras, on his arrival there after his first trip

(*Right*) At Pamul, which he visited in 1961, the author stands at the foot of a pyramid topped by a ruined oratory
(*Below*) Part of the semicircle of pyramids at Chunyaxche

Before and after the unveiling of a Mayan ruin at Chunyaxche. These photographs give a precise idea of the thickness of the vegetation

The author and Coba-Cama standing on the platform of the "pink palace" at Chunyaxche. It is hard to believe that under the rubble of the platform lies a completely unspoiled underground palace of the ancient Mayas

Marie Claire peers into the low entrance of the temple found at Chunyaxche within the semicircle of pyramids. Roots are slowly breaking through the structure

Marie Claire examining a giant black pheasant shot by Coba-Cama near Chunyaxche. Bagging the bird meant not a trophy, but a welcome change in diet!

The author with the large idol he discovered at Chunyaxche

thing that struck me, and which also had attracted the attention of Landa, was the chastity of the women and the considerable *pudeur* of both men and women, who can never be seen in, or even heard mentioning, any unchaste action—a considerable improvement over the rather vile Mexican poorer classes. The sexual habits of the Mayas are reported to be quite peculiar in that they are very much restrained. Although the ancient Mayas have left us many erotic statues, their behavior in matters concerning sex has always been recorded as being of the utmost correctness. Whether this comes from a particularly rigid moral code, it is hard to tell; many people think that this reserve arises from the fact that the Mayas have the lowest rate of metabolism in the world. Some have believed that they copulate only in spring, although I have not been able to check the truth of this rumor. It may, however, well be true, perhaps less because of low metabolism than because of the Mayas' former superstitions which required children to be born during certain auspicious months of the year.

The Mayas nevertheless have many children and in pre-Columbian days used to go to endless pains to secure the benediction of the Goddess of Fertility, Ix Chell, whose shrine was on Cozumel. At Tulum the children were very well cared for and parents would spare no effort to make them happy; the small children were all very well behaved.

Another strange custom of the Mayas that I noticed while living with Canche is that they have no set time for sleeping. They would stay up till very late, often sleeping only a few hours at night and catching up in the daytime. Nor do they associate sleep with silence, as we tend to do. People would chat unrestrainedly beside a sleeper's hammock. This probably comes from the fact that, living in close quarters, they rapidly become accustomed to sleeping surrounded by noise.

After the meal that evening Canche's two eldest children were put to bed in the same hammock, wrapped in the mesh like two small bundles. When it gets cold they light small fires below the hammocks. Once the children were in bed, Canche took his bath and, having finished, asked me to come over to his father-in-law's hut.

There, to my surprise, were gathered all the men of the village, a few more having in the course of the evening returned from their *milpas*. They were all squatting on their heels with their backs to the oval walls of the large hut. In the center, as if supervising the assembly, an old woman lay in her hammock. I later gathered she was the headman's wife, Pablo Canche's mother-in-law. The men all sat in silence, occasionally addressing the matron; as they came in or as they silently rose and left, they held out their thumbs to be kissed by the woman, a gesture of greeting also performed on most of their encounters with each other.

In the flickering flame of a small oil lamp I could see the shiny faces of the men of the community, their piercing eyes and rather savage looks accentuated by their long hair. I had no trouble recalling that these were the Chan Santa Cruz Indians, a dangerous tribe who, up to 1935, had been the terror of Quintana Roo and masters of a greater part of their ancient region. I could not gather exactly the meaning of the ceremony, and my entrance into the room caused no more stir than that of a fly. I squatted silently beside Pablo Canche and looked on, as a slow, strange, practically whispered conversation would sound across the room, the voices coming from the dark squat figures of the men, whose faces glowed dimly in the light. The great reverence paid to the old woman, her air of importance as she swung gently in the hammock above the heads of the squatting men, made me think of some religious ceremony, and I wondered for a moment whether she was not the true chief of the village. I soon discovered the meaning of this reunion, which was no more than a routine gathering of the men prior to a religious day. I had been told by the old priest that he was preparing candles for a ceremony the following day; we were therefore on the eve of some great feast.

Some of the men were smoking small, rough, handmade cigars,

and on my arrival I was offered one. Being an inveterate smoker, I did not refuse and smoked the strange, leafy-tasting cigar.

It was only the following day that I found out what I had smoked—nothing less than marijuana, a drug which I found grows in great abundance in Quintana Roo. Pablo Canche explained to me that very little was smoked solely for the purpose of intoxication and that most often the cigarettes would be smoked to acquire a new burst of energy on the long treks that the Mayas frequently made from one village to another through the jungle.

I was quite disappointed. Never having taken any drugs whatsoever, I felt that I should have had hallucinations. I had none, and after the strange gathering broke up, my one desire was to sleep, for it was extremely late and the strain of the day had been considerable.

That night in the dark I strung up my hammock beside the three hammocks in Canche's hut. But I could not sleep, as the events of the day kept flashing back into my mind. Looking through the stake walls of the hut, I could see the village square lit by pale moonlight, an oasis within a sea of jungle. A strange feeling crept over me as for an instant I felt totally assimilated into my surroundings, to the point of wondering whether I too was not a Maya. Here, lost within the jungle, lived man, and never before had I felt so close to the meaning of survival, to the meaning of life, that of primitive men of all times.

I was awakened the following morning by Pablo Canche. The sun had just risen.

Pablo told me to hurry and come to the temple. Having slept as usual in my day clothes, I was up in a second and making my way across the clearing toward the white-painted hut in its center. By the hut grew three tall pine trees, three "sacred" trees which Canche had pointed out to me the day before. Most of the villagers were now approaching the temple, all bearing calabashes full of what I found out was called *atole*, a thick, porridgy drink of corn and water. The entrance of the hut had been decorated for the occasion with two large palms. As I was about to step into the small sanctuary, Canche told me to take off my sandals; it surprised me that, as in the case of a Mohammedan mosque, one could not enter the temple of Tulum with shoes on. Already a row of six or seven pairs of sandals stood beside the entrance—typical Mayan sandals composed of simple leather soles and henequen straps. Taking off my shoes, I entered the temple, probably the first white man to do so.

The interior of the small hut was dark. A veil and a small stake partition divided the hut in two. Already a cluster of people stood in the antechamber, passing to the priest on the other side of the curtain their calabashes full of *atole*. I was later informed that this was a ceremony of blessing of drink that was held every fortnight, the same ceremony for food being carried out on great festive occasions. I was ushered beyond the veil into what must have been the inner sanctum, a dark room with a table (the altar) made of a large piece of wood secured to a tripod formed by upturning a tree trunk with three branches stemming from it. Many similar natural tripods were lined against the wall of the inner sanctuary, supporting small planks that formed little tables on which had been placed the scented beeswax candles I had seen the priest preparing the day before.

On the altar table stood half a dozen small crosses with their peculiar triangles; some were veiled in white or red cloths, others were bare; in the center stood three roughly hewn wooden crosses, the other crosses representing each of the ten families of the village and the three larger crosses, those of Chan Santa Cruz, the crosses of the Indian revolt. On the table in front of the crosses lay a dozen small bowls made of calabashes cut in two and resting on wicker rings. These ceremonial bowls had been filled previously with the offerings of *atole* brought by each of the villagers. The high priest, in his sacerdotal uniform consisting of simple, beltless, white trousers cut at knee length and a typical, bulgy, embroidered Mayan shirt, was busy reciting in Mayan various prayers, to which the assembly both beyond the curtain and from within answered. In the corners of the room were placed little flat drums and small chair-like contraptions that were used in carrying the three Chan Santa Cruz crosses about the village on special occasions; the small drums formed part of the band for these religious processions.

After many prayers in Mayan which invoked the Christian saints, San Lorenzo and Santa Rita, and also the Mayan god, Canche Balam, the priest then took the small calabashes and, drinking a little from each bowl, distributed the remainder of the *atole* to those present, children and grown-ups, who had all brought their own calabash bowls to partake in the ceremony.

It was a strange reminder of the Christian Mass interspersed with pagan rites. The ceremony I had seen was one of drinking, and after it all the villagers returned to their homes, where they drank more, this time a strange kind of mead made from fermented corn and honey. Pablo Canche had a large stock of this beverage and begged me to indulge in drinking some with him. The liquor was quite good, and when I had satisfied my host's desire to see me drink, I realized that my head was spinning and, like Pablo Canche and most of the villagers, I was becoming quite drunk. I eventually flopped down into a hammock, after many rather sense-less signs of appreciation and considerable improvement in my small Mayan vocabulary, and fell asleep. When I awoke, it was around three in the afternoon and Mrs. Canche had prepared a much-needed meal which soon put me on my feet again. As usual I ate alone, with Mrs. Canche handing me one after the other the hot tortillas she was preparing.

Having gathered my wits about me, I tried to get from Canche more information about the village and in particular about the existence of ancient Mayan temples in the neighborhood. This took quite some doing, for Canche had no exact idea of what I could mean by ruins. "There are many," came his encouraging reply, when he finally understood. He then led me out of the village. We passed the palm-covered altar on which all the villagers

had placed their gods to keep away evil spirits, and crossed a
small clearing in the jungle that Canche pointed out to me as the
cemetery. In amongst the tall grass and small trees were tombs,
each marked by two concentric rings of heavy stones—a simple but
grandiose burial ground for the Indians whose whole lives, like
their resting places, had never occupied more than a small clearing
in the ever-destroying jungle. Past the cemetery we came upon a
small side trail; following this for a few hundred yards, we came
upon a low stone wall that led into the broken-down remains of
what had been a minute ancient Mayan oratory. Its roof had caved
in, and leaning over the top I could see, laid out in the rubble, the
broken pieces of an idol. Canche explained that this was a sacred
statue. Dead flowers and little bundles of leaves strewn around
the idol showed that the Indians paid reverence to it. I wanted
to pick up the pieces of the idol to examine them, but Canche
stopped me, saying that no one could touch it, for it was sacred.

Having seen the small shrine, I questioned Canche about the
existence of other ruins. Canche was apparently reluctant to talk
and it took a great deal of coaxing to persuade him to tell me about
the other ruins. These, he said, were far away, at a place called
Chunyaxche, which means in Mayan "trunk of the ceiba tree."
There, said Canche, stood many ruins, one so high that from its
summit one could see the sea. It was, he assured me, taller than
the Castillo of the coastal ruins of Tulum. It was there, I gathered,
that the annual procession from Chumpom stopped for the night
on its way to Tulum with the original sacred crosses.

I gathered that these ruins were situated south of Tulum and a
fair distance from the coast. I immediately tried to persuade
Canche to bring me there. But at first he was reluctant, saying that
it was too far and would take two days' walking. For hours that
night I tried to persuade him to take me, and finally, to my delight,
Canche agreed.

I also took this opportunity to inquire whether Canche could
help me on my route south, explaining that I had very far to go

and badly needed his help to go down the coast. Canche agreed to take me a little beyond the ruins of Chunyaxche to a spot on the coast called Capechen, meaning "four *cenotes*," where, I gathered, lived some Indians he knew.

I therefore made plans to leave in two days, hoping beforehand to gather as much information as I could about the strange Santa Cruz village of Tulum. As far as I knew, I was the only foreigner to have stayed at the village, and I intended to make the most of my visit. Canche was delighted at my wanting to stay and seemed most flattered at my interest in all the affairs of the village.

The next day in a less formal manner he took me again to all the houses to meet the other villagers. Although I felt rather like a lion in a zoo, I nevertheless enjoyed these visits. Mothers would come and show me their sick infants, and after I had given a pill to a child that seemed to be suffering from dysentery, all the villagers came up to me with various sores and ailments, having their personal symptoms translated to me by Pablo Canche, whose strange Mayan Spanish I could now manage to understand. I was already beginning to master about half a dozen vital Mayan phrases and three or four dozen words.

My attempts at being a doctor brought me great popularity, and late that night many women came over to Canche's hut carrying presents of fresh eggs for me, which, to Mrs. Canche's delight, I turned over to her.

I spent the afternoon filling out my little notebook with observations. My writing intrigued Canche tremendously and, with his habitual curiosity, he asked me if I could teach him how to read. As if to show his serious intentions of learning, he went to a small wooden chest in one corner of his hut and came back ceremoniously carrying a magazine which he proudly displayed to me as a great treasure. It was a brownish dirty copy of a 1944 issue of a popular Mexican magazine. Having had no reading material for the past two weeks, I fell upon the old magazine with the enthusiasm of a culture-starved scholar. It made excellent reading and I could not help but laugh when in my hammock I read about the invasion of Normandy; it seemed so strange reading a magazine so old in so remote a land, and I mused as to whether I was really reading of the past or whether, isolated as I was among primitive Indians, I was not really reading science fiction about the future.

My interest in Canche's prized magazine, the only printed matter in Tulum, induced Canche to go to his chest again, and this time he returned with a still stranger treasure, a small tin box full of nails and containing a small photograph of a Negro and three ten-centime coins of Guadalupe. When I asked where he had found these, he simply said he had found them on the coast. Then, as if to show off the wealth of the village and satisfy my curiosity, Canche left his hut and returned with his neighbor, carrying a large brown pot with "Graphite Grease" lettered on the lid, which had also been found on the beach. In all, the treasures of the outside world which had drifted to these shores of Quintana Roo, and which were almost the only marks of exterior civilization, amounted to one pot of graphite grease, a piece of a life raft with the words *Batte Rock,* and a box of pills with no name on it, but which the owner certified were very good for stomach-ache, although she admitted having found them on the shore. At Tulum I had not seen the end of all the strange objects that the Yucatán Straits current washes onto the shores of Quintana Roo.

In the afternoon I went back to see the old priest and attempted to get more information on his strange religion. Language being such a problem and Pablo Canche being unable to understand any Spanish words that dealt with such sophisticated problems as theology, I had to limit my questions to rather elementary ones. I gathered that the main function of the Chan Santa Cruz priest was to say the kind of drink-masses that I had seen the day before, with occasional great orgiastic ceremonies in which he would bless not only drink but food. On those days, as during the eight-day yearly festival of the transportation of the crosses from Chumpom, all the inhabitants would stuff themselves with food till they were sick, an occasion that Canche greedily recalled with great pleasure and yearning. I had already noticed how greedy the people I had met on the coast were, which is understandable in a country where people do not always have their fill. When someone was lucky in hunting or killed a pig on a festive occasion, no one would think of putting anything aside (this would have been impossible anyway, as there are no means of keeping meat in the tropics). They would stuff themselves until they practically burst. I reflected that temperance was a virtue only for those blessed with plenty.

No matter how hard I tried, I could get no proof that the Chan Santa Cruz Indians recalled or knew anything of their great past beyond the names of their ancient gods. No songs or music remained from the times of their great ancestors, and beyond their pride at simply being Mayan, the villagers would probably have been surprised if they had been told the history of their forefathers.

This history, going back countless centuries, would last till the death or dispersal of the last proud Mayas, who would, I sadly reflected, be destroyed more rapidly by the inescapable effects of contact with the civilized world than they could have been by warfare.

My stay in Tulum village and the strange things I had seen there had made me temporarily forget that there still lay ahead of me two hundred miles of unknown territory that somehow I had to cross. Canche proved of little use when it came to enlightening me about what lay to the south, for I gathered that thirty miles south of the village was the limit of the area inhabited by the Chan Santa Cruz Indians and that in fact most of the zone I was to cross was completely uninhabited.

I nevertheless felt quite confident. Had I not been able to gain the confidence and friendship of the fearful *Indios sublevados*? I felt very brave and sure that mattters would turn out all right.

Canche had agreed to accompany me to Chunyaxche and from there to Capechen, where a small group of Chan Santa Cruz Indians had settled for a few months. From there I hoped one of the

Indians could guide me farther south, although, as Canche warned me, in that rainy season there was a great deal of water in the lagoons I would have to cross, and it might easily reach above one's head.

Gathering together my belongings, among which was my blue blazer, now green with mold, I packed my henequen bag and slept for the third night at the village.

When Canche woke me, it was before sunrise and all was dark. It had rained and the ground was wet. I silently followed Canche as we slipped out of the village into the pitch-dark, mysterious jungle. I was sad to leave behind the strange isolated world of the Chan Santa Cruz Indians, a world that had by now become my own, an oasis of hospitality in the jungle and also in the modern world of civilization, a village still so close to the earth and so remote from the artificial intrigues of modern society with its jungles of telegraph poles and neon signs.

Canche had taken my pack on his back, but nevertheless I had trouble following him, as he advanced almost as if he were running; his fast step, similar to that of Chinese coolies, was in fact a step dictated by his load rather than by any great hurry. Later I was to find out that carrying a load is made easier by running slowly, because by never straightening one's knees, one does not receive the jolts that are customary when walking, thus easing the strain when a load is bound to one's forehead.

We made our way along the narrow tunnel of a jungle path to the rhythm of Canche's machete, with which, every now and again, he would take a quick and accurate swing at an obstructing branch.

VII

Citadels of a Vanished World

We were heading south but away from the coast. As far as I could gather from Canche, we were going to spend the night at the *milpa* in the jungle where Canche and his immediate family (father-in-law and brother) had their corn plantation. The *milpa* was, I gathered, some twenty-five miles away and it would take us most of the day to reach it.

The jungle became stickier as we advanced, and the terrain, instead of being perfectly flat, was now an endless series of small ups and downs of sharp coral limestone, in which somehow gigantic trees had managed to take root. Some of these were chicle trees, and Pablo showed me where their trunks had been cut so as to let the sap drip. Others were giant ceiba trees with immense roots that sprang out like tentacles making their way into the soil, giant snakes conforming to the shapes of the rocks. Huge vines dangled from these trees, coming from somewhere above where the sun shone. As for us, we were in the dark shade of the narrow trail.

Every few hours Canche would stop, and squatting down, we would rest for a while. My sandals had by now lost much of their original shape, and this made progress most difficult; every five minutes the loose straps would slip off the end of my feet, requiring a brief stop while I readjusted them.

Canche had brought along his *escopeta,* an antiquated shotgun whose stock had been mended with a clumsy binding of henequen cord. On two occasions he silently set down my bags and, signaling me to stand still, stalked some game that was entirely invisible to me. On one of these halts he disappeared silently into the jungle, making his way like a cat until he was out of sight. I then heard a terrific report and a few seconds later he came back jubilantly holding up an immense black feathered bird with a bright yellow beak, a large specimen of the rare Yucatecan pheasant. Never had I looked upon a dead carcass with such envious and greedy anticipation. This was something, I thought, that would go well with tortillas! Canche plucked the bird on the spot, scattering the feathers about the path, retaining the small bluish-black feathery crest from the top of the bird's head. I had seen many of these hung up in the village huts, and even nailed to a post in Puha, without knowing whence they came. The Indians kept trophies of all the game they shot, small bunches of feathers, teeth of wild boars, and the skins of small jaguars. Although in our modern, distorted civilization, where hunting is reduced to a game, the important part of having a trophy is to be able to show it off afterward, with the Mayas, as with many other primitive people, keeping a token of the animal one has killed is done for the purpose of warding off bad omens by showing respect for the slain animal. In ancient Mayan times, as today, this is a way of eradicating the feeling of guilt that accompanies killing, whether for food or in war. An animal once shot is revered and part of its body preserved to ward away its spirit, which could seek revenge. With the smoking carcass of the giant pheasant slung over his shoulders, Canche continued on his way.

To me the path soon became one endless little stream, along which I flowed mechanically, unthinkingly repeating the movements of placing my feet on the proper stones and rocks that slowly slipped by. As we walked I could see the jungle assume different aspects, now low and dry, now lush and opaque; in general, as we advanced, the trees became taller, the vegetation thicker and damper, the vines more numerous and the undergrowth but one thick impenetrable hedge. We came to a fork and, turning to the left, took a narrower trail, the trail to the right being that to Chunyaxche. We were now making our way to Canche's *milpa*, which lay deep in the jungle away from the path connecting Chumpom with Tulum.

The jungle was now incredibly thick and the path no more than a small gully which it took an experienced eye to discover. We wound our way around large tree trunks and up and down rocky mounds, occasionally passing a small natural well in a hollow among the rocks. At one of these wells we stopped to drink. At first I dared not, for the water was covered with a thick, slimy foam. This Canche cleared away, before drinking what seemed like stagnant water. After walking for six hours, I could no longer refrain from drinking and I tasted the water, which to my surprise was very good. At this last stop we sat down and ate some cold tortillas, a frugal meal which nevertheless quieted my stomach for the rest of the afternoon. Toward four, utterly exhausted, we suddenly came out into a large clearing, a desolate ocean of charred tree trunks dotted here and there with immense trees. This was Honco Poc, the *milpa* of Pablo Canche. Amid the desolate-looking and rather messy clearing could be seen small shoots that looked more like weeds than corn. Surrounding the edges of certain zones marked out in the *milpa* were small barricades made of fan palms half buried in the ground. This was to keep iguanas and other small animals and insects from moving in and eating the small shoots. With some difficulty we picked our way through the *milpa*, and Canche let out the strange cry I had first heard on the *Lydia*. It was soon answered by a distant guttural voice from somewhere on the other side of the clearing.

We walked in that direction and came upon an old Indian who I learned was a cousin of Canche's. He greeted us with a smile and led us out of the *milpa* along a narrow path to a small hut composed only of a roughly made palm roof supported by four stakes. Under the roof hung two hammocks and smoke rose from a small fire attended by a tiny, plump young Mayan woman. This was where Canche and his family lived when working on the *milpa*. The open hut was the only shelter and sign of human habitation for miles around.

Soon after we had arrived we were eating warm tortillas and the plump woman was busily cutting into minute pieces the pheasant Pablo had shot on the way over.

After eating, Canche invited me to follow him to see his *"santo* of the *milpa,"* literally "the saint of the fields." He led me past the hut, down a small path to a sunken cave formed by a large rocky outcrop; in the hollow of the cave could be seen a small puddle of water. This was nothing else but a *cenote,* the one from which water was drawn for the needs of those working at the *milpa.* Going under the overhang, Canche proudly pointed to a small, square, stone altar at the edge of the water, and there, to my amazement, stood a delicately carved head in stone on the end of a six-inch-long neck.

The idol was in perfect condition, and in my excitement I could hardly listen while Canche explained that it was sacred and protected the *milpa* so that the corn would grow well and made sure that no one would be sick while working in the jungle. My mind raced madly as to how I could acquire the statue, for it certainly would have had considerable importance to the Mexican Department of Archaeology, and I felt sure that, if left at the *milpa,* it was bound to get broken or stolen.

I therefore rather dishonestly looked at the statue with disapproval, saying that from its looks it could not possibly be sacred, and asked whether I could examine it more closely. To this Canche did not object. And I picked up the strange idol. It represented a bald-headed character with immense round eyes, on its head a diadem projection that rose above the forehead, its long cylindrical neck being pierced at its base with a large hole. It was of a very hard and heavy stone which seemed very much like marble. What first struck me was that the stone, if it was marble, could not have come from limestone Yucatán; secondly, none of the features of the idol bore any resemblance to those of the Mayan figures I had seen previously either at Palenque or in the Yucatán peninsula. Where the strange idol had come from, I could not tell. Was it a vestige of some civilization prior to the Mayas? I did not know but could easily tell that the idol was not a forgery.

Canche explained to me that his father-in-law had found it at the entrance of the *cenote*, in the ground not far from where it now stood. All my coaxing could not lessen Canche's beliefs in the sacred and miraculous virtues of the statue. And no matter how hard I tried, it soon became evident that for nothing on earth was Canche ready to part with the sacred idol. I argued with him about the idol till late at night in the flickering light of the small fire. And it must have been close to ten o'clock when I finally got into my hammock.

From where I rested I could see around me, beyond the wall-less hut, the immense mysterious jungle; the large looming forms of the gigantic trees cut out blackly against the pale sky illuminated by a great moon. And I reflected on the ancient sacred land of the Mayan gods, on the lonely spot where I was sleeping, so remote, so far now from the outside world, the world in which I had always lived but which now seemed but a dream, a faint memory, the world somewhere beyond the unknown world of the jungle. Strangely, I had no yearning for it, and looking upon the other hammocks in the shelter I imagined myself a Maya. That night I finally fell asleep under the protective watch of the small mysterious stone idol whose round eyes, to this very day, still guard the cornfields and protect the Indians as they wage their battle for food against the encroaching jungle—the strange stone face from the deep well in the unknown region of Quintana Roo.

When I awoke the following morning the sun had risen, and from the summits of the giant trees floated up a gentle mist, slowly disentangling itself from the vegetation and disappearing into

the radiant blue sky. I will always remember the beautiful sight of
the mist rising slowly and the small open hut that for one night
had been my resting place, a shelter in the harshness of the giant
forest, a small foothold, a foothold of man, in the midst of the vast
expanse of crushing vegetation.

After a brief meal we went on our way, Canche with my bags
on his back, his head gripped by the forehead strap, his machete
at his side, and his shotgun swinging loosely in his hand. Winding
our way through the dense undergrowth, we left behind the Mayan
idol to guard the *milpa*, where, under its severe auspices, corn
was about to grow that would feed, back in the distant village of
Tulum, the children of Canche, who were among the last of the
countless generations of Mayas, those mysterious people who, outside Christianity, beyond our world, in their own strange jungle
universe, thrived on corn and gods.

My thoughts were cut short by a loud report from Pablo's gun,
followed by another. Stopped dead in his tracks, Canche had fired
two successful shots at some chachalakas, whose weird, panicky
cries had been echoing in my ears for some time. More food, I
thought, surprised at my already conditioned reaction to what a
few years ago had been for me an amusement, a pastime. I remembered how far I was from gastronomical considerations when
at fifteen I had shot my first game bird, or on those innumerable
times when I had shot at clay pigeons or gone hunting just for
amusement.

A few hours away from the *milpa* we arrived at an immense
cenote nearly two hundred feet wide, a great pool sunk deep into
the limestone ground with sheer cliffs descending all around to the
water. This *cenote* seemed like a deep green eye in the jungle. The
dark water was clear enough for one to see fish swimming in its
depths, the mysterious fish of the *cenotes*, fish that in a way live
underground. The water was far too low for us to drink, and walking around the *cenote*, we came upon an abandoned thatched
shelter with a few crudely made benches of logs set upon forked

posts. This was a small camp where a few *chicleros* lived during the season, ganging together to boil their chicle, the white latex of the *zapote*.

After passing the wrecked remains of the small camp we then proceeded south through the jungle. Here there was no path, and with great blows Canche cut a passage, making a beeline for Chunyaxche. How he found his way I can never tell. Progress was very slow indeed as we cut through grove after grove of palm bushes and around dead trunks and large trees. But less than an hour later we came out onto a narrow mysterious path, the one Canche had been seeking, and continued south at a good rate.

By the end of the morning I was completely exhausted and dying with thirst, repeatedly bothering Canche with the same question: "How much farther?" He answered each time with the simple and indicative phrase: "Not yet," and continued on. There are times when one hates the paths, the unknown trails that have no beginning and seemingly no end, but which continue forever, refusing the final turn that will announce arrival, and rest. Often in Quintana Roo I was to feel desperation at the paths that never ended but would simply go on and on, always carrying farther what I had thought must be the last bend. Each time I was disappointed and each time, having new hope that the next bend would be the last, was deceived, till my mind was tired of being tired, tired of worrying, tired of hoping, and I just trudged on with the measured pace of eternity, only to realize that, when I was least expecting it, I had finally arrived.

This was the case when, toward one in the afternoon, we broke out, sweating and tired, from the jungle into a clearing. After the suffocation of the jungle I could at last breathe, and I now fully understood what had been described to me in Mérida as the claustrophobia of the jungle.

We had reached Chunyaxche, three poor huts on the edge of a marshy piece of jungle. Two women were drawing water from a small well, and having refreshed ourselves, and Canche having chatted with them in Mayan, we both sat down exhausted in the hut of one of the villagers.

After a while I remembered my prime purpose for coming and asked questions about the ruins. I was so tired that the last thing I felt like doing was getting up. I nevertheless managed to drag myself out of the hut, and, along with the Indians in whose house we had been, I proceeded down the clearing past the other huts. The man then stopped and pointed with his finger to the treetops. And there to my amazement, soaring skyward above the summits of the tallest trees, and glaring at me through a narrow dark opening amidst them, was a small temple-like structure standing on what was to prove a mighty pyramid, the famous temple Canche had spoken to me about, the one higher than the Castillo of Tulum.

I could not believe my eyes, and asked the Indian to take me to its base. A small path led from behind one of the huts into the jungle, and in a few minutes I was standing at the base of the pyramid—a truly awe-inspiring structure rising out of sight through the mass of vegetation. Trees grew on its flanks and on what were the remains of a very steep and wide staircase. This was the most extraordinary building I had seen so far and I could barely contain my excitement as I scrambled up the great mass of rocks and cut stone, hanging onto vines for support. The monumental stairway led to a steep, crumbling wall, which I scaled, landing on a small ledge that had once been a narrow covered gallery going around the pyramid. Two sides of this gallery remained in good condition. Crawling, I made my way around the pyramid till I came upon a sheer drop where part of the side had crumbled. The ledge on which I stood was about two thirds of the way up to the summit. Finding footholes among the disjointed stones, I climbed up above the ledge, reaching a strange conical wall that formed the top of the pyramid. This too had partly collapsed but proved easy to climb. Crouching on the summit, I stood dazzled by the intense sun. It was as if I had changed worlds, leaving that of the damp and humid dark jungle for a dazzling landscape of shining water and the billowing waves of treetops. To the east stretched an immense lagoon, a lake seemingly endless but interrupted here and there by the contours of small islands and marshy grass patches supporting tattered, finger-like palm trees. A stiff sea breeze blew in from over the lagoon and made the summits of the large trees that extended to infinity to the west dance and shimmer in the strong sun.

Canche had been right: the pyramid was taller than the Castillo of Tulum and from the summit one could see the sea, although it was more than twenty miles away. In the fresh breeze, as I eagerly observed the horizon from the summit of this venerable ruin from which, many years back, the ancient Mayan priests had looked out over their domain, I forgot the damp, humid jungle and felt that to stand here and survey the vast panorama below and around me more than made up for all the effort of our trek that day. From the summit the jungle seemed tame, and I felt that from now on it would be at my feet, a small obstacle to my future progress—an idea that another twenty miles of walking that same afternoon were to dampen slightly.

When I crawled down the pyramid after having meticulously examined its wall for signs of sculpture, and drawn a sketch, I found the Indian who had brought me there busy picking what seemed like grains of dust from his skin. And to my horror I realized that they were ticks, thousands of them, and that I myself was literally covered with swarms of these minute gray insects that had spattered on my clothes and body from the branches on which they had waited ready to jump, as it were, on the first moving being to pass by them. I hurriedly attempted to brush away as many as I could, before they had time to dig their small heads into my skin and start sucking my blood, which many were already doing. There were, I later learned, a considerable number of old recipes as to how to get rid of ticks, but at that time I knew none and had to give up after having desperately tried to tear away as many as I could, being careful not to break off the heads, which would otherwise stay in the skin and get infected.

My excitement, though, was too great at first to worry a great deal about the ticks, and by signs I urged the reluctant Indian to show me more buildings. He accordingly led me on through the jungle, cutting a narrow and low path as he advanced. About a hundred yards away we came upon the extraordinary sight of a vast square temple or palace looming up behind the vegetation, its summit and walls interwoven with great snaky vines and giant roots. It was a large pinkish-stuccoed structure perched upon a high platform. Cutting our way, we slowly went around it. Its western end had the remains of a large stairway that led to the summit of the platform, on which was erected the square palace, with two large circular columns that had once supported the now partly crumbled roof of the main entrance. Beyond the entrance were three small rooms, now but a pile of rubble, one being filled with a giant anthill.

There were no traces of paintings on the walls of the building, which I called the "pink palace," but at the entrance where the lintel had partly collapsed could be seen a great, ancient wooden beam, possibly a thousand years old. Many such wooden lintels had, I knew, already been discovered, and are priceless when found in that they help date a site through carbon tests. I took a small specimen from the dry rotted beam.

The extremely large proportions of the first two buildings I had seen urged me to look for more. My guide led me back down the way we had come, past the clearing with the three huts, and down another little path from which he again entered the choking vegetation, soon stopping and proudly pointing toward what at first seemed only more leaves. Advancing, to my amazement I saw another pyramid, then another and still another, till finally, climbing up the sides of one of these structures, I realized that there were five in all, forming a rough semicircle around a small, partly destroyed square temple in the center.

In my excitement I did not know at first what to do; immediately visions of hidden treasures, of vases and jade objects, flashed into my mind. But there was little or nothing I felt I could do; thousands of hours of patient work would be necessary to carry out a thorough archaeological survey of such a huge site as this.

Was I the first white man ever to stumble across the ruins of this magnificent city? Later, as I shall describe in another chapter, I learned that an expedition had been there before me, although in the dense jungle vegetation they had found only some of the city's buildings. It was obvious, in any case, that here was a great complex of Mayan ruins worthy of further exploration and study.

The structures I had so far seen were larger than those of Tulum. Excitedly I ordered the Indian to cut away as many branches as possible, so that I could take photographs of all the buildings. Running back to my bags to get a new roll of film, I found Canche anxiously awaiting me. Coming toward me, he said that I had to hurry, for we still had a long way to go before reaching Capechen. I myself had not thought of leaving, and told Canche that the buildings were so extraordinary that I wanted to stay. But Canche would hear nothing of this, explaining that he had to get back as soon as possible to Tulum. And no mattter how hard I attempted to persuade him to stay, he refused, facing me with the alternative of being left alone or accompanying him to Capechen, where he had planned to arrange with friends for my going farther south. Had it not been for my anxiety about what lay ahead, my complete helplessness without Canche, my only friend, and the only man to whom I could make myself understood, I would certainly have stayed at Chunyaxche. But in view of the circumstances I had little choice. I decided to go on, promising myself that I would return here and explore this fantastic city in more detail. I therefore rushed back to the ruins to take some last photographs, and then joined Canche, reluctantly setting out for Capechen.

It was to be only three years later, after further exploration and reading, that I was fully to grasp the huge size and importance of Chunyaxche. The trying circumstances of my first visit had not allowed me fully to realize the size of Chunyaxche, which, as I later determined, encompassed more than 108 buildings or remains of buildings.[1] Here I was to find idols and other temples and many signs suggesting that Chunyaxche may once have been the most important trade center of the Quintana Roo region. Even today its exact size has not been determined. For some four hundred years Chunyaxche was virtually the lost metropolis of eastern Yucatán, and had lain in the jungle, unknown to the outside world, the secret of the Chan Santa Cruz Indians, who once a year came to the great lost pyramids in religious procession on their way to Tulum from Chumpom. Situated on a large inland lagoon communicating with the sea through canals, Chunyaxche was beyond doubt a major hub of commerce and ancient Mayan marine traffic. Its sheltered waterways were better designed for canoes than Tulum itself, whose importance seems to have been mainly religious.

Reluctantly following Canche, I skirted the lagoon I had seen from the summit of the pyramid. We crossed an immensely high area of jungle, with great trees with slimy trunks and long wide roots digging into the spongy earth. Often our feet would sink into gluey mud and progress was slow and increasingly difficult.

We were now bound for the coast, but to reach it we were obliged to skirt the two large lagoons and the marshy approaches of the waterways that made their way inland from the sea up to the Chunyaxche lagoon. For lack of exact maps and there being no landmarks from which I could gather my position at any one

---

[1] This figure includes over 40 structures in either good condition or fair condition (i.e., easily recognizable, and only partly destroyed), the remaining structures forming the total including independent mounds, platforms, wall bases enclosing rooms, and badly damaged oratories. See chart, page 286.

moment, I was at a loss in attempting to estimate the route we were taking, and could only rely blindly on Canche, hoping that he would not get lost.

We advanced for four hours through this muddy terrain, and when Canche would turn his stooped head, bent under my load, I could see the sweat as it ran down his cheeks. I thanked heaven for having provided me with such a kind man, for alone, with my own luggage, I would never have managed to walk more than ten miles in such terrain.

Toward six in the evening we came upon a narrow peninsula that headed south, caught between the sea and an inland lagoon. Here at the beginning of this narrow strip of land we came upon Capechen. Capechen was a sort of camp where the villagers from Tulum had settled for a few months. The huts were of the same kind as at Canche's *milpa*, with no walls. When we arrived, three men were lazily stretched out in hammocks, and around them were playing half a dozen small children, while some women were crouched before an open fire. In the characteristically dispassionate Mayan manner, we were greeted by the men, who sat up in their hammocks. The dark-eyed children clustered around us and stared. I was so exhausted that I let myself down into a free hammock while Canche kindly opened a coconut for me. Apparently one of the men of Capechen worked in a *cocal* down the coast. He had brought a few coconuts back with him at the end of his day. It was at Capechen that I finally understood a little of the Mayas' detachment and love of solitude. They think nothing of leaving their villages and changing domiciles, staying absent for long periods of time while working their jungle fields.

Having refreshed myself with the cool coconut milk, I was then offered tortillas and a broth made of much pimento and odd bits of game cut up into minute chunks full of bone. Canche's chachalakas were a welcome dish, and no sooner had we arrived than a machete was busy turning into mashed chachalaka what would have made a good small roasted fowl. But I was already too thankful to find any food and shelter to worry about indoctrinating the Indians with French gastronomical customs. And chachalaka stew, although it tasted only of pimento, was that night the best dish I had ever eaten in my life.

While Canche was engaged in long conversations in Mayan with the other men, I took out my notebook and wrote down the extraordinary happenings of the day.

It was delightful to be near the sea again and the air smelled fresher and the mosquitoes were not so bad. That night I rapidly fell asleep.

The following day at dawn Canche came to tell me that he was leaving for Tulum immediately and that he had spoken to one of the men at the camp and that they said that one could not go farther south because of much water in the lagoons and in a particular channel that connected the lagoons with the sea. This spot was known as Boca de Paila, the "mouth of straw," and during the dry season the water was shallow enough to wade. But one of the Indians knew a man down the coast who had a small dugout canoe in which he could probably take me across Boca de Paila. The men at Capechen could not tell how I could cross, farther south, the other lagoons and the great muddy bay of Ascensión. There were, I remembered, more *cocals* farther south, according to Don Jorge Gonzales, and I thought that possibly I could find there an answer to my transportation problem past the muddy Ascensión bay.

I wanted to pay Canche for his services, but feeling that this might hurt him, I gave him instead in token of my gratitude two shirts and one of the two small miniature machetes I had bought in Mérida. Canche was delighted, although I had scarcely considered that I was giving him treasures. My shirts, I reflected, would look funny on his back and certainly would not last long, being two "Oxford" shirts with button-down collars and French cuffs. But this did not seem to worry Canche and, enchanted, he thanked me profusely, repeating over and over that I should come back to live a long while at his village and maybe teach him the things in the books.

When Canche disappeared, his elegant figure walking lightly through the vegetation, I felt that I had lost a real friend. Though I had known him only five days, the circumstances had made it appear an eternity. How much more I would have liked to have given him! Many times since have his pleasant features haunted me.

At Capechen I felt entirely lost; no one there spoke a word except Mayan. If this was unpleasant in a way, it was most amusing, and my attempts to make myself understood or to understand others brought peals of laughter from all those present and from myself. It is remarkable what good actors men become when faced with the necessity of explaining their thoughts by actions and gestures. And in such circumstances one realizes that speech is only an additive to expression, which in ordinary conversation plays a far more important role in conveying one's ideas than one would think.

It was late when one of the men, taking my load, led me down a path that followed the lagoon. Less than a mile farther along I could see the sea, with its familiar brilliant blue colors and jagged reefs. We were now walking south on the narrow strip of land, surrounded by water on both sides. The lagoons to my right, cut up by mangrove swamps, seemed endless.

Less than two hours later we arrived at a hut in a *cocal* stretching along the sea, its back to the marsh. This was Paso Juana, a *cocal* belonging to a wealthy Cozumeleño. It even sported a rickety plank hut. A half-caste Indian came out of the hut at my approach and seemed most suspicious of me. Before I could speak, my guide had explained my intentions and the reason for my presence.

Addressing me in Spanish, the man said that it was futile to go farther south, that the recent hurricanes had destroyed all the *cocals* save two small ones and that the water was high in the lagoons; as for the Bahía del Ascensión, he did not know about conditions as far away as that, but doubted I could find anyone to take me across, for there were no inhabitants at the *cocals* toward the bay.

Having come so far, I took little notice of his warning, confident that my luck would see me through. Upon further questioning the man as to what lay south, I soon found out that he really did not know, having never been beyond Ascensión bay and having never left his *cocal* except, on rare occasions, to go by sea to Cozumel. The man nevertheless suggested that if I wanted to he could have a small dugout put at my disposal and that two young Indian boys of the *cocal* could pole me past Boca de Paila, which would be too deep to pass on foot. Boca de Paila was about one mile down the coast from the *cocal*, I gathered.

I thanked my Indian porter from Capechen with a gift of a rather old undershirt, which he carried off with great pleasure. I was then led down by two young boys, around fourteen and fifteen, to the edge of the interior lagoon on the other side of the narrow sandbank on which stood the *cocal*. To reach the water we took a narrow path cut through the thick mangroves whose tall roots shot out, from high on the stems of the bushes, down into the water. Mangroves themselves are not very thick bushes, but what makes them impenetrable are their rocky hard, numerous roots.

At the end of the narrow passage lay a tiny Indian dugout hauled up in the mud. It had been crudely shaped from the trunk of a tree, as in the days of the ancients, although this craft was much smaller than the Mayan ones and was really made only for one person. However, we all three managed to fit into it, but to cough was enough to roll the canoe on its side, making it ship water. I feared considerably for my camera and films, as wobbling from side to side we slowly slid through the shallow muddy water.

The younger of the boys was poling from the bow, standing astride the canoe, his brother no doubt doing the same from the stern, while I lay on the bottom, my bags between my knees. I dared not move, and froze in perpetual expectation of what seemed to be an inevitable dunking. Three minutes after gliding out of the mangroves one of the poles got stuck in the mud, the boy leaned over, clinging to it, and made the boat dangerously tip to one side. Both I and the other boy leaned to the other side, and when the pole suddenly got free we swung right over and slowly sank. Fortunately the water was only fifteen inches deep, and I held my camera above my head, crouching with one knee in the mud and the other clumsily astride the canoe. As for my films, they were in the henequen bag which now looked like a sack of wet fish. Getting up in the mud, I hurriedly hauled out my bag, which although soaked had not had time to become waterlogged, and my films had not been wet at all, I found out later, due to the layers of protective envelopes, the plastic bags furnished by Kodak, and my useful blazer.

The two young men soon straightened out the canoe and with an apologetic burst of laughter dismissed the whole incident as a terrific joke.

I was wet through and paralyzed by cramps; I could not move or shade my eyes, much less ease the cramps. In such conditions I had little to do but look up at the sky, the vast, strange sky of Quintana Roo, seemingly supported on the two flimsy poles of my shipmates, who with grace and harmony slowly repeated the endless and difficult movement of lifting the poles, swinging their tips forward, contacting the mud, and slowly sinking them until finally the hard bottom of the lagoon would make us silently creep forward.

Watching poles moving slowly and a sky that is endless and blue, and giving way to considerations of self-pity, are little occupation for a day, and from the dugout my thoughts drifted to gondolas, and this made me sing. The setting was right; the analogy with gondolas easy to bridge. I therefore surprised the two young Mayans with tentative bursts of various arias. *"L'amour est un enfant de Bohême"* and my homemade version of *"O sole mio"* (I've never known more than those three words of the song) managed to draw tears from my gondoliers, who roared with laughter. I needed no more encouragement and soon the lagoon rang out with what in Europe would have been considered a more efficient way to bring rain than the bloody sacrifices that the Mayas offered up to the Chacs. But either the Mayan rain gods were deaf or poor opera critics; it did not rain, and my voice came back to me over the still waters of the lagoon.

My vocal cords having finally broken down, I took to watching the water; occasionally we could feel the bottom as in great swirls of muddy water we oozed through particularly shallow spots. Sometimes we poled right up to the edges of mangrove islands, so close that the branches would scratch the sides of the canoe, delicately brushing my face as they went by. When near these islands I could see large fish working their way back and forth along the edge of the mangroves. Many of these fish were the dangerous barracuda. Periodically from within the mangroves and echoing over the water one could hear loud splashing noises made by big tarpon beating around with their tails in quest of small fish in the shallow obstructed waters under the mangroves.

As we glided slowly on, I could now and again catch a glimpse of a white heron, or see above my head the black streaks of birds flying in swift formations across the sky. From the marshes and lagoons arose an eerie silence, similar to that of an aquarium, in which lay the strange shapes of the mudbanks and the marshy islands. This, I felt, was the land of the Mayan gods, a land mysterious and unknown, whose tortuous channels were inhabited only by a mute population of creepy lizards, sly alligators, gigantic turtles, and strange, enigmatical birds.

All afternoon we had been making a serpentine route south, in and around mangrove islands and mud banks. At times it was as if we were sailing in a large, wide lake, but wide expanses of water would soon narrow into small waterways creeping between the mangrove islands. It was impossible to determine by sight what was solid land and what were only marshy flats.

Toward five in the evening the boys began poling toward the

long strip of land that separated the lagoon from the sea. Making our way among small marshy islands we finally came upon a muddy canal cut through masses of mangroves. The water was very shallow and soon the two boys jumped out and started pushing the canoe over muddy flats. Then they stopped and, showing me a cluster of mangroves, announced that we had arrived.

Sloshing through the water, I stumbled out on a muddy shore. The boys drew up the dugout canoe behind me and led me through the mangroves, picking their way where the bushes were not too thick, and told me to follow a small sandy trail until I reached a *cocal.* I paid them twenty pesos and they set off, apparently rather glad to abandon their slightly mad passenger; they must have greatly appreciated my singing.

I made my way slowly down the narrow trail. Somehow I felt at ease walking alone in the jungle and felt most confident for the future.

An hour later my thoughts began to change and I wondered how far I would have to walk to reach the *cocal,* and whether I should find food and water. Deep shadow drowned the trail and a cool breeze was rustling through the leaves from the sea.

The path finally led into majestic coconut groves and now seemed like some overgrown driveway making its way along the beach. Walking up to the water's edge, I could see at the far end of the *cocal* the familiar sight of a cluster of tiny huts snugly gathered under the palm trees.

But the sand was very soft, so instead I made my way through the coconut trees. To my left extended the sea; to my right there shimmered in the setting sun the pale waters of the lagoon, partly hidden by mangrove bushes. Before I came to the huts, I looked across the lagoon and there, standing in front of me, perched on a high mound, was a neat temple, shining golden in the rays of the sun. I was not expecting any ruins and this impressive pyramid with a temple on its summit appeared like something in a dream. But I was not dreaming, and as I made my way through high reeds toward the great mound I noticed that all around me were other buildings hidden in the reeds. At a glance I counted more than six. This too had been a large old Mayan city, and according to my map it had so far eluded the eyes of mapmakers.

In the sunset the ruins were a spectacular sight, particularly the tall pyramid which loomed above the palm trees as if guarding both the sea and the lagoon, a majestic sentinel, a proud landfall of the ancient Mayan kingdom. How surprised the two shipwrecked Spaniards must have been when they had encountered these cities, part of the realm of the great lord of Xamanzana, whose slaves they were to become. How surprised also, I thought, would be the archaeologists back in Mexico to hear of these ruins which they did not know existed.

I felt like a conquistador, in my own way, and the delight at being the first foreigner to set eyes on such marvels made me rapidly forget the dangers and hazards of the trip. Still today these impressive visions haunt me, the majestic structures of Chunyax-che, the mysterious temples in the mangrove swamps, and now the grandiose city of the *cocal* called San Miguel de Ruz, a city whose Mayan name has long been lost.

It was too dark to undertake any reconnaissance of the ruins, so taking a last look at the pyramid, I hurried on with my heavy bags toward the huts of the *cocal.*

I came up to the huts just before dark. Two Mayan women came out and looked me over with apparent suspicion. Not knowing exactly what to say I explained that I wanted food and would like a place to hang my hammock. One of the women spoke a little Spanish and answered that I could not spend the night there and she could do nothing for me until her husband returned from the *cocal,* where he was working. An hour later, dressed in blue trousers and a rough, patched, pale blue shirt, he came. He seemed a pleasant man, and when I told him where I had come from and that

I was walking down to Belize, he smiled and expressed surprise at the distance I had planned to walk.

He cordially invited me to his hut and said I could sleep in one of the smaller huts which served as a storeroom for the dried copra waiting to be shipped off to Cozumel.

His kind welcome made me venture to ask if I could remain for the following day to rest and investigate the ruins. He agreed and I smothered him with questions about the ruins. Had any foreigners been to see them? He said no, no one had seen them except his family, and since he had first arrived there seventeen years ago no one had come to those parts save occasionally *chicleros* and the men who lived a little down the coast at Chamax, another *cocal*.

The following morning I got up at dawn and went over to the ruins I had spotted the day before. The main pyramid was some forty-five feet high, the structure on the summit being a square temple like the ones I had seen earlier on the coast, but larger, with two great doorways leading into a central room. There were no signs of paintings. At the foot of the pyramid were a series of large piles of stones, the remains of what must have been fair-sized buildings. Some of these still had walls standing. Rummaging around in the vicinity, I came upon a series of columns lying on the ground half buried in rubble. Intensifying my search, I found a large rectangular structure with a great doorway with two large square pillars. Unfortunately, part of the heavy vaulted roof of this building had fallen down, filling in the interior almost entirely. In all, on the edge of the *cocal* and backed against the swamp, I ran into the remains of ten structures, all set around the tall pyramid on whose summit grew a large bush whose roots would soon destroy the top temple. It was little wonder that no one had come here, for this bush had hidden the summit of the pyramid from any ships that might have ventured close to the coast. And, in fact, it had escaped the eyes of the few archaeologists who had sailed along the coast in search of ruins. No one had yet thought or dared to do the coast by land.

I was filled with pride and all my childhood dreams of adventure seemed pale beside the excitement that ran through me each time I saw an unreported structure and peered inside its arched rooms. Was I not as close as one could get to the ancient Mayas? The gap of some four hundred years seemed to me to narrow down, and very often I approached the old buildings as if expecting to see an ancient warrior, his skin painted in red, come out of them.

At San Miguel de Ruz there was one small temple that had been built over a still smaller one, thus making up two small rooms,

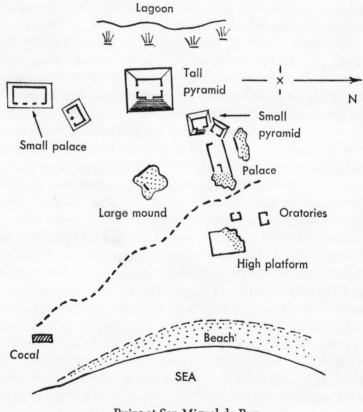

Ruins at San Miguel de Ruz

one just a corridor around the older, smaller temple that formed the inner chamber. Here was visible an ancient altar on which must have stood the old clay idols of the Mayas. A small raised platform a foot high stood against the wall of the inner room.

I searched around this temple attempting to find some object that would recall the ancient Mayas. I did not have to look for long, soon finding many pieces of old pottery, but alas, they were all so shattered that they seemed of little use or value. I nevertheless kept these, and fortunately so, for all the specimens of pottery that I brought back were most useful in dating the structures I had found; luckily I also thought of keeping the specimens separately in small paper bags, one for each site.

After returning to the *cocal* for a frugal lunch of tortillas and black beans, I returned again to the ruins to make a detailed map of the city, the largest I had so far found, as I then thought, for San Miguel de Ruz seemed much larger than Chunyaxche, where I had not had the time to investigate the area fully.

That evening, tired and scratched from crawling around the rough stone structures and clearing the bushes to take photographs, I had a chat with the owner of the small *cocal*. I asked him all he knew of the coast southward and the possibilities of finding a way through to Belize. His answers were similar to all those I had heard: there was no trail, only marshes and jungle, and no inhabitants save at a few more *cocals*. The hurricanes had discouraged all attempts to form new *cocals* since the others had been abandoned south of Espíritu Santo bay. As for crossing Ascensión bay, he told me that there used to be a lighthouse at the northern point with a keeper, a fisherman, but he had died during the last hurricane and the light had never been set up again.

When I asked if he could accompany me south at least to the last *cocal* before the end of the narrow peninsula on which we were, he refused, saying that it was more than a day's walk away and he was too busy and had to stay at the *cocal*. "But you will have no trouble," he added. "Just follow the coast. Three miles from here you will find another *cocal* called Chamax. There are some ruins there also, but I do not advise you to go there; the men that live there are *muy mala gente* [really bad people]." And he went on to explain that Chamax had once been a *colonia*, a village inhabited by Vera Cruz bandits who had taken refuge on the barren coast to escape justice and had thrived as *chicleros*. But every man of the once numerous colony was a murderer and they had feuded among themselves, killing each other off until their number was now reduced to five. These five still lived at the *cocal* called Chamax and engaged in evil deeds of robbery; they also smuggled whisky which they brought by boat from Belize, through the lagoons, and carried inland over secret trails.

Although slightly frightened by the prospects of meeting these renegades of the *colonia*, I was overcome with joy at thinking that maybe they had a boat and that, smugglers or not, they could take me on south at least past Ascensión bay, if not to Belize. After all, I knew one *chiclero*, Miguel, and he had really been a nice fellow. But the man of San Miguel de Ruz seemed to disagree with that.

"Stay away as far as you can from these men," he warned me. "I would not advise you to even stop and speak to them."

The following morning it was in a rather anxious frame of mind that I prepared to set off alone. This was to be my first complete day without a guide, and I had only a vague notion as to where I was headed.

After saying good-by to the *cocalero* and his two wives, or the two women who lived with him, I made my way down the *cocal*. In my mind I repeated the order of the day: to follow the coast to Chamax, where the crooks and smugglers lived, and then all the way down the coast until I got to a *cocal* called San Francisco. According to the man from San Miguel de Ruz, that was nearly twenty-five miles, although I was by now most suspicious of any estimate of distances by the people I encountered. After an hour's walk I began to worry as to whether twenty-five or maybe thirty miles was not a little too far with my load, which was already cramping my neck and proved heavier and heavier as I trudged on in the soft sand.

The sun was incredibly hot and I was wet with perspiration when I arrived, after about two hours and numerous stops, at the edge of the *cocal* of the smugglers. I could see a small sailing boat hauled up on the beach. Drawing near, I saw to my surprise a Negro sitting on the sand mending a tattered sail. One of the smugglers, I asked myself. I walked up to him, receiving a cool greeting in Spanish. "What do you want?" he barked, now joined by an unpleasant character who growled, "Who are you, an adventurer or a propagandist?" Quite frightened by my reception, I explained that I was on my way to Belize, adding that I was interested in ruins and had been told that there were some nearby. The Mexican with the unpleasant features cut me off, saying, "No, there are no ruins here." I did not insist, and fearing some more unpleasantness, I hurried on, bidding them a brisk good-by. A little farther down the endless beach, I decided to walk under the shade of the *cocal*, thinking that if there were some ruins there I might get a glimpse of them after all.

With my heavy pack I made my way through the high underbrush below the coconut trees. The *cocal* seemed quite abandoned and I wondered how bad the men at Chamax really were.

Here by sheer chance I came upon two large structures, one a pyramid smaller than the one I had seen the day before, but in a remarkable state of preservation. There was a square superstructure standing on a series of superimposed platforms forming giant steps up the pyramid. Dropping my load, I climbed to its summit. After having inspected the top structure on this pyramid, I descended and climbed up the partly destroyed second structure. This building must have been some kind of palace and stood upon a very high mound; part of the building had crumbled and what remained was a long, high, vaulted room with two doorways on one side and one on the other. One end of the corridor-like room was open where the wall had fallen down. Inside I found numerous traces of paintings, but all in very poor condition. What struck me most was that here and there upon the walls were hand prints in

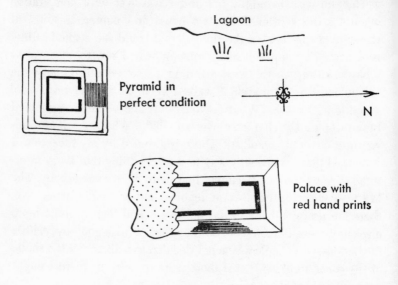

Pyramid in
perfect condition

N

Palace with
red hand prints

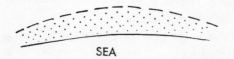

Ruins at Chamax

red, neatly outlined on the stucco. They were a frightening sight, seemingly of blood, and the neat outlines brought to life the person who had lent his hand to be printed on the walls of the temple, the age-old mark of someone who had lived there many years ago. Many such red hand prints have been found in Yucatán and nobody knows their exact significance. Were they the hand prints of victims sacrificed to the fearful Chacs, the rain gods? I did not know. Nor did I have much time to contemplate the ruins I had found, for having climbed the pyramid again I saw to my dismay three figures standing on the roof of the palace I had just looked over. Spotting me, the three men started shouting at me, and to my fright I noticed that two of them were the bandits who had crossed over from Cozumel with me on the *Lydia* and who had robbed the *cocals* on the coast; the third man was the one who had told me a few minutes before that there were no ruins at Chamax.

I immediately knew that they meant trouble, and with my heart pounding, and fearing the worst, I scrambled down from the pyramid, picked up my heavy bag and ran through the bushes, praying at every moment that I was not being followed, and not daring to turn my head. Three hundred yards farther on I ventured to look around; I could see no one. But this did not put me at ease. Through my mind flashed all the tales I had heard about *chicleros,* and I imagined for more than an hour that I was being stalked from behind the bushes as at an accelerated pace I made my way down the beach. At the end of the beach the coast became exceedingly rocky and it was impossible to follow the shoreline. I therefore tentatively tried cutting inland. The vegetation was quite low and mostly made up of large, bushy trees. After five minutes I found myself facing a watery marsh, a little arm that came in from the lagoon and practically cut in two the narrow peninsula I was on. I backtracked, taking a new course through the groves of spiny bushes and palms. Since I had no idea of the lay of the land ahead, all my directions were tentative. Never before had I realized how important a good map was. For although I had the sea to guide me, I could not tell whether the coastline I was walking along might not lead me later on to the edge of some deep bay that might require more than three hours to walk around.

Hesitatingly I made my way through the bushes, occasionally using my baby machete. Feeling safe at last from any pursuit by the ruffians from Chamax, I now started to feel the pangs of thirst and hunger. I had drunk nothing since dawn and had brought along no food, having foolishly counted on getting both food and drink at Chamax.

The sun was beating down on me in full force and from all around came the buzzing and screeching of thousands of locusts and crickets, announcing the hottest time of the day. In the northern hemisphere it is difficult for us to realize that the sun can represent anything but joy and pleasure. For northerners, a cold gray day is the symbol of despair and tragedy, but now I felt the full heat of the tropical sun, that crushing sun which is more often tragic than gay, all-consuming, blinding, a sun so powerful that all things under its glare lose their shape as if flattened out by that great ball that burns somewhere in the sky, that ball that no one can look at but which one constantly feels above oneself.

My bag was getting heavier at every step and my progress was slower owing to my thirst and the irritating fact that every four steps the now half-torn straps of my sandals would slip off my feet, making me hop around on one foot while I attempted hurriedly to slip the straps back into place.

Would the day ever end, would I ever find another human being, and some refuge and water?

Not being able to stand the thirst any longer, I started in desperation looking for something I could drink. There were no coconut trees in sight; I was now miles from any *cocal*. Nor could I expect to find any natural *cenotes* on the sandy strip of land where I walked. It seemed hopeless, and I struggled on, always hoping that perhaps I had walked faster than I had imagined; perhaps I would soon see the shape of a *cocal*, the refreshing coconut palms, the signs not only of the thirst-relieving nuts but also of life and food. Half closing my eyes, I wandered on hoping that I was on the right path, making my way again toward the sea, feeling that I might finally break out on a clear beach. Then I did find a very narrow beach on which, to my delight, I saw the familiar fronds of one coconut tree. It was small and bent and stood alone, its hairy roots like the tentacles of an octopus, half covered by the sea that lapped against the trunk. At least here was something to drink. The tree had probably sprung up from some coconut that had washed ashore. High up at the summit dangled half a dozen rather seedy-looking nuts. Having finally managed to knock one down, I then set about the difficult task of opening it. This finally achieved, dying with thirst, I took the nut to my lips and drank, immediately spitting out the foul salty liquid. Either the nut was too green or, more likely, the tree was too close to the water, but the milk was undrinkable. I nevertheless ate the meat with voracity.

Feeling better, I wandered on down the beach that stretched lazily in the sun, bordered by the growth of thorny bushes. The sun was at its hottest and I made slow progress on the sand, my feet sinking into the beach. At one point where the bushes thinned I made my way down the coast inland amongst vast, bare patches of rugged limestone rock that in its bony whiteness reflected, like an oven, the immense heat. Making my way over these flat expanses closed in like small, rocky fields by the hedges of palms and bushes, I came upon a small square Mayan structure, virtually unspoiled, unexpectedly standing in the middle of one such rocky patch.

This made me rapidly forget my thirst and the strain of my pack as I hastily made for the building. It was one of the dwarf-type structures, two yards high with the same characteristically slanted side doorway. It had, however, one interesting peculiarity at its summit, where two stone decorative ledges formed a double-barreled frieze. Around this frieze were rectangular sunken niches ornamented with delicate crisscross decorations of stucco plastered over thin, straight, dried coral sticks. It was an interesting motif and the first of its kind to be found.

It seemed incredible that here again could be standing, unknown and unexplored, another vestige of the ancient Mayas. Decidedly, the coast from San Miguel de Ruz through to Chamax and down to this point had been but one large settlement. Had these perhaps been the three towns so close to each other that Grijalva's chaplain spoke about? For in the ancient times all these three places would have been clearly visible from the sea. What again struck me as strange was the fact that no one had attempted to go down on foot and explore these areas. Was I not less than six hundred and fifty miles by air from Cape Canaveral, where rockets were trying to reach the moon and from where satellites were launched into space? While here man had not yet fully explored the earth!

I took a few photographs and made a small sketch of the structure, looking for any signs of pottery around it. As I did so, a brilliant stone caught my eye, and I found that it was a fragment of obsidian, the volcanic semi-precious stone the color of smoked glass that had been used by the ancient Mayas for making knives and razors and even spearheads. The piece I found still had the distinct flaked cuts where it had been splintered into a double-edged knife. This find enchanted me even more than the discovery of all the buildings I had found that day.

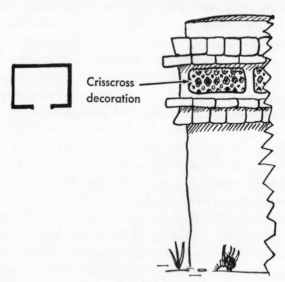

Ruin at Punta San Juan

I was nevertheless still exhausted when I started off again, down more stony fields and through bushes, occasionally catching a glimpse of the sea or of the lead-colored gray lagoon from which occasionally arose the strident cries of waterfowl.

I tried hard to see where the coastline led or what lay ahead of me, but I strained my eyes in vain. How far, I wondered, would I have still to go? Perhaps I had got onto a point that might lead out to sea. I could get no indication. The lagoon stretched away into the distance, dotted with flat islands and sandbanks covered with mangroves.

Breaking through a clump of bushes, I suddenly found myself at a short canal that joined the sea and the lagoons. Thirty yards away, beyond the arm of water, extended a low, flat island.

Wondering what to do, whether to swim or wade across the channel, or to turn back and look for another way which might take me into the lagoons by a sandbank, for the first time I felt really frightened. I had hardly the strength to walk all the way back from where I had come; furthermore, I feared a second encounter with the men of Chamax. I had not had a drink since dawn, the few pieces of coconut had not satisfied my hunger, and I felt weak.

I decided to go on, thinking that certainly the *cocal* I had heard about would be along the sea and not inland. A swift current flowed into the lagoon through the crystal-clear blue water of the small channel. I could not tell if it was deep. Wasting no time, I set down my bags, and slowly feeling my way across the sandy bottom, found that the water was in no place more than four feet deep. I returned to my bags, which I held above my head as I waded, but halfway across I felt my baby machete slide out of my pack and into the fast current. Once on the other side I returned and tried vainly to recover it, but soon gave up the hopeless search.

As I started off again I was by now quite exhausted. The sun had parched my lips and my neck ached from the strain of the clumsy henequen bag, which seemed to have gained hundreds of pounds. I was again on a narrow strip of land barely above sea level and lightly covered with bushes; here and there high sandy dunes rose to my left, obstructing my view of the sea. All was desolate and there was not the slightest sign that humans had passed by here, not the smallest or faintest footprint in the sand, nothing but small bushes, occasional stumps of miniature fan palms, and odd clumps of brittle grass.

In despair I sat down in the shade of a small bush. With some rest I would feel better, but getting up and continuing required an effort that nearly made me sit down again; I could hardly manage to raise the load and pass the strap around my forehead without being thrown off balance.

I tried this time to walk along the beach, taking off my sandals, which now were more of a hindrance than a help. But the sand along the water's edge was hard and the salt water stung the cuts and scratches on my feet.

I began to drag the load along the sand at the end of my hammock rope, but this proved no good as soon I was dragging great piles of sand in front of the bag. I felt weaker and more depressed than before, and now I seriously started to doubt that anything lay before me. Even if I found a coconut tree I would not be able to rip open the strong fiber shell, since I had no knife. It was getting late, and in a last burst of energy I decided to pull myself together and advance again as quickly as possible, sweat blurring my eyes as I made my way on ahead. At every step I postponed stopping again, repeating to myself that not the next clump of bushes but the next would reveal a palm grove and the familiar signs of a small palm hut where I could drink and sleep for the night. But bushes succeeded bushes with occasional bare stony flat fields, more sand and more rock, and the sun still burned as hotly even though it was going down.

There are moments when one feels ready to give up, and this was how I felt. My mind flashed with all the warnings I had received before leaving and all the advice I had been given and not taken; and suddenly it dawned on me that if the temples I had seen had not been previously visited, it was not due to a lack of adventurous spirit or to the hostility of the Chan Santa Cruz Indians, but simply to the fact that the coast was no more than barren rock, marshes and lagoons with high, inhospitable jungle inland. Had I not been stupid to attempt to walk down this coast where no one had been foolish enough to go before? Who would ever be able to give me aid here? Nobody knew of my whereabouts, for although, as I progressed southward, I had established a relay chain of names and places, none of these separate links had contact with each other. I had visited isolated spots one after the other: Puha, Tankah, the village of Tulum, the ruins of Chunyaxche, the *cocal* on the other side of the lagoons, and now I was on an island, a flat, parched piece of land stretching into the sea along a coast whose reefs had for centuries discouraged navigators. Here I felt I would die.

I now gave up hope, trudging mechanically on, fighting away the mosquitoes that began to rise in swarms from the marshy lagoon.

I would probably have stopped and thrown away my bags and abandoned the struggle finally, had I not come unexpectedly upon another Mayan temple. This one, in perfect condition, appeared like a hallucination, such an odd sight it was in such a barren spot. Seeing it made me forget my weariness; it now appeared not like a Mayan ruin but like a sign of civilization on the unfriendly coast.

Furthermore, it confirmed my idea that the whole coast south of Tulum was but a succession of towns, that the barren Quintana Roo coast was after all a rich treasure chest of unexplored archaeological sites. The familiar but always new excitement of the realization that I was making a discovery gave me fresh hope and energy. The small building that I had found stood, its sides covered with plants, directly behind a high sand dune that blocked the temple from the sea. Most intriguing was its peculiar shape; instead of being rectangular or square, like all those I had seen so far, it was oval. It was slightly larger than the building I had seen earlier, rising about three to four yards above the sandy ground. It had one narrow low, classical doorway facing the sand dune. The walls were in good condition; they formed a well-designed oval slightly more rounded than the shape of the Mayan huts I had seen at the village of the Chan Santa Cruz Indians. Around the tops of the walls it had the characteristic double-barrel frieze made of stone covered with stucco. In Mayan structures circular forms are quite rare save for a few examples of circular towers on top of platforms or the characteristic conical summits of pyramids like the one I had seen at Chunyaxche.

Penetrating the structure, which was dark as I blocked the narrow opening with my body, I had a feeling of violating a sanctuary. When my eyes got accustomed to the dim light I saw to my surprise that the interior was not empty. Nor did it have the slightly elevated floor that formed the ancient altars, but the interior was half occupied by a giant oval rock, an immense coral growth with its thousands of delicately chiseled designs. It resembled a giant fossil, with a surface like a huge sponge. The coral formation was so large that it could not have been carried in through the door and must have been there before the erection of the temple. Was this some temple to a god of the sea? Later the presence of the coral rock was to puzzle all the Mayan experts to whom I described the building.

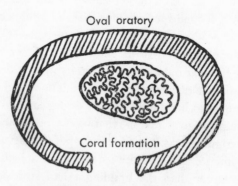

Oval oratory

Coral formation

Ruin at Recodo San Juan

The ceiling of the temple was dome-shaped, instead of being V-shaped with a traditional Mayan vault. Such dome-shaped ceilings are quite rare, and I was most excited at having found this one. I took photographs of the temple and continued, with a new burst of energy and hope, on my seemingly endless way south. The sun was very low; as I hurried on I made plans as to what to do if I needed to spend the night on the beach.

More than two hours later, as dusk descended over the bare island, I caught sight of one coconut tree and then another, and then to my relief, and hardly daring to believe my eyes, I saw the outline of coconut groves. I had arrived at the *cocal* where I had planned to spend the night. All my fears vanished as I now walked under the coconut palms and could look up and see the bunches of hundreds of giant nuts dangling from under the leaves. This renewed my thirst and hurried me on.

A mile farther down I caught a glimpse of a flickering light and then heard a dog bark and could see the familiar outlines of two huts nestled beneath the coconut trees in the sand on the beach, which sloped gradually toward the sea. Something moved and I caught the dark silhouette of a man with a shotgun on the doorstep. I let out the "U-ugh" I had heard so often, the noise that means "Can you hear me? I am here," and went up to the man in the doorway. Seeing me in the narrow beam of yellow light that filtered from the hut, he lowered his gun. Stupidly, not knowing exactly what to say, I said, "Good evening."

The man fortunately spoke Spanish and the first thing I asked him was for something to drink as I sat down exhausted on the sand, explaining that I had come from San Miguel de Ruz. The name of this place, and my looks, seemed sufficient to inspire confidence, and curious as to how I had managed to walk that far and get over the *rio,* as he called the stretch of water I had waded through, the man asked many questions about my trek. I gave a brief recital as to my purpose on the coast. With customary *cocalero* hospitality, the stranger ordered his wife to cook some food and he went out to cut a coconut for me. I drank like a pig, letting the milk run down my neck; at long last I had found food and drink and shelter.

If I had had the energy I would have hugged my benefactor. Never before had I looked upon a fellow man with such gratitude, for I felt that his existence here had saved my life. He went on to tell me that never had a foreigner come to these parts before.

Later, in my hammock, I realized that I had walked for sixteen hours that day under the blazing sun with nothing to drink, and my bag weighed forty-five pounds. It did not take long for me to fall asleep to the gentle rocking of the hammock and the drone of the coral reef.

When I awoke next morning the sun was already shining in yellow streaks through the stake walls of the hut. With sleep I had quickly forgotten the hardships of the previous day. I was now in a small *cocal* called San Francisco, very much like Puha. It was inhabited by its owner, a poor squatter from Cozumel.

Going over to the main hut, I had a chat with the owner and tried to get information about the ruins I had seen the day before. He apparently had never seen the ruin I had found after meeting the bandits, the one with the crisscross decorations. "I never go up the coast," he explained. "As for the circular building, I thought it was an old Spanish house from the days of the pirates." He seemed most surprised when I told him that these structures were hundreds of years old. He gave me the name of the sandy bays on which these ruins stood, Punta San Juan and Recodo San Juan. I entered the sites in my archaeological map under these names. Since Puha, the uncharted archaeological sites I had encountered now numbered as many as nine. More than ever I felt that in continuing south my mission should be to discover and explore as many archaeological sites as possible. Certainly I felt many more marvels of the ancient Mayas lay waiting for me to uncover them, and I was not wrong in believing this.

At San Francisco, I found out, there had also stood a ruin, but unfortunately the owner of the *cocal* had a few years previously destroyed it to use the stones. He brought me to a spot in his *cocal* to contemplate what an archaeologist would call a nightmare—the scattered remains of a small square temple, recently destroyed.

The existence of yet another ancient Mayan structure at the *cocal* strengthened my belief that the narrow peninsula and thin islands that stretched along the coast south of Boca de Paila had been a great ancient Mayan maritime settlement.

I also learned from the *cocalero* that the narrow island upon which we stood ended some ten miles to the south, projecting into the Bahía del Ascensión and practically closing its entrance to the north. At the end of this point had stood a lighthouse, or rather an automatic light beacon, which the recent hurricanes had destroyed. Furthermore, I was in luck, for although the coast was uninhabited, I was told that I might be able to find, at the lighthouse point, a fisherman who spent some time on the coast each year. Three weeks before, my host had seen his small boat sailing south, and there seemed a good chance that we could meet him and that he might be able to take me south across the great bay that now barred my route to Belize.

VIII

Jades of the Gods

Toward eleven we set out. I was greatly relieved not to have to carry my bag and to have stumbled onto such a pleasant person as the *dueño* of San Francisco—a small, scraggy Cozumeleño with a soft voice, a man to whom I felt greatly indebted, if only for the fresh drink he had given me when I stumbled unexpectedly into his *cocal* after the terrible day of thirst walking alone down the coast.

Three hours later we arrived in what were the hideous remains of a *cocal* through which hurricane Janet had recently passed. I had never yet seen the damage caused by the passage of the eye of a hurricane. What lay around me was a vision of devastation. Hundreds of bare stumps, coconut trees that had lost their plumed heads, were sticking upright like amputated limbs; the vision was more than ghostly. But if some trunks were still standing, literally thousands more lay on the ground as if pushed down by a giant hand, neatly arranged on their sides in a pattern that showed the curving passage of the eye of the hurricane. Here apparently not only the wind had blown, but also the sea had risen, covering the island and reaching the lagoon behind it. The *cocal* of San Francisco, although extremely close, had been spared and its owner had suffered the loss of only a few hundred trees.

Right within the graveyard of trunks and dramatic stumps, at the furthermost point of the island strip, stood a rickety hut that had been blown over and knocked around by the hurricane and then later patched up and righted with the help of great poles that now supported one of the leaning sides. Its occupants during the hurricane had all died. Now this was the home of the fisherman who I hoped would take me to the other side of Ascensión bay.

We were greeted at the hut by an old lady of Mexican blood, apparently the mother of the fisherman, who had gone out to set his nets and *trampas* (traps) between mangrove islands.

The old lady informed me that I would have to wait until the return of her son. The *cocalero* bade me good-by and made his way back up the beach. The old lady (contrary to most old ladies) was not at all talkative, so while awaiting the return of the fisherman I investigated the surroundings. We were on a sandy point: to the east extended the blue Caribbean; southward lay the muddy entrance to Ascensión bay, some twenty miles wide; the other side of the bay was invisible in the haze. Here and there in the muddy waters of the bay were small islands to which clung mangrove bushes, blocking, as it were, the entrance to the bay; to the west the bay stretched out of sight inland between other patches of mangroves that ran down from the north parallel to the sandy strip of land on which I had traveled down the coast. It was hard to grasp what was solid land and what was lagoon, and one could rightly say that all the coast behind the solid peninsula running north to south was but a succession of small lagoons eventually leading to the great inland lagoon at Chunyaxche.

All these lagoons, in the time of the ancient Mayas, must have been most active, with innumerable canoes that ferried back and forth from the settlements which I had discovered. It must have been a great, booming, coastal center, a giant Venice of canals and lagoons dotted here and there with mangrove islands and small, solid sandbanks clustered with tall pyramids rising above the low horizon and forming a frightening skyline. Now all was desolation —only the limitless succession of patches of muddy water alternating with pale green, low, flat mangrove swamps and little islands. There somewhere at the end of the bay had stood the small port of Vigía Chico, the only access the besieged General Bravo had to the coast. This was the bay of the Chan Santa Cruz Indians, now totally abandoned to nature and to a few intruding half-caste Indians from Cozumel. Ascensión bay had been also one of the great pirate harbors in the seventeenth century, a wild, isolated natural shelter, but one whose treacherous sand and mudbanks must have stranded more than one of the pirate vessels that waited here in hiding for the passage of Spanish ships as they made their way up the coast, fighting against the trade winds on their way to Santiago de Cuba.

The twisted rusty remains of the steel frame of what had once been a small beacon lay among the broken coconut trunks. The light had been a recent installation on the coast, judging from its modern design.

Toward noon the fisherman returned, announced by the barking of a dog in the hut with the old lady, and then confirmed by the appearance of a small sloop with a dirty triangular sail. It slowly rode up the coast and was steered in to the beach, where it came to a grinding halt. A strong, stocky man descended, drawing with him the painter of the boat, which he secured to a stake. He looked like a typical pirate, with pale blue, brine-hardened trousers rolled up to below his knees, a loose shirt of the same color much patched and open in front, a rugged face with a small thick mustache, and on his head, in pirate fashion, a red handkerchief. He even wore a gold earring. With a long fish-knife at his side he appeared a character from my dreams. I could not help imagining him putting his knife between his teeth. And although I expected this, he disappointed me by simply walking up to me and asking rather loudly in Spanish what I wanted.

I told him that I was going down to Belize on foot along the coast, that I was looking for temples and ruins, and that I needed his help. "Ah," said the man, "you are looking for treasures. I have already met a man of your sort. Do you have a map?" I was only half surprised by his question which so fitted his Long John Silver looks, but I quickly reassured him that I had no secrets and no maps. This seemed to satisfy him, and he went on to say that he could take me over Ascensión bay the following day for twenty pesos; he would take me to a place called Carmen-something, he said, pointing to the southern end of the bay. He added that he doubted that I could go farther south, since the hurricane had destroyed the *cocals,* and now that the water was high in the lagoons one could not wade them or cross on foot the many water channels along the coast. He nevertheless knew of a man who lived at the spot called Carmen. He might be able to help me.

Delighted that my problem of crossing Ascensión bay had been so easily solved, I thanked the pirate and asked for food and lodging until the following morning.

The next day I awoke at dawn to learn that we might not be able to leave, for the winds were unfavorable for the crossing. I had not planned on the winds and spent the first hours of the day anxiously looking at the sea and optimistically reporting anything that seemed like an improvement to my eventually irritated host.

Three hours later the fisherman judged the weather adequate and, asking to see my money, waved to me to board the small boat, which was no bigger than the *Lydia.* With a fair breeze we slid past the point, passing from the blue waters of the Caribbean into the shallow waters of Ascensión bay, making our way for the distant mangrove islands. The entrance of the bay, I could now see, was partly clogged by mudbanks, and I later learned that the bay had once been quite deep and navigable but now was inaccessible to large vessels. There are no adequate maps or nautical charts of all this part of the coast. In fact, the charts used by seamen today date from many years ago and are inaccurate surveys. It is believed that no check has ever been made of the coast's outline, which on all maps of the world is shown possibly as much as half a degree off true bearing.

This was of little concern to my pirate captain, who steered in silence a clear course across the lagoon, while I lay on my back occasionally looking up at flamingos that streaked across the sky. I was by now used to the feeling of loneliness and isolation, and meditated on the strangeness of the circumstances that had brought me to the coast and all the incidents which had led to my sailing across Ascensión bay.

The crossing took three hours, and toward midday we came in sight of the opposite side of the bay. We had steered a course that had taken us to the southwest end of the bay. The coast appeared as a jagged mass of dead trees interwoven with mangroves, and to my surprise I realized that all the dead trees were uprooted ones that had been carried about by the hurricane and finally planted upside down in a great tangle by the tidal waves.

We drew up to a narrow, sandy beach half swallowed by mangroves, and there stood a strange palm-thatched hut, or rather a steep, slanting, thatched roof directly resting on the sand, a primitive shelter with no walls but just a large roof with a hole for doorway.

At our approach, an old, tattered man crawled out of the doorway. He was dressed in a shirt of patches, so much repaired it was. As we slowly sailed onto the beach, startling a couple of black wild ducks that had been standing face to the wind, wings extended, on a dead tree, the old man came running toward us. He was uttering strange cries and shrieks. And he was completely mad, or at least had all the symptoms of gentle imbecility. He spoke Spanish, but to utter one sentence he went through thousands of guttural sounds and meaningless words.

My pirate captain explained to the man why I had come and asked him if he could take me down the coast to the next inhabited spot, if there was one. After much stuttering, the old man replied that it was unlikely that we could go any farther south, for all along the coast there were many water channels which the rainy season had probably swollen to a depth over the head of a man.

He added that the *cocal* of Punta Paharo, the point that closed Ascensión bay to the south, had been abandoned and that the only people living on the coast were a family of Cozumeleños established eight *leguas* away—approximately twenty miles. Hearing this bad news, I wondered what I could do. I had little choice, and thinking that if the worst came to the worst I could always swim the channels, I urged the old man to try to take me along, offering him a bit of money.

Money changed his mind and he agreed to try to bring me south, but recalled that the *rios* were very deep, also saying that he could not swim.

I bade farewell to the pirate, who slowly slipped out of sight in his small boat while my half-idiot guide went about preparing food to take on the journey.

I wondered whether my guide's strange stuttering and apparent idiocy were not the result of his being completely isolated from other human beings. He lived all year on the coast and had no boat and fed on the fish he caught in fish traps built of stakes. Stranded on the marshy shores of this great barren bay, most people would certainly have been driven insane.

Toward ten, the man loaded my bag on his shoulders and we set off along the coast, having to walk in the water of the bay when the mangroves overshot the narrow beach.

It was incredibly hot and the sun not only struck us from above but reflected violently from the water in which we trod, obliging us to squint. Fortunately in the hot sun there were no mosquitoes. All was silent and dead under the crushing rays of the midday sun that spread over the grayish waters of the marshy bay like molten lead. The sun was so brilliant that it faded all colors and the landscape seemed but one mass of white light and black shadows. Occasionally ripples on the water would turn into a thousand electric sparks, blinding us as we looked over the bay. Above the dense mangroves of the shore protruded the ghostly bones of dead trees thrown upside down in hideous positions by the hurricanes. If the suffocating effects of the jungle had at times been depressing, it was nothing compared to the wild barrenness and tragic void of the lagoons in the crippling sun.

After a short while we came upon a narrow channel that cut across our path and made its way inland through the mangroves. Advancing cautiously, we managed to wade across. The sun dried our wet clothes, which became rigid with salt.

Now and again my guide would turn around and mutter incomprehensible phrases for which, fortunately, he expected no answer.

It was not long before I began to feel the effects of heat and thirst, but here there was no water, and not even a chance of encountering a coconut. The sand of the shore was so painfully hot that often we had to rush into the surf to bathe our feet.

We soon came upon another stretch of water crossing our path, which we forded with no trouble, and then a third, this one much wider and swept by a rapid current. Here my guide hesitated and, leaving my bag on the shore, cautiously advanced to the middle of the *rio*. By then the water was up to his chest and he began losing balance, slowly being dragged along by the current, but he finally found a firm foothold on a sandbank and safely reached the other side. This left me with the unpleasant chore of carrying my own bags across, an operation that was not easy. However, as I was much taller than my guide, the water never came up to my chin as it had with him. Bracing myself against the current and feeling the sand being swept away under my feet, I slowly inched across, succeeding in what was to be our last difficult passage until we reached the southern point of the bay, whose sandy projection again separated the Caribbean from the muddy waters of Ascensión bay.

A refreshing wind blew over the desolate, sandy point, which was but one great scene of disaster and tragedy. Here had been a *cocal* and here had stood a couple of large huts that were now nothing but wrecked remains strewn among the twisted debris of thousands of trees that had been carried in by the tidal wave from some unknown and now uprooted jungle. A few dented and rusty pots lay about in the sand, the last tragic reminders that someone had once lived here. A family of four had all died here in a hurricane, and even archaeological ruins seemed to have disappeared: no matter how closely I looked for it, I could not find the ruin marked at Punta Paharo on the chart given to me by Dr. Alberto Ruz. I suspect that the last hurricanes and tidal wave had finally leveled the ruin which for more than a thousand years had miraculously escaped destruction.

Punta Paharo had been visited by the famous archaeologist Morley, who while cruising down the coast had also encountered ruins located between the two bays of Ascensión and Espíritu Santo. He had called these ruins Chac Mool, the name of a reclining god of the ancient Mayas that corresponds in statuary to the sphinx of the ancient Egyptians, a strange, enigmatical figure. This site of Chac Mool was, I found out, the place for which we were heading that night. There stood a half-wrecked *cocal* where a few men were still living. It is unfortunate that Morley and the other archaeologists who had been to Quintana Roo had explored the coast by boat, for thus they overlooked the many additional sites that I found. This accounted for the belief that there were no more than half a dozen ancient Mayan settlements on the three-hundred-mile-long east coast of Quintana Roo. Here again below Punta Paharo my walking down the coast was to reveal another small temple, which may also have had, like all those I had found so far, a counterpart of five or six additional accompanying structures deeper inland, beyond or in the midst of the mangrove marshes. I came upon the temple a few miles south of Punta Paharo, my not-so-stupid guide having finally understood what I was looking for. It was a small, broken-down, square structure, unimpressive but nevertheless significant in showing the former presence of ancient Mayas on this lonely coast.

According to my strange guide, the small temple I had discovered stood at a spot called Punta Arena. After a short rest we pursued our route southward along the beaches bordered by jungle and marshes that stretched away endlessly in the sun.

Never before had I fully understood the meaning of a beach, that place where land and sea meet. During that long afternoon I had ample time to reflect on the fixedness of the coast and the movement of the sea, which carried along with it objects torn away from distant shores. The sea that had brought the Spaniards in its drift and with its winds, now bore, as it must always have done, debris from far-off lands. Such strange objects as life jackets, bottles, and lamp bulbs lay insolently on the coast, carried ashore by the strong Yucatecan current. For me all these manufactured goods seemed like presents, the happy reminders of a world I had completely left behind me. I encountered a bottle of Bols, deodorizer tubes, French and American light bulbs, and a thousand and one other insignificant objects that nevertheless took on a sacred aspect in my eyes. What had the ancient Mayas found on this same beach many years ago? Possibly they encountered Roman objects and many other signs of Africa and the Old World.

In the same way the strong currents had landed the two Spanish citizens, Gonzalo Guerrero and the Spanish friar, on the Quintana Roo coast in 1511; in the same way a Jamaican had drifted to Mayan Cozumel; and in the same way the three French bandits had come to Quintana Roo. Prior to the Spanish conquest these currents and winds had quite possibly brought to the Mayas some mariners from the old continent who had been driven off their courses; and perhaps the first people of the Old World to have seen the New World were shipwrecked Turks or Portuguese swept by the Atlantic onto the shores of Mayadom.

Slowly we made our way along the coast, now stepping on rocks, now on sand, now on putrid red seaweed that crackled under our feet. My guide occasionally broke the silence with a comment or two that had no meaning. At one point I could see from a distance a large strange object looming dark against the pale sky. When we reached it it turned out to be the gigantic engine of some motor vessel that had been wrecked on the shore, a victim of the reefs.

Totally exhausted at nightfall, we came upon the tattered remains of a hurricane-struck *cocal*. All day we had not seen a living being. This was Santa Rosa, the *cocal* situated where lie the ruins known as Chac Mool. My strange guide vanished once we had arrived and I was not to see him again. A half-Indian Cozumeleño greeted me warmly, rather amazed at my presence on the coast, and full of good will and visible pleasure at seeing me. Already my experience of the coast allowed me to be a good conversationalist with the *cocaleros,* and for hours the *cocalero* of Santa Rosa asked me about the coast and friends he had not seen in years. I answered to the best of my ability, giving him all the information I could about the various *cocals* I had visited.

It was very late when I retired to an empty shed to hang up my hammock. This was an operation in which I had now become a master, and which, as I had found out, was very important in its effect on one's sleep. One has to be careful not to stretch the hammock too much, but to find the exact curve most favorable to one's comfort. Lying in my hammock under the pale veil of my mosquito net, I once more thanked the ancient gods for giving to the uncomfortable world the consolation of the soft meshes of a hammock.

The following morning I inquired about all the ruins in the area. The *cocalero* said he knew of none other than the ones beside the house. Listening to my questions, a small Indian (who I later learned was called Chuc and was of the Chan Santa Cruz group) interrupted my host, stating that while hunting a long time ago he had seen a large ruin far back in the marshes. The *cocalero* seemed skeptical and rather displeased at being contradicted, while I jubilantly cross-examined Chuc about the temple, asking if he could remember where it was and whether he could take me to it. He asserted that he could remember, but to my disappointment said that it would be impossible to go there without a dugout canoe, for the lagoons had deepened with the rains and could not be crossed on foot. To my annoyance there was no such thing as a

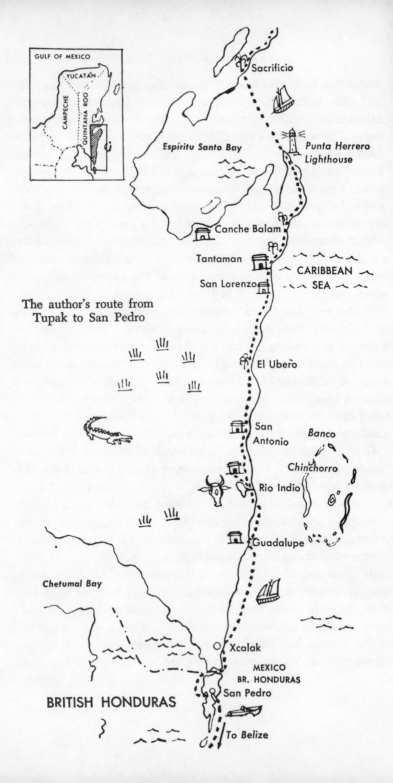

GULF OF MEXICO

YUCATÁN

CAMPECHE

QUINTANA ROO

Sacrificio

Espíritu Santo Bay

Punta Herrero
Lighthouse

Canche Balam

Tantaman

San Lorenzo

CARIBBEAN
SEA

The author's route from
Tupak to San Pedro

El Ubero

San
Antonio

Banco

Chinchorro

Rio Indio

Guadalupe

Chetumal Bay

Xcalak

MEXICO
BR. HONDURAS

BRITISH HONDURAS

San Pedro

To Belize

dugout canoe at the *cocal*. Thinking that nevertheless there might
be a chance of wading across the lagoon, I insisted on at least trying
to reach the temple. Chuc readily agreed to go with me but assured
me that it would be impossible.

Toward nine o'clock, carrying my camera, I left with Chuc to
go down the coast. Less than a mile from the huts Chuc pointed
inland toward the thick mangroves and jumble of dead trees that
bordered the sandy strip on which stood the *cocal*. Here he said
we should try to go inland.

It took more than ten minutes to advance a few feet through the
tangle of dead trees, mangroves, and vines, with Chuc hacking
away like a desperate Saracen in some Oriental battle. Chips of
hard wood flew all over the place and slimy mangrove trunks bent
with a squirmy thud as the machete repeated its attacks

Three yards farther into the bushes our feet began to sink into
water. Slowly the mangroves thickened as, sloshing through deeper
and deeper water, we came upon the edge of a large lagoon bordered with mangroves over which loomed a considerable number
of dead trees uprooted and overturned by some cataclysmic hurricane. Our feet bathed in putrid warm mud that sucked at my
shoes until they came off, obliging me to ferret elbow-deep in the
oozy slime in search of them. I finally took them off altogether and
proceeded, tripping on pointed stones and jagged branches,
through the marshy water, following Chuc, who progressed, hesitantly, seeking shallow spots in the large lagoon.

Stepping now on one foot, now on another, waving our arms like
tightrope walkers, we made slow headway, following the edges
of the mangrove islands whenever possible. On one or two occasions it was only due to desperate acrobatics that I managed to
save my camera from a fatal bath. I now considerably prized my
camera, the only witness to my discoveries. Humidity had turned
the leather case green and corroded many of the metal parts—signs
of the hard times we had seen together and which endeared it to
me even more. Its consistent presence around my neck was some-

times a considerable bore and I felt it was a rather touristy ornament. Nevertheless it had now become a habit, and eagerly (often
to the amazement of all I met who had never seen a camera) I
recorded every face and building I encountered in this strange
land.

For three hours we sludged our way through swamp and lagoon
or cut through thick mangrove islands clustered with dead trees,
Chuc ever straining his neck to find a way and taking personal
bearings to locate the temple.

While cutting through a shallow swamp cluttered with dead
trees and mangroves, Chuc called out to me to be careful; and to
my horror I could see a deadly water snake wriggling toward me
on the surface. I have rarely felt so panic-stricken, for the terrain
allowed of no escape, and fearing that movement would attract
the horrible reptile, I froze on the spot as the snake slithered by
in smooth, undulating movements within inches of my bare legs.

As if to make up for this unpleasant incident we soon came upon
the ruin. It first appeared as one large clump of bushes rising
above the swamp, but as we drew nearer it took shape—that of a
big rectangular building. On its summit, partly concealed by cactus and palms, was a second story like a small square tower a yard
high, pierced on all sides by little doorways.

The building was a strange sight, reflected in the muddy water
like some kind of Venetian *palazzo* of the Mayas. We had approached the temple from the east, and that side presented no
openings, but only a long frieze decorated with the crisscross coral
work as on the temple I had seen on the other side of Ascensión
bay after encountering the smugglers and bandits. This building
was some fifteen yards long, eight yards wide, and around five
yards high. It had no opening on three of its sides, but on the fourth
side, facing west, it was cut by a large rectangular doorway whose
lintel was supported by two large round columns with square
capitals.

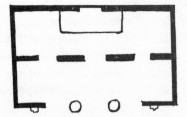

Plan of the temple of Tupak

All around the summit of the structure ran the crisscross frieze, there being no other decoration save two dragon-like heads carved in the stone wall, one on each side of the doorway. The temple was, to my surprise, undamaged, perhaps owing to the salty lagoon in which it stood.

This temple might have been the main building of a large settlement, judging from its size. Perhaps the settlement had been a commercial center—a seaport forming one of the links down the coast with San Miguel de Ruz, Chamax, and Chunyaxche. This port might well have been connected by long-gone inland canals with the other Mayan coastal settlements.

Hesitantly I made my way through the door. The floor was smooth and bare, occasionally showing small piles of rubble that had dropped from the roof. Inside I became aware of small screeching noises above my head, and looking up, I could see in the pale light hundreds of vampire bats swooshing around, while others dangled upside down by their large claws. A strange smell filled the room. As my eyes became accustomed to the light I could see that three low doorways opened into yet another room set at the back of the temple. Bending down, I entered the second room. This one was practically black and within its darkness I could hear the screeching of more vampires and feel them stirring the air above my head as they flew madly about. Both rooms ran the entire length of the temple, each was vaulted with a high, massive,

Mayan inclined arch. While I investigated the surroundings, Chuc stood hesitantly at the entrance, reluctant to go in. In the dim light that penetrated to the back room I could see that the raised floor formed a large, rectangular altar, one foot above the real floor. Here perhaps the nobles had sat and the statues and idols of the fierce Mayan god had stood. I was doubtless the first person from the outside world to penetrate the sacred inner room since the disappearance of the ancient Mayas. Nothing seemed to have disturbed the temple since its abandonment. Save for a large crack in the altar, all the interior of the second chamber was neat and dry.

I beckoned to Chuc to follow me in, so he could witness that I was doing no harm to the ancient building. He asked me what the structure had been, inquiring whether it was an old *rancho*. I explained to him that it was an ancient Mayan temple built many years ago, but he apparently did not believe a word. Squatting down by the altar, I began investigating through the crack what lay below. The altar had been made of wide flat slabs of stone covered with stucco. At first I encountered only stucco fill under the cracked slab, while Chuc gazed incredulously when I told him that I was looking for pottery fragments to bring back to Mexico. He did not stand still for long, though; for soon I brought out a small fragment of broken pottery with a clever torsade design on it. This intrigued Chuc and he decided to help me dig under the altar and through the crack. Soon we were bringing up a great quantity of pottery fragments, all of different clay, caliber, or finish, thus attesting that the fragments were not of some idol but had been included as rubble in the stucco. I had gathered about twenty small fragments, some with such designs as elaborate crisscross etchings or crown-like studs of pottery. I was about to stop, certain that I had more than enough to serve the purpose of identifying the period in which the temple had been built, when with the aid of his machete Chuc, who had dug deeper than I, suddenly produced a small bright red object which he handed over to me.

To my amazement and delight it was a cylindrical red stone bead. This spurred me on to dig for more, and soon, close to the spot where Chuc had found the bead, I came upon a beautiful hatchet-shaped jade about two inches square with a hole in the upper part by which it could have been strung onto a necklace. I now dreamed of glorious treasures, and waiving momentarily the counsel that no amateur should dig, I kept up the search, sifting through my hands the rubble of dry stucco, which gave up another jade bead. This one was smaller than the hatchet-shaped one, and oval. Nothing could have stopped me now, and Chuc was elbow-deep in the now widened crack under the altar. But all further search proved fruitless, and I felt the necessity of calling off the hunt, feeling somewhat like a man starving in front of a baker's shop. I did not think it could do any good to look for more, as excavations would have to be performed in a methodical fashion with all the necessary time and equipment. As had already occurred to me, I resolved again that I would return under better conditions and with competent archaeologists to fully exploit my finds. I contented myself with the treasure of being the first civilized foreigner to see these lost temples.

Already it was becoming unbearable inside the temple, the air being stuffy and laden with mosquitoes that had followed us in. The vampires continued to hover above our heads and for a moment I felt as if I were suffocating. The entire surroundings were strange and quite frightening. Here I was encircled by vampires in the back room of a forgotten temple set in the center of a marshy lagoon. Each of my movements was watched by the enigmatic Indian face of my guide Chuc, whose long machete, I thought, could serve him well were he to suspect that I was hiding something from him. Furthermore I had pocketed the jade beads without thinking. I decided to go outside, and Chuc followed me with apparently pacific intentions, explaining that it was time to start on our way back. I felt relieved to be in the open and, breathing in the fresh air, hurriedly set about examining and photographing in detail the exterior of the temple. Its square massiveness made it unique of its kind, and I had never before seen such a monolithic structure in other parts of Yucatán or along the coast. The rectangular mass of the building contrasted with the airy lightness of the minute tower on its summit. I wondered what could have been the purpose of the small open rectangular structure above the temple. Maybe it had been some sort of lighthouse of the ancient Mayas, since a fire inside the tower would have been seen from afar. This assumption may well be correct, judging from a similar four-posted stone structure I observed the following day. This was on a high mound beside the principal temple of Chac Mool, the ruins at Santa Rosa, where I had met Chuc.

Once Chuc cleared away the branches that obstructed the building I was able to get some good photographs before setting out again across the marshes and lagoon on our painful trek back to the *cocal*.

While we crossed the lagoons I imagined the inland waterways as they must have been in the times of the Mayas, full of large forty-oar canoes gliding back and forth between the coastal cities and those situated behind the lagoons. Tupak was the name the Indians had given to the ruin we had just visited, the Venice of Quintana Roo. I was extremely proud of this new find which, like a number of the other sites I had seen so far, had until now escaped being recorded by archaeologists.

Thinking of these things, I fell asleep on my twenty-third night on the Quintana Roo coast. In my dreams I vaguely remembered Ball and our plan to go to Colombia, but even this could not strike me as a reality. Already I felt as if I had always belonged to this strange world of temples, beaches, jungles, and marshes—to the world of the Quintana Roo coast. I could not even imagine that I had not originally set out to explore the coast, which was now no more for me the barren, frightening void of the map in Tepoztlán. Now it was a land of legends, faces, scenery, and temples, a land so rich in past and present that I treasured it like my homeland.

Discovering a temple had now become a normal experience for me—finding six was also familiar. If I feel it necessary to state this, it is because on my return to civilization I was greatly reproached for my lack of curiosity by those who saw in the happenings of every day of my stay on the coast events demanding all the energy and consecration of a lifetime. For many people to find one vase is a discovery so great that they cannot understand that in the profusion of all that Quintana Roo had to offer I was bewildered, and what would in another context have been truly extraordinary was to my eyes quite normal. For this reason, and because of trivial but vital things such as mosquitoes, thirst, weariness, insecurity, and fear, I did in fact tend to overlook certain details, certain facts of the ruins I discovered and of the men I met. My mind was perpetually occupied by the small problems of life, which left scholarly interest secondary and unimportant. There was the pressing problem of where to sleep as dusk descended over the lagoons, in itself a small problem compared to what one would drink or whether one would survive the attacks of malaria-carrying mosquitoes or of poisonous snakes. I felt anxious that I might never reach Belize, for during the first twenty-three days of working my way south I did not once receive the assurance that it was possible to attain my goal. Never was I certain that at any moment I would not have to turn around and retrace my steps, a task that I knew could have proven impossible. Day after day I had severed the links of the mysterious human chain, the relay of Indian to *cocalero*, *cocalero* to fisherman, fisherman to *chiclero*, and so on, that had seen me down the coast. . . .

The following morning I filled in my diary, in which already appeared the Indian names of places that I had been told of on my arrival in Mexico. Behind their difficult Indian syllables they now held for me immense poetical and musical values: Puha, Ak, Xcassel, Yalcou, Tulum, Chunyaxche, Chamax, and now Tupak and Chac Mool. Strange syllables, foreign to our tongue but pleasing to the ear when recited with the short melodious tone of the Mayas.

They were names which to me were images of hidden mystery that machetes had bared to the sunlight, for our modern eyes to have the pleasure of discovering. For me at twenty-one this was intoxicating, but nevertheless much less poignant than the people I had met, whom I had rather innocently taken into my complete confidence and in whom I was fortunately never to be disappointed.

I spent the following day investigating the ruins of Chac Mool, which stand a few hundred yards from the *cocal*. Since I knew that here people had been before me who were so much more competent than I in the skills of archaeology and classification, I felt that all I needed to do was enjoy the sight of the ruins, trusting that someone had already taken the trouble to analyze and measure them. For measurements are a precious tool of the archaeologist.

At Chac Mool, as already mentioned, I was able to note an open small tower similar to that of Tupak, and my theory of lighthouses seemed more and more probable. However the doubt remains, for I have no exact dimensions of the rectangular lantern-house structures.

I did learn from Chuc something that was to prove most interesting for the study of other ancient Mayan ruins and the religious history of many buildings. While with him at Chac Mool I pointed out to him some red hands that were imprinted on the wall of one of the structures, similar to those at Chamax. Chuc seemed a little surprised, and in his poor Spanish explained to me that at his village of Chumpom people made the marks in blue on the wall of the church as a votive offering. This explanation coming from a man as simple as Chuc could hardly be judged as scientific, but nevertheless offered a plausible answer to the old mystery of the red hand prints that cover many of the ancient Mayas' buildings in such a disorderly fashion. It seems more than possible that Chuc was right and the hand prints of Chumpom are for the same purpose as those all over the Yucatán peninsula, which recall today the vivid presence of some ancient Maya who left for eternity his personal ex-voto on the walls of the temples he visited—a far more touching sign than the marble plates and gilt hearts that cover shrines in Christian Spain and Italy, or the more pagan inscriptions that so many millions of tourists seem obliged to leave on the summits of tall towers or the pedestals of public statues. Man has this irresistible urge to leave a trace of his passage wherever he goes, and the Mayas found the most vivid of all traces in leaving their hand prints on their temple. Each print is so unique that Scotland Yard could no doubt detect the wanderings of one Mayan individual, as his grubby hand was successively applied to the walls of all the shrines he went to.

Altogether there were about seven structures at Chac Mool, all similar to those I had encountered but without elaborate decorations such as sculptured heads of dragons or other beings. One of the buildings held my attention. It was a structure that had no wall, but nine columns that I suppose had once supported beams and a thatched roof like the thousand columns of the Temple of the Warriors at Chichén-Itzá. The ancient Mayas used to cover many such stone structures with palm fronds, thus allowing more interior space than the rather heavy Mayan vault which reduced the size of the interiors. The wooden beams used by the ancient Mayas were most frequently of sapodilla. Many beams were carved and some have survived for over a thousand years, withstanding the rot of the humid climate and the attacks of thousands of insects which attempted to eat them. In the city of Tikal in Guatemala carved lintel beams were found decorated with very fine, well-modeled carvings, a feat all the more remarkable considering that the wood was so hard and that the Mayas had only stone and obsidian knives to do the carving.

It appeared incredible to me that the ancient Mayas could have had such a flourishing civilization without the knowledge of metal, although they did know of gold and copper, which they purchased in the form of jewelery from Panama.

In their memoirs, the Spaniards have left proof that the sailors who once lived in the cities I had visited sailed all the way to Panama in their great dugouts, and must have put in at places along the coast on their long voyages southward. But unfortunately for me, modern times have made the journey to Panama by following the coast nearly impossible. Reflecting on the strange turns of history, I realized that today it would take me ten times longer than it did for the ancient Mayas to go down the once-inhabited coast of Quintana Roo.

Chac Mool marked the halfway point of my journey and already I felt weary, as more than a hundred miles remained before reaching Belize.

However, I did get good news at Chac Mool. I would not have to worry about crossing the bay of Espíritu Santo, for farther down the coast at a place called Sacrificio (probably in memory of some sacrificial deed of the Chan Santa Cruz Indians) lived three fishermen who had two boats between them. Chuc agreed to go there with me and see me embarked on my way south. What lay south of Espíritu Santo was still a mystery. I was not able to get more information about the coast to the south except that the few *cocals* there had been destroyed and that the coast was barren until Xcalak, a village situated on the border of British Honduras. I could only hope I would meet isolated *solteros* and that some of the *cocals* had not been entirely abandoned after all. Total lack of communication barred me from being correctly informed.

In any event there was one landmark on my planned route—a large lighthouse south of Espíritu Santo. From there I could possibly get a boat south to Belize.

The following morning I set out again for an entire day's walk through the mangroves and bushes along the hot dry beach. My feet had become immune to rocks and more often than not I took off my sandals, which by now were no more than a pair of worn leather soles that were coming apart, attached around my ankles by odd pieces of henequen string.

There were no temples on our route and none that Chuc knew

of in the interior apart from Tupak, which we had already visited together. I was now beginning to feel the effects of my rather uneven diet of turtle eggs and tortillas, of long marches, little water, and less food, and of the perpetual strain and accumulated fatigue of strange circumstances on my walk down the coast.

My skin was completely burned and in the sun had already peeled off a dozen times. My beard was respectably long and my trousers and shirt so torn that I looked little better off than a beggar; this pleased me, as it was a guarantee that I would excite nobody's evil intentions. I kept rolling my trousers up higher and higher to hide the tears. When we arrived at Sacrificio they were rolled up to the middle of my knees, giving me an appearance that could have been fashionable in Bermuda, but remained rather strange to the eyes of those I met. I had forgotten what my face looked like (no great loss), not having seen a mirror for more than three weeks.

I often surprised myself by discovering how easily I had parted with all the familiar objects that had always been in my surroundings, things that I had thought were truly universal such as chairs, plates, and soap. My only nostalgia for civilization was for food and drink. Visions of Pantagruelian meals haunted my hammock at night, and when fiddling with a turtle egg I wished it were a sirloin steak. As for drink, I always craved cool fresh water, and even dreamed of Coca-Cola in my most desperate hours. How I would appreciate such things as water in the future, and I was already making plans for orgies and banquets after my arrival that would have seen me with at least enough food to survive on for five years.

But beyond the call of the stomach I felt little desire to return, save now and again for the sole reason of wanting company. I needed some civilized person to whom I could tell what I had seen and found and thus prove to myself that all this was not just a dream. The unreality of the things I had seen and done, the ease and naturalness with which I now performed various acts that a month before would have appeared to me as either inconceivable or comical, made me wonder whether it was really I in the present, or whether it was my ghost walking down the strange coast in the long-distant past. I began to doubt that Belize even existed, and could not bring myself to think that at the end of my voyage there would be English-speaking gentlemen drinking tea, or preferably gin and tonic. . . .

However, I had not seen the end of my troubles, for twenty more days of doubt and isolation still lay ahead, with the worst part of the trip yet to come. I did not know until I sailed across Ascensión bay how lucky I had been always to be able to walk within twenty-four hours the distances necessary to find food and shelter, and above all to meet friendly, hospitable people. My chain was now on the point of breaking and the links were not to be knit in the convenient relay they had so far presented.

Things had gone well until now. The tide had changed. . . .

IX

Outcasts of the Coast

At Punta Sacrificio we came across two fishermen who lived in a small palm-thatched hut erected on stilts at the edge of a mangrove swamp. For a small sum they agreed to take me across the bay to the lighthouse of Punta Herrero that stood at the other end of Espíritu Santo bay.

At Sacrificio Chuc left me, and I gave him as a parting present the last of my city shirts. By contrast Espíritu Santo bay was as blue as Ascensión bay had been brown and muddy, and the little double-ended boat of the fishermen glided silently over the clear water. I was now headed for the last stretch of coast that separated me from British Honduras. It was a barren, straight coastline that stretched due south from Espíritu Santo bay to the small village of Xcalak, which marked the border between Mexico and British Honduras on the Quintana Roo coast.

By crossing Espíritu Santo bay I was leaving behind the zone of the *Indios sublevados'* present occupation and entering the No Man's Land that separates true civilization from the primitive Indians. The straight coastline that I now planned to follow was the outer edge of a giant triangle of land that cut off the Caribbean from the broad inland sea that is Chetumal bay. This triangle ends in a point at Xcalak, where both waters meet through a narrow channel called Bacalar Chico. This wedge of land south of the

Ascensión and Espíritu Santo bays is one vast, barren expanse of swamps and occasional clumps of jungle, and consequently practically uninhabited. I knew that the only people I might encounter would all be of the execrable race of outcasts, stray bandits and isolated *chicleros*—those whom civilization uses as a spearhead in conquering virgin lands.

I have always wondered why, whether it be in Australia, Brazil, or any other vast new country, Western civilization must necessarily first present itself in a most unfavorable light by sending into virgin territories its outcasts and criminals, men who have by their savagery caused the "white man" to be classified in the eyes of the aborigines as a bearer of evil. Intellectuals, scholars, and missionaries alike wait till our discredit is total before daring to move in and indoctrinate the remaining natives who have escaped the unruly advance guards of the brilliant civilization we like to think is our own.

In this characteristic fashion, over the past twenty years efforts had been made to open up the southern coast of Quintana Roo. This operation still being in its first stages, I could expect to encounter few men besides bandits and outlaws. And, in fact, these hasty efforts had so far failed to change Quintana Roo. I was to find little more than the rusty corrugated-iron remains of these attempts to populate and exploit the coast. For this failure hurricanes are to blame—once again the elements have protected this strange part of the world from the despoiling hand of civilization.

The first trace of civilization was the tall lighthouse toward which we were sailing. Halfway across the bay it became visible, a great rusty tower looming some forty feet skyward. We landed on a small sandy beach at the foot of the lighthouse. Paying off the fishermen, I made my way toward it. Drawing closer, I could see what a pitiful state the tower was in. It stood upon a cement base that had once been firmly anchored to the rocks of the narrow point that separated the Caribbean from the waters of the Espíritu Santo bay. Successive hurricanes had slowly eaten away at the base and the rocks, so that now the whole lighthouse had keeled over to a dangerous angle which rivaled that of the tower of Pisa. At the foot of the lighthouse stood the leaning twisted frame of a wooden cottage which was now supported by large beams that prevented it from collapsing altogether.

Here lived a Yucatecan with his wife and two daughters. He had recently come to the coast to replace the last keeper who had died two years previously—washed out to sea by a tidal wave!

The keeper was a simple man but appeared then to me as an educated individual, since he was the first man I had encountered for three weeks who knew how to read. He eventually proved rather disappointing, having none of the acute intelligence that I had so frequently encountered among the so-called uneducated Indians and *chicleros*. He was a sedate bourgeois and of little use to me, since he knew nothing of the coast, in which he was not interested. He spent his days eating from the stores that a ship brought to the light once every three months, while his wife and daughters patiently made hammock after hammock for eventual sale in the markets of Mérida. . . .

The lighthouse itself was far more interesting than its keeper, and its history is certainly a strange one for a nautical beacon. It was built in 1905 by a company of French engineers who came to the coast from the sea. The construction of the lighthouse was an incursion into the territory of the *Indios sublevados*. Once the lighthouse was completed the Indians besieged it, killing the guardian, and the lighthouse was abandoned until the signing of the "great peace" in 1935. Since then more than three of its keepers had perished in various hurricanes. The light in fact shines for practically no purpose, for its beam hardly reaches out to Banco Chinchorro; in other words, to see the light one has to cross over the most dangerous reefs along the coast of Central America. The light could then only be expected to serve as a distant signpost to shipwrecked mariners, Banco Chinchorro being a deadly, circular string of rocks that stick out from the sea some thirty-five miles off the southern part of the Quintana Roo coast. On maps Banco Chinchorro appears as a cluster of black dots surrounded by a necklace of rocks the size and shape of Cozumel Island. Thirty miles long and twenty miles wide, Banco Chinchorro has been the cruel graveyard of thousands of ships over hundreds of years. Upon these deadly rocks still rest the carcasses of many modern cargo vessels, and against them many ships laden with gold must have foundered when, returning up from Panama, they hugged the Quintana Roo coast, fighting against the trade winds. In recent years attempts have been made to place two automatic beacons on the extremities of this island of jagged rocks, but hurricanes have defeated these attempts.

When I clambered up the lighthouse, to my surprise I noticed that from lack of practice I had forgotten how to climb stairs. As stupid as this may seem, it was true, and I managed to descend the stairs only with great caution, placing one foot voluntarily before the other and letting my weight go at each step, a movement that comes naturally to everyone in practice but which in fact requires habit and a certain skill. This is clearly demonstrated by the clumsy way most Indians in Mexico descend the only stairs they know—those of their village churches.

That evening I ate for the first time in four weeks seated at a table with plates and, of all things, a real spoon and fork! But being at the lighthouse solved none of my problems and I could get from the keeper no details as to the state of the areas I was about to cross or any clue as to the possibility of encountering some inhabitants on the coast.

Once again I was vague as to what lay ahead. Prospects seemed grim: more than a hundred miles of tornado-struck coast, no water, and no inhabitants save, said the keeper, "a chance fisherman" and possibly *chicleros*. The lighthouse keeper refused to accompany me even a short distance south, and according to him I had only a slim chance of making it on foot.

Having crossed Espíritu Santo bay, I could not retreat, and for the first time I realized that I had come to the point of no return, with no alternative but to sit and wait two months for the lighthouse boat or carry on. I did not hesitate and prepared to leave alone.

I felt certain that I would still encounter some coconut trees from which I could get water, and I estimated that if I purchased some food from the keeper, I could walk alone at least half the distance that separated me from Xcalak, some one hundred and twenty miles from the lighthouse. I therefore purchased a few pounds of dried turtle eggs and asked the keeper's wife to cook about a hundred tortillas for me. I also bought from the keeper a knife to replace the one I had lost.

At dawn the following day I set out, trusting to my luck. I felt quite confident, encouraged by the fact that until now I had come to no harm and was well acquainted with the ways of the jungle.

With my new knife slipped in my belt, the remains of my luggage, tortillas, turtle eggs, and the carcasses of two roast chickens, I bade farewell to the lighthouse keeper and set out once more along the lonely coast.

For a while, as I followed the sandy beaches, by turning around I could see the lighthouse slowly disappear like the funnel of a ship behind the horizon. Before me stretched the dark green outline of innumerable points of land, the ends of countless shallow bays overlapping one another until the last ones were but pale gray streaks that sank over the blue horizon of the sea to the south.

The beaches were barren save occasionally where they were littered with the remains of giant trees submerged in the pale sand. As I walked along the damp edge of the beach my footprints were washed away behind me as, with a crackling thud, small waves exploded on the still beaches. After walking for two hours I came to an abandoned *cocal*, a beach littered with the fallen trunks of dead coconut trees strewn about like matchsticks upon the sand. The jungle was losing no time in reclaiming the beaches and had already covered the fallen trees with a green blanket of vines, still and silent tentacles of the jungle. There is something tragic and animal-like in the trunk of a coconut tree, its gray, smooth, round surface looking like the leg of some giant pachyderm. The hurricane-struck *cocal* looked more like one of those mythical elephant graveyards where thousands of great tuskers had come to die. But occasionally one or two hideously bent coconut trees had managed to survive after having been knocked down. After being blown across the sand, these trees had righted themselves and, thanks to painful-looking bends in their trunks, still held skyward half-torn crests of large green palm fronds. From these trees I cut some nuts and they solved my water problem.

Toward nightfall after a day in the sun I came upon the remains of what had been a large *cocal*. The sand was littered with the tragic leavings of civilization—the sad-looking modern archaeological debris of rusty pots and empty bottles. This had been in all appearances a large *cocal*, and two huge warehouses lay flattened out among the dead trees. An explosion could not have disintegrated the huts more completely, and grim-looking, battered remnants of the settlement rested in the tangled boughs of the stacks of dead trees that bordered the edge of the jungle behind the beach.

I found a battered door which I propped up to make some kind of shelter under which I strung my hammock. After a short swim in the cool sea I set about making camp in the ghostly décor of the *cocal*. All was silent around me, and as the warm tropical night darkened the *cocal*, I lazed in my hammock listening to the murmur of the distant reef and the occasional startling shrieks that arose from the dark jungle. Having walked at a good pace all day, I felt much closer to Belize, and for the first time I wished that I had arrived. I wondered whether a search party had been sent after me, although this seemed most improbable, and I hardly dared believe that there still existed an outside world with motorcars and electric lights. I fell asleep to the thought of at last seeing an end to the solitude of the Quintana Roo coast. . . .

The sun had just risen the following morning when I set out

again along the coast. All morning it seemed to me as if I was making little or no progress, as the coast stretched farther out of sight, as if it would never end. I began worrying about my meager stores. Would they hold out until I encountered human beings? Judging from the sun, it was toward two o'clock when farther down the coast I came upon the remains of yet another *cocal*. Like the others I had seen it was but a tangle of fallen trees that stretched along the coast for miles. In the distance I saw a small hut that still seemed in good condition, and I was wondering whether I should spend the night here when to my surprise I spotted, rising through the palm-thatched roof of the hut, a thin column of smoke.

As I approached a squat man in his fifties came out of the hut. Stripped to the waist, the fellow had on his chest a ghastly scar some twenty inches long. A smile on the man's face put me more or less at ease. He came forward to me, asking in Spanish from where I hailed and where I was going. In turn I asked him who he was and he proudly declared, "The owner of the *cocal*," showing off the torn and twisted coconut groves. He went on to explain that he had been a *chiclero* and that now he had settled in the abandoned *cocal*. Despite his rugged looks I was too pleased with this chance encounter to be concerned for the time being with the true origins of the rough-looking *chiclero*.

I gathered that I was dealing with a man who most certainly was a bandit, although he boasted that he was an *aventurero* like myself! He kindly suggested that I spend the night at "his *cocal*" and share his evening meal, to which I readily agreed. On entering his hut I was surprised to see that, unlike all those I had visited so far, it was furnished with roughly made chairs, a table, and—strangest of all—a bed, a box-like contraption so unfamiliar and unusual to this part of the world. It was with evident pride that my host took note of my surprise.

Inside his hut the old man put me through a thousand questions as to the exact purpose of my presence on the coast. I soon became suspicious of his curiosity, especially when he became exceedingly interested in my camera, wanting to know its cost and its value. I played the role of a very poor man on my way to Belize in search of work, adding casually that the camera had been given to me and was unfortunately broken, and in any case it could not have been worth more than a few pesos even when new.

I offered my host a cigarette and this made him a little kinder. In characteristic Mexican fashion he came up to me and, slapping me on my back, declared, *"Estamos amigos,"* in a rather insincere sort of a way. I recalled the evenings I had spent with Ball in Tepoztlán where these same exterior signs of friendship had more often than not preceded the drawing of knives. *"Estamos amigos"* means "We are not yet enemies" more than it means "We are friends."

Whatever may have been the afterthoughts of my host, it was evident that above all he was delighted to have company, and he generously shared with me his crude evening meal, which consisted of the large bony head of a fish swimming in some nondescript ooze. I learned from my host's rapid monologue that besides having been a *chiclero* he had also been a woodcutter in mahogany camps both at Chetumal and in Belize. He had left Chetumal for the coast of Quintana Roo to "retire for personal reasons"—reasons, I felt, that must have been linked with the horrible scar on his chest.

On learning that he had been to Belize, I lost no time in cross-examining my host about how one could get to British Honduras. To my delight he gave me highly detailed information about the country that lay ahead of me and about what I would encounter farther south along the coast.

I was now apparently some forty *leguas* from the end of the Quintana Roo coast, marked by the lone village of Xcalak (roughly ninety miles away). There were, I gathered, four inhabited spots on the coast before the village on the border of British Honduras—two *cocals* just south of where we were, a *colonia*, and a *rancho* called Rio Indio, a small estate on the mouth of a sea channel that cut the coast just north of Xcalak. According to my host I should be able to reach Rio Indio in four or five days. I was warned that at one of the *cocals* called El Ubero there lived a "bad man" who had charge of looking after the remains of the partly destroyed plantation. From El Ubero to Rio Indio would be a matter of two days. I prayed that I could trust the word of the old bandit. For the first time since I landed on the coast I had a clear picture of what lay ahead of me, my only concern now being the *colonia* that stood on my path. And I remembered all that Don Jorge Gonzales of Tankah had told me about these small villages of fugitive criminals from central Mexico. The reputation of these settlements was not one to inspire confidence. Even in their own villages the bandits keep up their tradition of crime by fighting among themselves, and for them sudden death is as common as breathing. I did not like to imagine myself passing through or, worse, stopping at such a place. I recalled the unpleasant reception I had had at the small *colonia* of Chamax from which I had been chased away.

I was also slightly suspicious of my newly acquired friend, whose ungracious scar and sardonic looks seemed to mean no good. I repeated again the story about how poor I was and must have slightly overdone it, for my host eventually got up and, sighing with sympathy, said, "Are we not all poor outcasts?" I managed to muster a timid "Yes." Had I then had a mirror, I would have thought this statement less surprising, for with my scraggy beard, torn pants, and shredded shirt, I could have seen for myself that I looked every inch a young and dangerous murderer's apprentice.

With an undertone of "birds of a feather flock together," my friend who proudly called himself an *aventurero* explained in gory detail the more sinister episodes of his "career," and he seemed disappointed and offended when I refused to share with him the details of the numerous crimes that he was persuaded I had committed.

From the old man's enlightening monologue I gathered much information about the true life of a *chiclero*, on how to distinguish between rival gangs, and what were the rules of the cruel life of those dedicated to gathering chewing gum. I was once more informed that, being tall, I had all the makings of an excellent *chiclero*, seeing that I would have little trouble climbing up the chicle trees to make the cuts that would yield the precious sap. To survive the dangers of the jungle the *chicleros* have many strange recipes. One of these consists in chewing while in the jungle a special herb that gives the *chiclero* a perpetual colic but prevents him from catching amoebic dysentery when he drinks contaminated water. I was also taught how to blow in the barrel of a shotgun to make the characteristic calls that the *chicleros* use among themselves when they get lost. For the first time I heard about the much-feared "chicle fly." The sting of this insect, one of the greatest menaces to *chicleros*, causes a cancerous growth, which eats away and rots ears and noses. I was later to see the terrible effects of the chicle fly's bite, which can disfigure a man for life, for the infection spreads in a fashion similar to leprosy.

My friend also gave me many confidential tips on how to prepare the bales of boiled-down chicle that one sells to the chicle companies. The white milky sap is boiled by the *chicleros* in the jungle and reduced to a hard rubbery paste which, rolled up in balls, is carried out to the chicle camps where it is weighed and sold. One of the most common frauds—used by all "honest" *chicleros*—consists in introducing sand into the caldron in which the chicle is boiled. Stones can also be inserted into the bales, though this last technique is less desirable in that it can be easily detected by the purchasing agents of the chicle companies.

On learning that I was French, my host told me of the fate of a compatriot of mine, Pierre, one of the three criminals who had escaped from Devil's Island and drifted on a raft from Jamaica to Cozumel. From Cozumel, Pierre had set out to the Quintana Roo coast where for a time he worked as storekeeper in a large chicle camp. One day he was accused of cheating a *chiclero*, who threatened to kill him. Apparently Pierre was "quick with a pistol" and he shot the man who had accused him. A whole gang of *chicleros* thereupon vowed to kill Pierre, who was consequently shot down.

It was in a gang feud that my new friend had received the terrible machete blow that had scarred his chest. I finally took a great liking to this solitary rascal who had so kindly opened his heart to me. Like most *chicleros*, his life of danger, and the perpetual battle he waged against the jungle for survival, had developed in him an acute intelligence and a profound wisdom.

I began to understand the murder and violence carried on by *chicleros*, crimes as justifiable in the context of a *chiclero's* life as are wholesale wars in the light of patriotism. A *chiclero* knows no country and has no possessions beyond his shotgun and machete. His principal possession is his pride and honor, and this he defends with his life on the slightest provocation. Most of their so-called criminal acts are performed not through greed but in an often justifiable spirit of vengeance for offenses against their pride. In a gang an offense to one member becomes a personal offense against the gang, and in a land with no police it is up to individuals to make their own laws and punishments. The *chiclero* knows only one immediate expedient: death.

Seated on a makeshift chair, I watched my friend prepare his evening meal. I felt as if I were in the hideout of the devil as inside the hut I watched the lined face of my host in the dancing red light of the small fire on which he was cooking supper. And once in my hammock I could see by the light of the dying fire the heaving chest of the old *aventurero* with its frightening scar. What struck me most was with what ease I had accepted such strange and frightful company.

The following morning we set out together down the coast, my friend carrying my bag. All along the coast the effects of a giant tidal wave were visible; the sea had swept over the beaches uprooted trees and bushes that had been carried out to sea when the first wave had withdrawn, all these objects later rushing back with the second tidal wave and crushing anything that had remained standing. It is hard to imagine the force of a battering ram made up of thousands of large uprooted trees carried upon the crest of giant waves.

Few of the people who had been on the coast at the time had survived, and at the village of Xcalak, for which I was headed, half of the one hundred and fifty inhabitants had perished when a wave covered the entire village with twelve feet of water that crossed overland from the Caribbean to Chetumal bay and then back over again into the sea. Those who survived found themselves sitting on top of standing coconut trees or stranded high and dry above great piles of debris.

An example of the force of the winds of these hurricanes is given by a leaf that I once saw in the West Indies. This leaf had been so hardened by the force and pressure of the wind that when it was hurled into the door of a house it buried itself in the wood like a razor blade.

We trudged down the desolate coast until sunset, stopping but twice on the way to eat some of the dried tortillas that remained from the stock I had purchased at the lighthouse. The coast had practically no rocky outcrops and we followed the water's edge all day. So doing we came upon many varied and often strange objects that had been washed ashore by the Atlantic currents. Walking along, I picked up on a whim a small, brown, sealed medical bottle. Looking through the dark glass, to my surprise I saw a piece of paper inside, which of all things was a message written in pencil which read:

Caribbean

26/1 1958

Knut Fullinglo

S/L Lundys Lane

Oslo Norway

I also came upon a tattered life jacket with the inscription "s.s. ANGEL HORATH." Whether it was the last remains of some secret and terrible maritime tragedy, I could not tell.

Every five hundred yards or so my friend, who was walking in front of me, would bend down and pick something from the sand; to all appearances he was gathering gray and beige rocks which he carefully dropped into a small henequen bag tied around his waist. When I asked what these rocks were he answered that they were lacquer, and that he could get eight Mexican pesos for a kilo of such stones. I then did not know exactly what lacquer was made from, but it struck me that surely lacquer did not come from the sea. Examining the rock-like fragments that my friend had collected, to my surprise I found that they were so light as to float. Further examination revealed that some of the fragments showed the clear imprint of what must have been a saucer-like mold. I was quite mystified, and it was only much later that I discovered the strange truth about the lacquer that is found on the Quintana Roo coast. For I discovered that this lacquer can be picked up all along the coast and is especially abundant after a severe storm. The "stones" were in fact true lacquer, and if they came from the sea, it was only in a backhanded sort of way. Apparently in 1942 a large cargo ship laden with lacquer ran aground and sank on Banco Chinchorro. Lacquer is made from the sap of a special type of dogwood tree, and like most resins, it floats. Year after year as the valuable sunken cargo is shaken about by storms small quantities of it break loose, are washed free from the sunken hull, and drift onto the Quintana Roo coast. The *chicleros* who occasionally pick it up are far from knowing either its origin or its true value, which far exceeds the price of eight pesos a kilo set by chicle companies. There must have been many hundreds of tons of this lacquer, since for eighteen years reasonable quantities have been periodically swept ashore on Quintana Roo, and even in British Honduras.

Another valuable kind of jetsam is the *ojo de venado* or deer's eye, an oval seed with a hard, light-brown skin marked with a dark-brown line. These seeds, which resemble the eye of a deer, are much sought by the Indians, who polish them and use them as decorations, beads, and pendants. They originally come from inland Venezuela and drift down rivers into the sea, later to be swept ashore on the Yucatán coast. According to my *aventurero* friend, who collected them, they were worth a peso apiece in Mérida. Beachcombing, I thus discovered, is not such a new hobby after all. And it can readily be assumed that these seeds were carefully collected by the ancient Mayas. Bamboo poles are also encountered on the beaches, and since bamboo does not grow in Yucatán these poles are collected by the few inhabitants of the coast to make punting poles for their dugout canoes. They also serve as booms and masts on small sailing craft.

Toward the end of the afternoon we reached a large *cocal* that had apparently escaped much of the devastating effects of the recent hurricanes. In the center of the *cocal*, which was called Cuyche, stood a small stone house of crude construction. This was the first stone hut I had seen since the house in the *cocal* of Tankah. When we approached we found an old man lying on the front steps dead drunk, surrounded by half a dozen young children. He was the owner of the *cocal* and they were some of his ten offspring. On our arrival the drunkard rose up on an elbow and started to swear at us, till he fell back vomiting. He was a pitiful sight lying there prostrate before his own children, who looked on with awe and a certain respect that reminded me of what I had always imagined should have been the attitude of the sons of Noah.

The drunkard's wife, a fat half-caste Indian, cordially invited us to never mind her husband. My friend told her about my destination and then came to bid me good-by, saying that he would return up the coast by night. Not being anxious to arrive alone the following day at the *colonia* of bandits, I asked him to stay with me, which after some hesitation he agreed to do.

The following morning I was shaken out of my hammock by the drunkard owner of the *cocal*, and I left Cuyche with my friend under a torrent of profane words which fortunately I could not understand.

Three hours later we reached the tattered remains of a *cocal* that used to be called Tantaman. Here, my guide informed me, were ancient ruins. But searching around I could not find them, and wondered whether I could trust my companion's word. Later, on a detailed archaeological map (more complete than the one I had brought along with me) I found a site marked on that part of the coast under the name of Tantaman. A few miles down from Tantaman at a spot called Tampalan we came upon the remains of a stone structure, right on the beach and half washed over by the sea. I was not able to ascertain whether this was truly an ancient Mayan site, although the square foundations seemed to be those of a small classical oratory like many I had seen. My guide informed me that here had been hidden a treasure, pointing out to me that on one of the stones was a carved arrow, which according to him had indicated the treasure's position. I added another dot to my map, with a question mark.

At four o'clock we finally reached the famous *colonia*. On a very wide, barren, milky-white beach stood five huts made of logs and flotsam crudely nailed together. As we approached the huts two men came out toward us, both wearing knotted red handkerchiefs over their heads. They looked thoroughly unpleasant and as dangerous as I had anticipated. Of Mexican stock, they both had quite respectable beards, and made an ugly pair. They greeted my friend with calm indifference and looked me over with cheeky, hostile eyes.

It took me little time to grasp that we were unwanted callers. Apparently the *colonia* was in a great state of excitement. A big row was on, pitting five of the men who lived there against their "head man." The gang leader was being given a rough time because the men of the *colonia* were practically starving owing to the failure to arrive of a small boat from Xcalak which had been expected to bring food for the men, but was fifteen days overdue. Despite the pleas of my *aventurero* friend, the men of the *colonia* refused to give me hospitality for the night beyond a hut in which to hang my hammock. As for food, they said curtly that I would have to do without, since they were now without corn and were living only on turtle eggs and what they were able to hunt.

It was in such company that my friend left me, after having refused any form of compensation for having carried my heavy bag for two days. When he marched away up the beach I felt that I was losing yet another good companion whom I would probably never see again. This time I did not even know his name, although in a strange sort of a way, having slept two nights side by side and having shared the common hardships of two days' walking together, I felt that I really knew the man well. Our mutual isolation from other contacts with humans had brought us together to a far greater degree than such a short acquaintance would have done in another context.

I suddenly found myself alone within earshot of five angry men who were screaming and menacing their gang leader for his poor arrangements for the provisioning of the camp. For the first time I felt like a fly in a spider's web; I was in a den of thieves and what made matters worse was that I knew it. No Hollywood producer could have imagined more typical-looking jailbirds than these men with their half-rolled-up patched trousers, their hairy chests and red scarves. Long machetes gave them the last touch of piratical menace.

Having strung up my hammock, I ventured over to the main hut where the men were all involved in a discussion. Nobody seemed to take any notice of me, and I sat down in silence, attempting to grasp the thread of conversation. The men still apparently had some food, and on noticing me, the head of the gang asked one of the other men to give me one of their last tortillas. This act of generosity caused a good deal of grumbling from the others. It was very late when I fell into my hammock, and I could still hear shouting in the hut next to mine when I finally dozed off, exhausted from the day's walk.

I was too nervous to sleep well and was up before sunrise. I prepared to leave without any more contact with my unpleasant and dangerous-looking hosts. As I crept out of my hut I had the unpleasant shock of running into one of the bandits. I explained that I had to be off early, and feeling guilty over my silent leave-taking, I asked whether one of the men would be willing to accompany me to carry my bag. His only answer was that I was crazy if I thought they had enough energy to waste on a son-of-a-bitch like myself. On these parting words I hurriedly made my way down the beach.

Having eaten nothing that morning, in a few hours I was already exhausted. I was just out of sight of the *colonia* when I made my way to a small rocky outcrop to sit down and rest. I felt most depressed, and as I trailed my toes in the water at the edge of the rocks I came upon a light bulb. I picked up this distant reminder of civilization and to my delight read that it was made in France. This bolstered my spirits, and as if in gratitude I decided that I would not throw away the light bulb but would bury it. This I did, and set about erecting a small pile of stones above the light bulb. In most people's minds such an act of whimsy would no doubt seem simple stupidity, and so it was, but this stupidity was to save my life.

As I was seated lazily erecting my small shrine to a French light bulb that had drifted to the lonely shore of Quintana Roo, I suddenly spotted, to my horror, five men coming down the beach. I immediately hid behind a low rock and nearly died of fright when, as the men approached, I could see that they were the bandits from the *colonia* and that all of them had shotguns. Had I not been making my shrine I would not have noticed their silent and rapid approach. They were coming down the beach at a rapid pace, heading straight for me. Fortunately I had stopped on the water's edge among rocks, for just twenty yards in front of where I crouched in hiding, a narrow path left the sandy beach, cutting inland around the rocky outcrop which formed a small projection into the sea. With machetes swinging and their shotguns held loosely in their hands, the men sped past within a few yards of where I hid. Had they spotted my tracks they would certainly have spied me. For a moment I remained crouched in terror. What could I do, I wondered. I knew that if I tried to flee up the beach I would encounter the man who had remained at the *colonia*. I could not continue southward in that direction; more than twenty miles separated me from the nearest inhabitants. There was no ambiguity as to the intentions of the crooks; they were after me and I would certainly be robbed if not shot to death. It suddenly struck me what an easy and desirable prey I made for these men. All the tales of horror that I had heard about the coast suddenly came back to me, and I remembered the young archaeologist who had been murdered. These criminals were no fools and they must have realized the true value of my camera.

There was nothing that I could do but remain crouched between the rocks of the shore. I settled down for a long, anxious wait, by far the longest I have ever had to endure. After what seemed an eternity I heard the distant report of a shotgun. Heart pounding, I then heard the noise of footsteps and buried my face in the rocks. The cutthroats were coming back. Had they given up the chase or were they beating the bush? I could not tell and dared not look up. They finally passed on up the coast, and when I ventured to raise my head I saw them disappear in the direction of the colony.

I did not look twice but, getting up, ran down the path, every now and again turning around to look behind me. The sun was incredibly hot and my bag weighed more than usual, but panic gave me wings. I feel sure that I broke some kind of Olympic record.

Exhausted from walking and nervous tension, and having eaten nothing all day, I finally arrived, toward five in the afternoon, at the remains of an immense *cocal* that had once stretched nearly six miles along the coast. This I presumed rightly was El Ubero. I was still not too reassured, however, for my *aventurero* friend had warned me that the keeper of the *cocal* was a "bad man." Coming from my scarred companion, this was no mild characterization. El

Ubero was a most depressing sight, grove after grove of amputated coconut trees, and in the midst of these the ghostly skeletons of wrecked warehouses. Among these structures stood the image of a haunted house—an immense bungalow on stilts covered by a large, half-torn, rusty roof. Part of the bungalow had been broken off its stilts and lay upon its side. A few coconuts had nevertheless survived the hurricane and the *cocal*, which had been the largest of the coast, was still being exploited but now produced only a small percentage of what had been its previous crop. A large twisted wharf snaked out into the sea; oil drums littered the beach about the bungalow.

I made my way to the partly destroyed house where I was greeted by a young man. It took me little time to find out that he was the keeper. He refused to give or sell me food, and only upon my insistence did he consider showing me where there was a pail so that I could get a drink from a large wooden vat that collected rainwater from the bungalow roof. I could sleep in the remains of one of the sheds, said the keeper.

I was too tired to argue and set up my hammock in a warehouse full of dry copra. Picking up some of this, I ate for the first time that day a rather filthy meal of moldy, greasy coconut. I soon felt sick and made for the bungalow in a second attempt to get food. Still the keeper refused and for the first time in my life I truly wished to commit murder. My arguing had attracted the attention of some Indians who had camped in a thatched hut next to the bungalow, and once I had given up arguing with the keeper, they kindly bade me come to their hut where I was immediately served tortillas and beans. These men had been hired to clear the *cocal* of debris, and proved good company. With great pleasure they joined me in cursing the *encargado* (man in charge).

It soon appeared that El Ubero had been a much greater *cocal* than I had thought and had once had a drivable road that followed the coast all the way to Rio Indio. This road had been washed away, but the going, I learned, would now be easy as far as Rio Indio, from where I could certainly find a boat to cover the short distance that separated the *rancho* of Rio Indio from Xcalak. One of the workers volunteered to take me down to Rio Indio the following day, a generous act, for he would lose a day's wages. That night I slept well, dreaming of sweet revenge against the *cocal* keeper. Later I forgave him when I realized that his job must not have been an easy one for a young man alone on an isolated coast. I myself felt that one could not be too cautious about strangers in such an area.

After having taken so many innocent people for bandits, it was now my turn to be taken for one. And nobody would believe my story that I had walked all the way down the coast. In fact I was very soon to be suspected of being a murderer and later, under different circumstances, taken for a criminal and placed in prison by the first so-called civilized people I was to meet.

The following afternoon I arrived with my new guide at Rio Indio. Here lived a man about whom I had heard much: Joaquin Aguilar, one of the great pioneers of Yucatán, a one-time big opera-tor of mahogany camps, and a man greatly feared. In the course of his adventurous life he had made quite a few fortunes, but his last venture, Rio Indio, had, because of hurricanes, been a failure. At Rio Indio he had had a *cocal* that was now completely destroyed. He also had there a concession of thousands of acres of jungle in which he bred and raised cattle, if one can call it raising cattle to let them roam about in the jungle and through the swampy, snake-infested savannas. Uncounted, the cattle were only occasionally disturbed when the arrival of a boat required rounding up a dozen head to ship off to Chetumal or Cozumel. When I arrived the cattle were in poor shape, many of them standing on the beach starving, the poor animals having been driven there by mosquitoes. These pests were so numerous that the cattle preferred to come onto the mosquito-free beach and die there of hunger than to search for food in the interior of the jungle. Already on the beach lay the smelly carcasses of two bulls, rotting in the sun and fought over by hundreds of *zopilotes*, the morbid Mexican scavenger birds. Here at Rio Indio ended my walking. Somewhat prematurely, I rejoiced at the news that Señor Aguilar's son, who had just arrived from Xcalak, would be sailing back in a few days and could take me along. At long last I was safe on the threshold of civilization, all my worries vanished, and I looked back with pride on the two hundred and fifty miles of trackless jungle and coast that I had crossed on foot. How far away Puha now seemed, and how many extraordinary people I had encountered since the morning when I set off with Miguel of Ak.

My rejoicing was overconfident, for the following day a strong wind blew in from the east and prevented us from setting sail. The sea grew higher and higher and a storm started blowing. This would close the reef of Xcalak and prevent us from reaching that village at the border between Mexico and British Honduras. For five days I had to remain at Rio Indio. Fidgeting with impatience, I was constantly looking up at nature's weathervane, the bent and distorted fronds of the coconut palms, good scales by which to tell the force of the wind. I felt like Ulysses stranded because of contrary winds. I had to put up with five more days of tortillas and turtle eggs. The first three of these days of waiting I spent in my hammock sleeping almost all day, feeling at last the sum of weariness and tension of the past month on the coast.

The fourth day I finally woke up and found enough energy to pester Señor Aguilar about the presence of ruins in the jungle surrounding Rio Indio. Señor Aguilar at first said that there were none, then after having ascertained that I was not a government official and that his property would not be confiscated in the eventuality that there were ruins on his concession, he admitted that he had encountered ruins on his land.

No one, he declared, had seen them except his son. With the same feeling of excitement as had accompanied my first discoveries I set out into the jungle with Aguilar, Jr. The ruins were set deep inland beyond the marshes and savanna that bordered the coast.

The jungle was fairly low and thorny, and for the first time it struck me that I was really at home now swinging a machete and making my way through the tangled vines.

On our way to the ruins we caught sight of a deer and Aguilar, Jr. took a shot at it. Unfortunately he only wounded the animal and we lost considerable time stalking it, finally losing the tracks as the deer had made for a small swamp.

The ruins were composed of five low platforms set out in a rough circle. Access to each of these platforms was provided by a wide flight of five or six steps. I was immediately struck by the fact that the stones that formed the sides of these platforms were of a different size, and better carved, than those of the temples I had previously seen. The stone blocks, narrow and about two feet long, were very accurately fitted together, with practically no stucco binding them. In the center of the largest of these platforms I uncovered a small column that lay hidden under a lacework of vines and many inches of leaves and mold. Wanting to dig out the rest of the fallen column, I started to clear the platform. After five minutes of searching I found, to my delight and the amazement of Aguilar, a carved stone. Once it had been cleaned of the earth that covered it, it proved to be a delicately sculptured stone "pig" of the same exact design as the one I had seen at Puha. Aguilar immediately joined in to help me clear more of the surface of the platform, and he soon found another stone that showed definite signs of having been carved. A few minutes later I located a second piece and both pieces fitted together, making up the head of a dragon with open jaws and extended tongue. Finding no more sculptures, I began looking for pieces of pottery that would eventually serve for dating the site. We found innumerable odd bits of vases, and later in Mexico these pottery specimens were to prove that the ruins of Rio Indio were of a period prior to all the other archaeological sites I had found along the coast. Rio Indio had been settled around the year 700 A.D., before cities of the Ancient Empire like those of the interior of Yucatán and Guatemala had

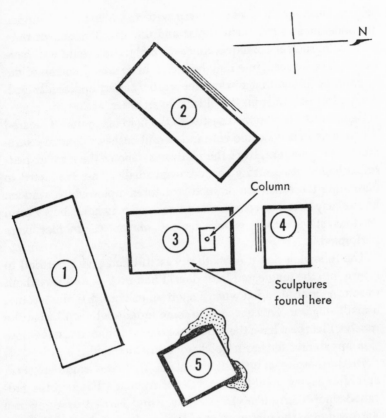

Ruins at Rio Indio. 1, 2, 3, 4: Platforms; 5, Crumbled platform

been abandoned. The ruins at Rio Indio, Tankah, and Xelha are the only known Mayan ruins on the Quintana Roo coast going back to the Old Empire, or classic, period. Tankah was settled in the Late Formative period, before the Christian era, and its maximum occupation came during the Old Empire period. Could it be, then, that after the abandonment of the large interior Mayan settlements a mass migration took place, a migration that, going toward the sea, led up through Rio Indio?

Perhaps Rio Indio will yield more secrets in the future that will help to clear up the greatest mystery of the Mayas: the sudden disappearance of the early Mayas and the abandonment of their great cities such as Palenque. Any such emigration could well have taken place by sea. Here may be a clue as to what became of the large populations that toward the year 900 had apparently suddenly disappeared from the older Mayan cities.

Before returning to the coast with the help of Aguilar, I cleared the ruins as well as I could of branches and bushes, taking measurements and photographs of the platforms. One of the smaller platforms had in its center a second, even smaller one. It is hard to determine the exact use of such structures, upon which wooden houses may have been constructed, or which may have simply been used as stages upon which ancient Mayan ceremonies were performed.

The following day the weather was still bad and I decided to return into the jungle and hunt deer. I had no luck and was about to return empty-handed when I spotted, on the edge of a swamp, a small alligator. This gave joy to some Indians who worked at the rancho. I let them have the reptile, whose meat they eat and whose skin apparently fetches a good price in Chetumal.

On the morning of my sixth day at Rio Indio the wind slackened, and after saying good-by to old Señor Aguilar I boarded the red-sailed sloop of Aguilar, Jr. A strong wind carried us through a narrow gap in the reef in front of the rancho and for the first time since my arrival at Puha I could once more contemplate from afar the low, jungle-bordered coast of Quintana Roo as it slipped by. How different it seemed to me now from when I had first seen it as I sailed from Puerto Juarez to Cozumel. The coast was now no mystery to me and it had become my coast, the one from which I had torn away so many secrets, and on which I had spent forty exciting days.

The trip to Xcalak was to take ten hours, including a short stop at an abandoned cocal called Guadalupe, where we went conch fishing—a sport that consists in diving to the bottom of the sandy shore and feeling in the blurry sand for the giant rock-like conch shells that one brings to the surface.

It was dark when we came in sight of the small lighthouse that marked the village of Xcalak. Drawing closer and closer to the foaming reef, the helmsman lined up two small beacons set there to indicate the narrow barrier through which one had to pass to reach the sheltered waters of the coast. Never had I been more excited than when we drew up against a wooden pier at Xcalak. For a moment I was stunned by the noises and the animation of the wharf. There stood a large crowd of men, the first crowd I had seen in more than six weeks. I felt strangely ill at ease and hesitated to step off the boat in amongst all the men on the wharf. I felt depressed; this was at last civilization, and how I already regretted the barren Quintana Roo coast and its solitude. Everything around me seemed ugly and unnatural: the din of a distant generator, the flicker of bare electric bulbs that lit the dirty sand of the streets of Xcalak, the wail of a radio in the dark, the large dock and the crowd. Gone were the distant roar of the reef and the whisper of the wind in the trees; even the sky seemed dimmer as the town lights veiled many of its lesser stars.

On the dock stood many unusual and forgotten objects: a bicycle, cases that smelled of factories, a rubber hose. I began wishing I had not arrived. Although my stay on the Quintana Roo coast had been short, I could not remember, and did not wish to recall, that this modern world was in fact mine. I could still take thought only for the problems of the jungle, for my friends of Tulum and the lonely *cocaleros*.

Up on the dock I overcame this first reaction when I realized that for once I would not have to bother about where to hang my hammock or what to eat. Food at its most elementary level, along with water, had been my preoccupation for so long now that I could not yet imagine a world where these two items were not scarce. Thinking about food, I then remembered all the things I had craved; now, I thought, they could be mine: a gin and tonic, ice, sweets, meat, and thousands of other things.

I was to be disappointed, for if Xcalak had at first appeared to me like a large settlement, I soon had to face the fact that it was only a small village, still showing the ravages of the hurricanes and the loss of half its original population, who had died in the tragic wake of a tidal wave. It had none of the small gastronomical surprises that could have reconciled me to civilization. Upon my request for an iced drink I was taken to the ugly cement house of a man called Caldwell, the former millionaire of the area (before the hurricane had ruined him). Half Mexican and half English, Mr. Caldwell welcomed me in a dirty kitchen around which he shuffled in slippers. He had no gin or tonic, but from a battered freezer he produced an ice-cold bottle of Pepsi-Cola, a rather poor substitute. Was this, I wondered, the prize of all my efforts—an ugly world (our own) with an artificial flavor? I felt very lonely having nothing to share with all those around me, and I made my way to the wharf to look out at the sea and recapture the beauty of what had now become *my* coast.

I had made arrangements with Aguilar, Jr. to sail me down the following day to British Honduras. Only sixty miles separated me from Belize. Aguilar could take me half that distance through the canal that separated Mexico from the British colony. This would bring us as far as San Pedro, a village on one of the many British islands that close the southern entrance to Chetumal bay, San Pedro being on the island known as Ambergris Key.

When I reached the wharf, to my surprise I noticed that a great argument was raging between Señor Aguilar and the crowd that still stood about the dock. As I approached, everyone turned around to stare at me and all stopped talking and opened a passage before me. When I reached Señor Aguilar he explained to me in two words what was the matter. The villagers had learned that Señor Aguilar was to take me to British Honduras the following day, and they were all trying to dissuade him from doing so, claiming that beyond doubt I was a bandit and that I would surely murder him. I soon learned that the villagers of Xcalak had a reason for being suspicious of foreigners like myself, for five months before I sailed into Xcalak three foreigners had come there from Chetumal. Like myself they had asked a fisherman to take them to British Honduras. When the fishing boat was out at sea the three bandits shot two of its three crewmen through the back of the head. They then ordered the surviving man to steer the boat to a barren spot on the coast of the British colony. Such a tragedy had of course made the other inhabitants of Xcalak suspicious of all foreigners, especially those wanting to go to Belize. Apparently the young crewman who had not been shot had managed to escape the criminals by jumping into the shark-infested waters of Chetumal bay.

There was little I could do but hope that Señor Aguilar would not fail me, and attempt to persuade as many people as possible of my innocence and inability to carry out any murderous intentions. I even went so far as to produce my passport, which was of little help for faithful to passport photographs my portrait, which decorated the front page, had an evil and sinister air about it.

Nevertheless at dawn we set sail and glided past the now silent village, which in daylight proved to be nothing more than a dozen sorry-looking, battered, wood and cement houses stretched along a dirty beach flanked on three sides by mangrove swamps.

We made our way down the coast until we came upon a narrow channel that cut inland. This was Bacalar Chico, a seemingly man-made channel that separated Ambergris Key from the Quintana Roo mainland and thus marked the border of British Honduras with Mexico. This channel led into Chetumal bay. The waters of the passage were crystal clear, and its bed was swept by a swift seaward current that bent the thin weeds that grew in it.

Through this channel had sailed vessels carrying much of the commerce of southern Quintana Roo, for Bacalar had carried on a flourishing trade with Belize in mahogany, dyewood, and other products before the War of the Castes. Bacalar also has associations with Gonzalo Guerrero, the Spaniard who had landed in Cozumel eleven years before Cortez's arrival. He had later refused to return to Spain or join Cortez, and had, at the head of Mayan troops, led the resistance of the Mayas against the Spanish invaders. Through the channel of Bacalar Chico, Guerrero had directed Mayan war canoes against the Spaniards. Later, at Bacalar, Gonzalo Guerrero had died at the head of his Mayan forces.

I wondered what would have happened had he won, and I could not help but compare the pitiful village of Xcalak with the mighty cities of Tulum and Chunyaxche. Had the condition of the Mayas progressed since the arrival of the Spaniards? I do not think so. The lot of the American Indian today is one of poverty. From Alaska to Tierra del Fuego, the Indians of the New World have received from the white conquest only disease, destruction, and distress. The present-day Indians of the New World seem to have gained nothing that could excite the envy of their forefathers.

Toward midday we emerged from the narrow channel into the blue, shallow waters of Chetumal bay. We then proceeded to sail down the lee side of Ambergris Key. I was now contemplating English territory, and felt at long last that all my worries had come to an end. From here, I knew, in a few days I could reach an airport and from there would be in contact with the rest of the world.

I suddenly became concerned with a thousand and one little matters that until now had fled my mind. I would have to cable upon my arrival to the French professor in Mérida, and to my anxious and probably desperate parents. I also remembered Ball, and the university, all that awaited me in that strange world beyond the sandy beaches and the mangrove swamps. How sad, I thought, to leave the Quintana Roo coast.

A red roof with two gables suddenly appeared from above some palm trees. As we were about to pull into San Pedro a very wet and British rainstorm came down on us. Shouting with joy, I set foot in British Honduras.

That night I was in prison. . . .

X

Of Dragons and Policemen

Upon arriving at San Pedro, unaware that civility and civilization are not synonymous, I had marched proudly through the main street of the small town to the police station. On my way I had passed the general store, snubbing for a moment all that it must contain. And what was to be my undoing, I made my way immediately to a dirty, white, wooden building in front of which floated the Union Jack. All the village was silent save for the pitiful wailing of a trumpet in the slow pace of a funeral march. A child had died, and on my arrival the whole town, led by an amateur band, was marching behind the coffin. The majority of the population of British Honduras is colored, and the procession was composed largely of hundreds of small black children in gaudy muslin dresses.

On the veranda of the police station I paused next to a tall, half-Negro, half-Mayan policeman who was standing respectfully at attention watching the procession go by. Before us lay the village, an incongruous assemblage of British colonial architecture and palm-thatched huts. This was the colonial Britain of my childhood story books. How disappointed Nanny would have been!

The dirge of the funeral still echoed in my ears when the policeman turned to me.

"Yes, man?" asked the policeman with a strange Carib drawl. I could have hugged him, it had been so long since I had heard

English spoken. For an instant I was taken by surprise, not knowing where to begin in what I had to say, or even what to say. I finally managed to stutter in English that I wanted to inform Her Majesty's servant that I had arrived in British Honduras. Upon hearing this the "friendly policeman" changed his attitude and, straightening himself, began to fumble in his pocket for some keys. He then proceeded to open the door of a small office, and without a word entered, picked up his cap, placed it upon his head, and slowly sank into a steel swivel chair. He was now the perfect caricature of an inhuman civil servant, and from behind his large desk he repeated his simple phrase: "Yes, man?"

By then I should have been on my guard, the batteries of complicated civil administration having now been laid out before me. But not heeding this, and with the candor of a *chiclero*, I proceeded to relate my story. I felt slightly ill at ease inside the neat office, blackened as I was from exposure and still shod in the tattered sandals in which I had walked the coast. I had not seen an office in months, and I was greatly impressed by the chairs, the desk, and the shiny chromium face of a large new radio transmitter that hung on the wall behind the policeman. The gaudy calendar of a local soda manufacturer was the only light note in the place; as for the royal coat of arms, it seemed to sneer down at me, along with piles of important-looking files neatly placed in steel racks.

After muttering something about my walking two hundred miles, the policeman abruptly asked, "Have you a visa?" I confidently replied in the negative, recalling my interview, which now seemed centuries ago, with British officials at the Embassy in Mexico City.

"No," I explained. "I am French and the French do not need visas to enter British colonies." I then mumbled something about the Franco-British Act extending to the colonies.

To all this the policeman's reply was firm: "You cannot enter British Honduras without a visa. You'll have to go back where you came from."

Beyond this he was inflexible. Orders are orders. No one may enter British Honduras without a visa, and no one may enter the colony via San Pedro. The policeman then went on to give me a detailed account of how the three murderers had crossed over from Mexico into British Honduras, the same ones who had caused me trouble in Xcalak. Apparently they had robbed a large bank in the United States and after killing the two crewmen of the boat they had hired in Xcalak, had crossed British Honduras unnoticed and fled to Honduras proper. Since then orders had been sent out stating that no one was to enter the colony via San Pedro or at any other point of the border save Chetumal.

In other words, I was being accused of border crashing, besides the fact that I had no visa.

"Go back where you came from!"

"Orders are orders," repeated the policeman, mimicking, I imagined, his stubborn instructor, probably some "old India" fellow back in the town of Belize. I explained in full detail the impossibility of my returning from whence I had come. I told all about the swamps and the forty days of walking, but the policeman was unimpressed, and for a moment I felt as if I were to lose the last battle of my expedition.

I gave another push at the Franco-British Act, but to no avail; the act was recent and it would take years to reach San Pedro, I thought. The policeman then handed me a yellow, leprous piece of paper, one of those forms that blot up ink as fast as one can write. On minute dotted lines I was asked to give my life history, and the why, when, and where of my presence in British Honduras. I made a mess of it, judging from the looks of the policeman as he read aloud, with great difficulty, such words as "explorer" and "foot," which later I admitted did sound like an incongruous profession and means of transportation.

The policeman swallowed hard and tried not to appear surprised. When he asked what funds I was carrying I had to fumble inside my old moldy pack, which exhaled a damp, unpleasant smell. From this I withdrew some crushed traveler's checks and a handful of dirty Mexican notes long past recognition. "Forty dollars." The small print of some nasty bylaw decided that I had not enough funds.

"Sorry, man, you will have to go back where you came from," repeated the policeman, jubilantly spelling out the law that condemned me. I pleaded my father's diplomatic immunity, forgetting that I had just turned twenty-one. I asked to see the French Consul; there was none. Finally the policeman softened up. "I'll call Belize by radio tonight," was his final answer. Then, as if dismissing a court, he rose and left the room.

His duties finished, the policeman became more human, and I ventured to ask where I could hang up my hammock, saying that all I needed was a shed. With this remark I was debased forever in the eyes of the Law, and treated with scorn. I left my bag at the police station and made a beeline for the general store.

Once again food was to reconcile me with civilization. I drowned my anger and disappointment by stuffing myself with as many of the wares as I could lay my hands on in the store. I had dreamed of a royal reception, triumph in a British fashion, myself standing with a drink in hand, my back to a large fire in some comfortable club. Instead, I swallowed raw sardines and chocolate standing at the wooden counter of the shop, where all the villagers stopped by to see the freak who had just set foot on Ambergris Key.

As I stood stuffing myself in the store, my thoughts flashed back to the coast, to the hungry *cocaleros,* to the poor small village of Tulum, and I felt ashamed. How much one of these tins would have meant to them. It seemed unfair that such an array of foodstuffs should be so accessible to a few, while others existed on a hard-earned diet of corn and turtle eggs. For the first time I enjoyed the freedom of civilized people to choose what they will eat at the movement of a finger. I was headed for trouble when I began attacking chocolate bars along with olives, and was not long in discovering that my stomach was still accustomed to the primitive food of the coast.

I paid for my purchases in Mexican money which was exchanged for British Honduras dollars. When I returned to the police station I found the policeman playing with the dials of his radio transmitter and uttering the cannibalistic and ritual phrases that seem necessary magic to obtain answers from radio sets. "Loud and clear," he was saying. "Loud and clear," came the answer, along with much gargling and buzzing. "Needs a visa, cannot admit, also not enough funds, must return." A dry click turned the receiver off.

"We," said the policeman, "cannot admit you. You have neither a visa nor enough funds to guarantee your repatriation to France." I argued that I had all necessary funds available once I reached Belize and a bank, and that if I had but a few dollars on me, it was purposely, for if I had carried more I would have exposed myself to being robbed.

The policeman smiled; he had heard similar stories before.

"I'm sorry, man," he added. "Till I see you out of the country you will have to remain here in custody."

There are times when one feels helpless; this was one of them. I now rocked the wooden police building with my protests, appealing again for the French Consul. Although there was none, I discovered fortunately, rummaging through a small directory, that there was a consular agent. I persuaded the policeman to call Belize again. The answer came back that the weekend had begun and that it was impossible to reach the Vice Consul before Monday. After the final click of the infernal machine the policeman fumbled again for his keys and opened a thick, steel-barred door.

"You're not going to lock me up," I protested.

"No, man, just keep you in sight," answered the policeman jubilantly.

Uncertain of my eventual fate, I thus spent two days in jail, sorting out my thoughts, and my belongings. In jail I emptied out my henequen bag, which I had not cleaned out once since my departure.

Glued with mold, out came the odds and ends that I had either brought along or gathered en route. Half of what had composed my heavy pack had been useless to me on my journey. There was a bath towel and my blazer, which now was but one green mass of home-grown penicillin. I gave my blazer to be cleaned; it came back the following day blue again, along with a bill: 15 cents for labor and 75 cents for the two gallons of cleaning fluid that had been necessary to rid the thing of mold.

Out of my bag also came a host of small parcels, my rolls of film, little bags of pottery, the jade beads, the obsidian blade, my notebooks, incredibly battered and torn, and my map of the coast, with its outline now completely blackened with the dots that showed the ruins I had encountered.

Of these there were sixteen archaeological sites that had not been shown on the map Dr. Alberto Ruz gave me in Mérida—sixteen sites which I then believed I had been the first person to record. Later, when I was able to examine more closely all the data available on Quintana Roo, I realized that, of all the sights I had found, there were two that had already been sighted before but had not been marked on the official map that I had in my possession. This nevertheless left fourteen archaeological sites which I had been the first to record, a number sufficiently large to have made my efforts well worthwhile. In all, on my first and second trips I would be the first to register well over one hundred oratories, temples, pyramids, and mounds, structures of the once powerful though little-known civilization of the eastern Mayas, a civilization of seafarers.

Having been the first person to inspect the Quintana Roo coast on foot, I now brought back valuable information on its Mayan settlements, the first clear picture of the ancient Mayas' coastal domain. My picnic to Tepoztlán had ended in the opening up for further archaeological research of a number of unexplored zones.

From my bag onto the floor of my prison fell a wad of paper and three small clay figures, those Gustav Regler had given me. I picked up a pencil and on the sheets of paper crossed out the Gothic lettering of the word "Darién." There remained the words "Expedition Quintana Roo." My first expedition was over.

As for the clay figures, I could now easily see that they were all forgeries. . . .

The French Vice Consul was duly contacted on Monday, and having for the last three weeks been pestered by desperate telegrams from my parents about my disappearance, he willingly put up the bail necessary for my entry into British Honduras, and I was soon whizzed off by motor launch to Belize.

XI

Return to Quintana Roo

It is quite easy to discover ruins hidden for centuries in the jungle, or at least a lot easier than to make one's way through the maze of the archaeological department of a museum. This I learned as soon as I returned to civilization.

I had naïvely believed that the chart of ruins I had brought back from Quintana Roo, along with the specimens of pottery and my photographs, would rock the entire archaeological world. To my surprise I was wrong. And even when I resigned myself to more modest claims, I was confronted with the inevitable barriers that exist between professionals and amateurs in any field. I felt more alone in the musty antechambers of museums than in the jungle. I had discovered ruins no one had seen, but soon I was faced with the fact that nobody had seen me discover them.

Thus lay before me the task of proving what I had found, and nursing my own archaeological baby among investigators who tended to believe only in the interest and importance of their own personal projects.

In this way I came to know a considerable amount about various other projects as my own went unattended and often unheeded. I felt, nevertheless, that it was my duty to see that my trip should not prove useless, and therefore I set about making sure my finds would be duly recorded and, I hoped, eventually revisited by competent archaeologists.

My first step toward this aim was to carry my charts and specimens triumphantly to the Archaeological Institute in Mexico City. There I was kindly greeted by Dr. Ignacio Bernal, the director, who had seen me off some three months earlier and to whom I owed my introduction to the Mayas.

My discoveries pleased him considerably although in no dramatic way did they surprise him. He explained to me that of the various pre-Columbian civilizations in Mexico, of which the Mayas were only one, many new archaeological sites were discovered each year. And every new discovery was but a little more work added to the considerable burden of the Institute, that of registering the many hundreds of yet unstudied archaeological sites of Mexico.

My finds, though, did attract particular attention among Mayan scholars, in that they covered an area that had been all too blank until my journey along the coast.

It so happened that the Institute was about to publish a new and detailed map of Yucatán State and Quintana Roo. On this my sites were recorded, thus in one stroke considerably modifying the archaeological picture of what had once been believed to be a largely barren coast.

In the offices of the Institute the specimens of pottery I had brought back were analyzed by experts, while I became familiar with the *Mayan Pottery Dictionary*. This work includes sketches of the designs of thousands of fragments, and by referring to this I found that my small pieces of pottery gave valuable information.

Among many other things, I was to learn that one cannot claim to have discovered a place unless one can prove that no one has been there before. In archaeology, as in many other fields, to discover is to find what has been forgotten, the important factor being to determine what can be considered memory. Before I could claim with certitude the value of the discoveries I had made, I had to become acquainted in great detail with the expeditions and travels performed in Yucatán over the past one hundred years. To my relief I found that no one, or at least no one on archaeological record, had made the trek by land that I had undertaken. This hardly came as a surprise, since experts on the Central American jungle considered it a miracle that I had escaped catching malaria and amoebic dysentery, diseases which, in my case, might have proved fatal.

There had, though, been a fair number of incursions onto the Quintana Roo coast by sea, the first of these having been performed by John Lloyd Stephens and Frederick Catherwood in 1843, which led to the discovery of Tulum. This expedition had passed along the coast prior to the revolt of the Mayas in 1847. The next important expedition was performed eighty years later, in 1922, by Dr. S. G. Morley and Dr. Samuel K. Lothrop. This expedition also approached Quintana Roo by sea. I had the pleasure of meeting Dr. Lothrop at Harvard and of learning that apparently very little had changed on the coast since his journey. Dr. Lothrop had mostly worked with Dr. Morley at Tulum, where, after barely escaping assassination by the Chan Santa Cruz Indians, he had made the first serious study of the city.

I learned also that at Tulum there were two carved stelae with dates engraved on them. Unfortunately, the boat which had been chartered to transport them from Tulum to Cozumel sank during a storm in the Yucatán Straits and the cargo has never been recovered.

In 1926 an American expedition set out to explore by boat the coast of Quintana Roo. Led by Gregory Mason and the archaeologist Herbert J. Spinden of the Peabody Museum at Harvard, this expedition discovered many yet unrecorded sites on Cozumel and on the coast, in particular the sites of Pamul and Xcaret, and the small temple of Yochac which I had believed I was the first to encounter. But more interesting still to me, the Mason-Spinden expedition had gone with a small motorboat inland from Boca de Paila to the large lagoons that cut deeply into Quintana Roo at this spot. They had followed a narrow channel that led them to a large lagoon, then through another channel to a smaller one. On the edge of the first channel they had discovered an elaborately carved temple, and on the edge of the smaller of the two lagoons they had found large temples and a tall pyramid. This site they called Muyil, although I have every reason to believe that its name should be Chunyaxche, the name of the Indian settlement at the very foot of the ruins. This site was beyond doubt the one I had visited. Gregory Mason reported this find and many others in his book *Silver Cities of Yucatán*. Regarding Muyil, he mentions that they found twelve temples and ceremonial buildings, and "mounds too numerous to count where others had crumbled." They left Muyil (or Chunyaxche) feeling that the city deserved "much further study." The need for such study had determined me to return one day and investigate Chunyaxche and the network of waterways that led to this large city. I had not been wrong, I felt, in assuming it to be the center of the Mayan coastal settlements.

This same expedition also studied the site of Santa Rosa, mapped under the name of Chac Mool, the reclining deity whose mutilated statue I had seen on the coast. They passed within a few hundred yards of some of the coastal sites I had found, without seeing them.

As I delved into the subject I found that Quintana Roo had fascinated and attracted other explorers and adventurers. One of these was Charles Lindbergh, who made an aerial survey of the coast in 1929. This survey yielded photographs of many yet unknown temples. Looking at these aerial photographs, I spotted the tall pyramid of Chunyaxche, easily recognizable by its position close to the lagoon. I could also see the site of Yochac, and among the photographs I recognized the ruin of Puerto Chile, which no foreigner had reached by land until my passage some twenty-nine years after the photographs had been taken.

But aerial photographs are not adequate for discovering ruins in the rain forest. The tall trees and bushes make a dense canopy, forming a camouflage no camera could pierce.

From my research it became evident that the part of the coast extending north of Puha up to the northeastern tip of the Yucatán peninsula, and the area immediately around Tulum, had been studied quite intensively by various scholars, especially the coast at Xcalet. There, for over ten years, a New York businessman, Mr. Loring M. Hewen, has been painfully exploring and discovering ruins. A member of the New York Explorers' Club, he works in close contact with various museums. Mr. Hewen is one of the last of a series of gentlemen explorers, a member of that wealthy, educated elite with a great curiosity for archaeology, who spends much of his time and money investigating problems of cultural importance. Unfortunately, like many "non-professionals," Mr. Hewen does not get the assistance he deserves, although he himself is more experienced in actual fieldwork in eastern Yucatán than most professional archaeologists.

From the pamphlets of Carnegie Institute I also became familiar with the works of Dr. William T. Sanders, a young archaeologist who had spent quite some time studying the ruins of Tankah, near Tulum. Dr. Sanders had also carried his research inland toward Chumpom, encountering many new sites on his way.

Over a period of two years, through the assistance of the Peabody Museum of Harvard, directed by the amiable Dr. John O. Brew, and with the help of Dr. Samuel K. Lothrop, Dr. Gordon R. Willey, Dr. William R. Bullard, Jr., and Mr. A. Ledyard Smith, I managed to determine which of the archaeological sights I had found were unrecorded, and was able to judge that my finds were of definite importance in providing a more continuous and clearer picture of Mayan settlements along the Quintana Roo coast. They also confirmed that the Mayas were active seafarers.

By the time I had completed my investigation the number of archaeological sites I could claim to have been the first to register was reduced from sixteen to fourteen, a figure that was still large enough to encourage me to carry on in Quintana Roo. From the start I had felt that Quintana Roo must still hold many secrets, and I was not so foolish as to imagine that during my perilous and hasty passage I had seen even half of what must still lie in the jungle, as yet undiscovered.

At the Harvard Library, I unearthed such strange documents as the *Album Monográfico de Quintana Roo*, a political pamphlet in magazine form that had been written with a view to inducing Mexicans to move into what was called the "new frontier." This pamphlet, printed after the last Mexican revolution and the signing of the peace treaty with the Indians in 1935, gave much precious information on the Chan Santa Cruz Indians, their leaders, their victories, and their battles, although needless to say, in the pamphlet the Indians were given a rather biased treatment. From this publication and the works of the archaeologists Alfonso Villa Rojas and Thomas Gann, of Belize, I managed to patch up the episodes of the little-known history of the Chan Santa Cruz Indians, a history most of which is yet to be written.

The more I became acquainted with Mayan archaeology the more apparent it was that to make any thorough archaeological expedition to Quintana Roo would require considerable funds, funds in fact far greater than any university would be ready to expend. To consider an archaeological site thoroughly explored and excavated required many dozens of workers, skilled technicians, and archaeologists. To transport such a crew into Quintana Roo would prove not only a dangerous task but also a highly costly one. To draw up precise ground plans of the fourteen sites I had discovered would take many years and would cost a fortune. Furthermore, many hundreds of other projects still had priority in the eyes of the Mexican Government and universities in America and abroad. I had to abandon, although reluctantly, the idea of seeing my finds analyzed and studied in detail in the near future. If I intended to set out for Quintana Roo again I would have to go at my own expense, accompanied by a few friends and possibly by an archaeologist.

From the start I knew it was impossible to hope to do any clearing of the jungle. If it was necessary to clear away the vegetation around some of the sites in order to see their exact layouts and structures, it would also be necessary to solidify the buildings, which might crumble when the vines and roots that held them together had been destroyed. Paradoxically, what destroys the temples (trees and vegetation) also preserves them. To resolve this problem an ingenious technique has been invented by archaeologists. When confronted with a ruin that would collapse if the trees that grew upon it were cut, archaeologists now set fire to the trees; gently, for several days, the trunk of the tree and its roots smolder, burning themselves out. When the roots are entirely burned away cement is then run down the channels left by the charred roots. Thus the ruins are consolidated by veins of cement that, like the roots of the trees, hold the structures together. But alas, this method, clever as it may be, requires technicians and material that would have been too costly for me to employ.

From the photographs that I had brought back, and also the pottery specimens, it appeared probable that all the archaeological sites I had encountered, save that of Rio Indio, were of the Mayapán period. The Mayapán era was one of prosperity in the history of the Mayas that extended from the years 1250 A.D. to about the year 1450 A.D. At this time in Yucatán the leadership of the Mayan people rested in the city state of Mayapán. The League of Mayapán incorporated most of the cities of Yucatán. This era was in a way a Mayan "renaissance," and saw the erection of many fine cities and the embellishment of many temples with Toltec-influenced designs. It was during this period that the Quintana Roo coast knew a tremendous development, favored no doubt by a flourishing commerce.

As for Rio Indio, the exception in my finds, according to pottery specimens and as confirmed by the architectural style of the platforms I had found there, it belonged to an earlier period—often erroneously called the Old Empire—which flourished between the years 200 and 900 A.D.

My studies were to interrupt any further work in matters archaeological, as I explored the rather more arid surfaces of balance sheets and financial reports at the Harvard Business School. Every day my hopes to return to Quintana Roo became more dim. But very often I would think of the coast, the mysterious jungle and beautiful barren beaches. How far away I felt in Cambridge from the simple life of the village of Tulum and that of the *cocals*! What had become, I wondered, of Canche and the families that I had left behind? I could also not forget the early sunrises upon the misty giant ceiba trees, the cries of the birds on the edges of the lagoons, and the friendly but fierce faces of those who had shared their food and few belongings with me, so that I might survive.

If my resolve to return was firm, fate was to delay it for some time. In Quintana Roo I had tasted adventure and known the thrill of exploring virgin land. I now yearned to travel far to even more remote areas of the world.

When I had been studying law in Paris I had accidentally purchased a Tibetan grammar. Starting with this grammar, I had become most interested in all matters Tibetan. At the end of my first year at Harvard I found myself with sufficient time on my hands and the necessary funds to do what had long been but a dream. Now, thanks to the generosity of a Boston gentleman, and with the aid of the Peabody Museum and Yale University—and the fact that because of my trip in Quintana Roo I had been branded with the ambiguous title of explorer—I was able to set up an expedition to the Himalayas.

A year to the day after having set foot in Quintana Roo I boarded a plane in New York with an anthropologist bound for Nepal and the Himalayas. This time, well equipped and prepared in the best manner for what lay ahead, I set out on an adventure that was to keep me away from Yucatán for yet another year.

But the Tibetan monasteries and the grandiose beauty of the greater Himalayan range were not sufficient to make me forget Quintana Roo, the land where, for the first time, I had felt the thrills of those who leave the beaten path to push into the unknown. In Nepal, with my companion Alain Thiollier, I had walked more than seven hundred and fifty miles over rugged mountains and up yet unvisited valleys situated on the summit of the world on and around Mount Everest. There, assisted by porters, a liaison officer, and qualified Sherpa guides, I had lived an adventure according to the rules of Himalayan travel and exploration.

When I returned I knew that in the future my life would be spent investigating and studying little-known or unknown areas.

After this expedition I was able to consider returning to Quintana Roo. I realized that it would be impossible to go there financed by a museum, and therefore planned a second trip of reconnaissance on my own.

My intention was to return to the sites I had already visited in the hope of finding structures I had overlooked. Better-prepared and with the experience of my first journey, I felt sure that I could investigate the ruins of the coast more thoroughly.

In Paris I started the first preparations. Looking over the map of Quintana Roo, and remembering the difficulties of my last trip, I decided that the best means of studying the ruins I had found would be to go to Quintana Roo by boat, and to use the boat as a sort of roving base camp. Thus, I felt, I could set out in maximum comfort and search for more temples.

For this trip I had to find companions, and this, I knew from my Himalayan expedition, is the most difficult thing to find for an expedition, especially when one's funds are limited. In Paris I had several volunteers, among whom were a young French journalist (a girl) and a young lawyer—a rather strange team, but two good friends who had both the time and the means to come along.

From Paris I flew back to New York to set up the expedition itself. There I spent three fruitless months trying to raise the funds we needed in order to set off. I wrote articles on the Himalayas, but they were not of popular interest at that time. The only thing that seemed to interest magazines and newspapers was the Abominable Snowman. As it happened, we had brought back from our expedition information that proved that the Abominable Snowman did not exist, which made me even more unpopular with the numerous publications that had been capitalizing for many years on headlines about the Snowman, based on rather thin and often imaginary evidence of "his" existence.

Toward the end of September it seemed that I would never be able to get under way. I received a letter from my lawyer friend in France informing me he could not come as his free time had run out. I was about to despair when all of a sudden my hopes materialized.

Thanks to Jim Drought, the young editor of *This Week* magazine, a large American weekly, I obtained part of the financial backing I was seeking. And at about the same time I ran into the owner of a yacht who was prepared to charter his schooner for the expedition at a very reasonable rate.

The yacht, called *Caroline*, was a fifty-six-foot schooner with sleeping accommodations for ten in luxurious oak-paneled cabins. Her skipper, Count Grabowski, a friend of my younger brother, was an appealing adventurer who had crossed the Atlantic from Gibraltar to New York singlehanded in eighty-four days. I could have found no more competent a skipper than Grabowski, and he was ready to take me on the four-thousand-mile journey by sea to the Quintana Roo coast.

Since I could not afford a paid crew for the trip I had to search for companions who would not only be interested in "roughing it" in the jungle but would also be ready to undertake the long ocean passage that, we hoped, would eventually bring us to the blue waters of the Yucatán Straits.

From Paris I now had but one favorable reply, that of Marie Claire de Montaignac, a friend whose eagerness to come was equaled only by her good looks and lack of experience. Just out of finishing school, she was trying her hand at journalism. At first I had refused to accept the idea of taking a girl along, Quintana Roo seeming the last place for a woman. As for Marie Claire's experience at sea, it consisted of a sun-bathing party in a small sailing boat on the French Riviera. Grabowski seemed rather appalled, and I had much trouble in persuading him to accept Marie Claire in the crew of the *Caroline*. "At least she can cook," I suggested hopefully. In fact she could not.

Wasting no time, Marie Claire jumped into the first jet for New York, and arrived on board the *Caroline* the following day, bringing along seven suitcases, the contents of which were as strange to jungle expeditions as fur coats to Mayas.

Along with Marie Claire came hurricane Donna, which battered the eastern coast of the United States and nearly sank the *Caroline* as she lay at anchor off City Island near New York. We were still short of at least two crew members. All my friends were unfortunately busy acquainting themselves with the intricacies of the Stock Exchange on Wall Street or otherwise engaged in starting their careers as businessmen.

Finally, a Belgian princess recommended a French artist, an inveterate globe-trotter called Bruno. Like Marie Claire and me, he had never sailed a large yacht, but his great physical strength persuaded Captain Grabowski to accept him on board the *Caroline*. As time was running out and all of us were eager to go, we decided to leave without recruiting further crew.

The day before we left was a hectic one; the docks of the shipyard where we had had the *Caroline* repainted were covered with crates of food which Marie Claire had purchased in a supermarket where, with her French accent and the quantity of her purchases, she had driven the manager crazy. For three hours she had caused congestion at all the cashier desks while dozens of New Yorkers stared in awe at the French girl with the gigantic appetite.

Crawling all over the stacks of food on the dock at City Island was a photographer from *This Week* anxious to catch a photograph that did not reflect the panic and disorder of our departure. Captain Grabowski was busy studying the charts for the first leg of our voyage which was to take us non-stop sixteen hundred nautical miles down to St. Thomas, the most important of the American Virgin Islands.

As for my parents, resigning themselves to the idea that their son might not be a businessman after all, they provided us with whisky and French wine.

The *Caroline* was a beautiful and elegant boat, but when she had been constructed in Holland her builders had not designed her for expeditions in the tropics or to be handled by a very small crew, especially by one as incompetent as ours. As for myself, I shared the anxiety of Marie Claire and Bruno as to how well we might fare during our first experience as sailors.

Fortunately Captain Grabowski was what is known in sailing circles as a "singlehander," for we fully realized that this trip, as far as he was concerned, would be a singlehanded passage. As for weather forecasts, they could not have been any worse. Hurricane Donna had only just passed through and was being followed by a hundred storms and the usual meteorological disturbances that occur in the wake of a hurricane. As for the Quintana Roo coast, not having heard about its condition, I could only pray that Donna had not done too much damage to the ruins we were off to study.

The 16th of October we weighed anchor, and then there commenced a series of technical disasters. As we left the dock at City Island the gear box of *Caroline*'s powerful engine broke down, facing us with making the decision whether to return for repairs, which would have delayed us considerably and involved extra expense, or to sail on with no motor. Captain Grabowski, being master on board, after God, decided to sail on. We therefore had to beat up the one-hundred-twenty-mile-long Long Island Sound instead of cutting down the East River alongside Manhattan into the Atlantic, and from there sail sixteen hundred miles without an engine.

Little did this worry us at first, because at last we were off. Bruno, Marie Claire, and I stared as Grabowski rushed around the deck doing all the necessary maneuvers. By mid-afternoon we had barely moved five miles and lay becalmed off Execution Rock in the Sound. We all felt rather stupid waiting for wind within twenty minutes by car of the center of New York, one of the world's largest cities. The day before we had said good-by with the glow of those about to take off for sudden danger and adventure; now we drifted helplessly in windless waters, surrounded by the fast motorboats of the hundreds of weekend sailors who throng Long Island Sound. Quintana Roo seemed farther away than ever, and Marie Claire expressed our unspoken thoughts: "At this rate we will take two years to reach even the West Indies." The wind must have heard her remark, for as night fell a storm blew up, chasing away the Sunday sailors and leaving us alone. We went on deck to take our first lesson on how to reef a sail, steer a course, and keep a watch. With night and the storm we were but a ghostly shadow sailing jaggedly between the coast of Long Island and the mainland of Connecticut. To the west of us we could see the great halo of lights of the city, and when the wind dropped one could hear a distant roar—the motors of thousands of cars—which drifted over the water to us. The sinister horn of Execution Rock resounded in our ears all night, while I fought with the wheel, turning it this way and that, in great panic of jibbing while the inconsistent needle of the compass fluttered all around the quadrant, an ever-shifting proof of my incompetence.

By the following afternoon we all agreed that thirty tons of boat was a lot for three men and a girl to handle. Nevertheless, two days later, as if celebrating a major triumph, we welcomed the Atlantic. Grabowski's face lit up. This was the Atlantic he had known, alone, for over eighty days. "Wait," he said, "now you will have real sailing."

He was right; from the moment we lost sight of land and for the following twenty-four days, we sailed. We sailed without stop, often without sails, without sleep, and without food. The Atlantic had prepared its worst for us, and only he who knows the North Atlantic in October can imagine what we saw during the series of four gales that followed hurricane Donna. It took us thirteen days to reach Bermuda (instead of five); we did not stop, but battered on through the calms of the Sargasso Sea and the squalls of the doldrums. We lost two sails and ripped the heavy mainsail a dozen times. In those four weeks Bruno, Marie Claire, and I went through the most arduous of sailing schools one can imagine. The *Caroline* was gaff-rigged and her sails were so heavy that it took all four of us to perform the slightest change in canvas. In the Gulf Stream a howling gale chased us north, then east; soon we were but a cork among gigantic waves some thirty feet high. Seasick Marie Claire prayed, Bruno moaned, and Grabowski groaned about the weather, the crew, and the boat. . . .

It was with a sigh of relief that on our twenty-fifth day at sea we sighted Sombrero Light. Our provisions had all but run out when we sailed past Anegada reef into the Caribbean Sea, and on to Charlotte Amalie, the capital of St. Thomas.

Our epic sea voyage had been a considerable strain on both us and the *Caroline*. In St. Thomas we were obliged to reconsider our plans. The *Caroline* needed an entirely new set of sails and work on her engine. This involved time and expenditure that we could not afford. Furthermore, it was now evident to us all that we would need at least two more crew members to carry on south.

Our trip from New York to the West Indies had taken us ten days more than what is considered average time, and we were as yet only one third of the way to our goal. Considering the expense involved in carrying on by ship, and seeing that we would also have to sail the vessel back north after the expedition along the Quintana Roo coast, we thought it advisable to change plans. On top of all this the political situation in Santo Domingo and in Cuba had so deteriorated that we could not consider sailing to Yucatán without running considerable risks. We were faced with no alternative but to leave the *Caroline* in St. Thomas. There Grabowski hoped to be able to charter the yacht to tourists and thus make enough money to mend the sails and engine.

Bruno, who had seen enough adventure on the way down from New York, decided that he would leave us and stay in the West Indies and paint.

I thus remained alone with Marie Claire, who still insisted on going to Quintana Roo. As nothing could dissuade her, I resolved that we would go together, flying from Puerto Rico to Miami, then on to Yucatán. Again, as at the beginning of my first trip to Quintana Roo, boats had let me down as a means of transport. Stranded in the Virgin Islands, I now seriously doubted that my return trip would come to any good.

As I would again be going to Quintana Roo on foot, I decided that I would go with Marie Claire to Cozumel and leave her there, letting her pay a few well-planned visits to the coast, sailing out from Cozumel on a reliable boat. But this did not agree with Maire Claire's idea of an expedition; at all costs, she decided, she would not miss an inch of the coast about which I had told her so much.

Our flight to Yucatán was to prove eventful, for soon after we took off from Miami we learned that our plane was to land in Havana. This was three days after the rupture of diplomatic relations between Cuba and the United States; our plane was in fact the last American plane to land in Havana during the three weeks that followed Cuba's general mobilization against a ghost U.S. invasion. Being held up at Havana airport, we both decided to leave the plane and pay a small visit to Castro's land. As the only foreigners, other than Russians, in Havana, we had a delightful time being indoctrinated in the machine-gun-packed streets of Havana. It so happened that we had to wait eight days before another plane left Havana for Mexico.

The sun was setting over vast expanses of flat henequen fields when, with Marie Claire, I finally reached Yucatán.

I was soon to learn that since my first passage three years earlier many things had changed on the Quintana Roo coast. To begin with, shortly after my return to America three years before, Mexico had changed presidents, and once more Quintana Roo had been declared the "land of promise," the "new frontier." Great efforts had been made to open up Quintana Roo, and a road for trucks had been built from Mérida to Chetumal. With a road into Quintana Roo, projects had been started to open up the coast north of where I had begun my long trek. At Puerto Morelos the army was considering building a road over what had long been the only approach to the sea, the small mule-drawn railroad.

The Cuban revolution had also affected the coast, for in closing Cuba to American tourists Castro had opened up a boom on Cozumel island. Three years earlier Cozumel had no hotel, and now I learned that four were in operation and two giant hostelries were under construction. There was a daily flight from Mérida to Cozumel, which had become but another name in the world of Caribbean resorts.

The invasion of Cozumel by tourists was, I felt, the end of the Quintana Roo I had known. What had been the effects of such modernization on the coast, I wondered.

While in Mérida with Marie Claire I purchased the essentials for a short stay in the jungle—hammocks, mosquito nets, and medicines. I was determined to live again with the Indians as I had done during my first trip, and this time I voluntarily reduced to a minimum what we should take along. As the day drew near when we were to fly to Cozumel, I burned with impatience, anxious to be once again among the people who had been my friends. Would I find Pablo Canche and the Mesoses? What would be their welcome? Had they forgotten me or did they remember me as well as I remembered them?

Again, while in Mérida, the few people I encountered spoke of Quintana Roo with the same dramatic tones and prophecies of disaster. But this time I did not heed their remarks. I knew where I was heading, and it was with relief that I left Mérida for Quintana Roo.

On landing in Cozumel by plane, I had to admit that things had changed. There were a few hotels, but they had not completely spoiled the island yet. I found Professor Perez still as jubilant and as eager to indoctrinate his fellow islanders as before. And on the dock I had the pleasure of meeting Samuel Mesos, who greeted me as a lost brother. Mr. Chamberlain also remembered my passage and in his now successful night club, called the Mayaluum (Land of the Mayas), offered us a most hearty meal to the rhythm of his eternal guitar and bongo-drum band.

I spent two nights in the house of the village cobbler, a cousin of Samuel Mesos. Asleep once again in a hammock, I knew that I was at last back in Quintana Roo. Three years of anticipation were now done with and I was filled with the same feeling of excitement as when I first set foot on Cozumel.

From Samuel I learned that the coast had been visited quite frequently since my first passage. First, a large expedition under the patronage of an American weekly had gone to the coast to dive to the wreck of the Spanish ship at Matanceros, where I had been shown the cannon. This expedition had been assisted by an adventurers' society known as the CEDAM, which specialized in underwater exploration. This expedition had caused quite a stir on the coast north of Tulum, the party being equipped with a helicopter. From the chief diver and leader of the expedition, Bob Marx, I learned that the ship had originally been a cargo vessel from Spain and had been wrecked in a storm off the coast in the 1780's.

Further, an American sportsman had found out that the waters of the lagoons of the Boca de Paila district produced the best bone fish and tarpon fishing in the world. This had started a small rush of keen fishermen to the coast and a "tent camp" had been set up on the edge of Boca de Paila some twenty-five miles south of Tulum. From this camp numerous fishing parties had gone by flat-bottomed boats up the lagoons of Muyil and Chunyaxche, visiting the Mayan ruins of this last spot.

At the thought of Chicago dentists who, with the aid of modern motor craft, had been able to penetrate where I had gone only at the risk of my life and after days of hard walking, I told myself the coast would never be the same.

At midnight on the second day after our arrival in Cozumel, Marie Claire and I boarded the *Maria Fidelia* (still faithful to her job) with Samuel Mesos, bound for Pamul, a *cocal* with a Mayan temple situated some twenty miles north of Puha.

By dawn we were in sight of the Quintana Roo coast and the familiar outline of low jungle up on the edge of the beaches appeared in the first rays of the sun. Soon we could hear the roar of the reef that protects the coast. But our luck was out; the waves were so big that the *brecha* (the gap in the reef) was closed by foaming water and we had to turn back to Cozumel and hope that the weather would clear before making a second attempt to land on the coast.

For twenty-four hours more we were obliged to fret about in Cozumel till the next scheduled departure at twelve o'clock at night.

At midnight the wind had dropped and the sea was calm when the *Fidelia* slipped away from the dock. This time we were really off. Little did Marie Claire and I anticipate what lay ahead of us. We planned only to spend a short while on the coast, but in fact it was to be six weeks before we saw Cozumel again.

The fiery columns of the sunrise were casting their eerie light upon the sea when the coast of Quintana Roo came in sight. In no time we had drawn up close to the reef and without much trouble

the captain of the *Fidelia* steered us through the narrow opening
into the calm, sheltered waters that gently lapped the edge of a
pure white crescent of sand. An anchor was dropped and a small
boat lowered to land us on the shore. We were among the palm
groves of the *cocal* of Pamul. No sooner had we counted our bags
than the *Fidelia* was off, chugging slowly up the coast to Playa del
Carmen where she was to pick up a load of copra. From the
thatched hut of the *cocal* a man came out to greet us. A good
friend of Samuel, he invited us to eat a few tortillas and an egg.
While we ate and Marie Claire discussed the eventual effects of a
tortilla diet on her waistline, Samuel arranged our luggage so that
it could easily be carried, Indian fashion, with a band around our
heads.

We did not tarry long at Pamul, wanting to walk as far as we
could before the sun reached its hottest, and we soon set off south
for Puha, Samuel in the lead and Marie Claire in the rear. Half a
mile from the *cocal* we made a halt at the foot of a tall pyramid
that stands guard on the coast, a few feet from the water. Marie
Claire was amazed at the sight of this, a vivid reminder that we
were entering the land of the Mayan seafarers. I myself had
seen the pyramid from the sea on my first trip on the *Maria Fidelia*
from Isla Mujeres to Cozumel. From its summit we had a clear
view of the coast stretching endlessly north to south in a series of
sandy crescents like a gigantic garland bordering the shiny sea.

To my relief Marie Claire seemed to take well to walking along
the coast on the rough coral, and apart from a few false alarms of
her seeing imaginary snakes, we made rapid progress. By eleven
we arrived at the *cocal* of Samuel's uncle, where I was greeted as
one of the family and Marie Claire given a warm and sympathetic
welcome, although her blue jeans seemed to astound the women of
the *cocal*. After drinking a few coconuts we set out again in the
torrid sun. Our path now led through the jungle, skirting rocky
points, and progress became slower. Soon we were calling a halt
every half hour to catch our breath and mop our brows.

By one o'clock we arrived at the lagoon of Chakalal, at the edge of which stands the charming, well-preserved temple of Yochac that I had seen the day after my arrival on the *Lydia* at Puha.

We now had but a short walk before we entered the welcome shade of the first rows of coconut trees of Puha. I felt as if I were returning home. Nothing had changed and I was not disappointed; Puha was still everything I had remembered—a little paradise stretched out along the turquoise blue sea. From the small thatched huts nestled under the palms we were greeted by Samuel's younger brothers. At first they approached us cautiously, looking me and Marie Claire over with a certain naïve curiosity, then one of the children recognized me. I could not have been greeted with more enthusiasm in my own family, and as Señora Mesos explained with tears in her eyes, "So few people come here that we never forget." Marie Claire was greeted with a certain reserve, especially by the younger children, who shied away from her, staring at her from behind the palm trees. It was half an hour later when I understood why—they had been greatly intimidated by her light-colored hair and considered her something from another planet. Even Señor Mesos became charming, abandoning his habitual dry tone and stern face to muster a smile of welcome.

I was soon informed about the little news of the coast. An Englishman from Cozumel had come and taken away the stone pig and foot of an idol that I had found and left behind.

But the greatest news of all was that a helicopter had landed on the beach of Puha with members of the diving expedition that had been prospecting the wreck at Matanceros.

Marie Claire and I sat in turn in Indian fashion by the fire while Señora Mesos handed us hot tortillas for our lunch. We got news of new temples that Señor Mesos had discovered while hunting in the jungle since my last passage. Thus no sooner had we arrived than we were making plans to go out and visit them. Marie Claire was particularly excited at the idea of seeing ruins that no foreigner had seen before. We decided to spend a week at Puha, after which

Samuel and his brother would take us down in the *Lydia* to Tankah and the *cocal* of the Gonzaleses.

While at Puha I got an explanation as to why the *Lydia* had not come back and why Señor Mesos had sent me down the coast on foot. Apparently, bad weather had held up the *Lydia*; sensing this and being slightly skeptical as to my true intentions, Señor Mesos had asked me to leave. He had not once thought, he now explained, that I would go all the way to Belize on foot, for he had sincerely believed that at Tankah I would find a boat. My return, Marie Claire's charm, and the fact that I was now so well acquainted with the entire coast and all the *cocaleros* from Puha to Xcalak, had dissolved the restraint that had been shown toward me during my first visit. Further, I learned that I had been the talk of the coast for some time, especially when many of the *cocaleros* had gathered in Cozumel during the fiesta of San Miguel. There they had swapped notes on me, and I had been accepted as someone not to fear.

The ruins Señor Mesos had sighted were within two miles of Puha, and during our stay I spent three days examining them with Samuel and Marie Claire. The first of these sites was in terrible condition but our visit proved rewarding for Marie Claire, who, her enthusiasm having given her the energy of a mole for excavating, unearthed the foot and the arm of a clay idol, a feat that in no way dampened her enthusiasm or her pride.

The second site, situated south of Puha and a few miles inland, was but an extension of the site of Puerto Chile that I had seen during my first trip. What Señor Mesos showed us was an ancient stone wall half closing a low cave. As this proved rather disappointing, we spent some time clearing the three small temples of Puerto Chile, one of which bore the carvings of a human head and a dragon carved around a stone ring that I had seen on my first trip. Here, at the foot of one of the smallest structures, we found the fragments of two delicately adorned clay hands. But here again we could find no other parts of this ancient idol.

The winds being unfavorable, we delayed our departure south for two days. This allowed Marie Claire to perfect her suntan on the beach which, she agreed, rivaled the best beaches of the Riviera and the West Indies.

Finally, after many signs of affection we bade farewell to the Mesos family. Señora Mesos gave Marie Claire advice and recommendations while at the same time she filled our bags with food for the journey.

We sailed down the coast with a northeasterly breeze, out of sight of Puha. The *Lydia* rocked gently on small waves, while with a henequen line we attempted to catch barracuda from the cramped and narrow deck.

Gone was the fear that had accompanied my first voyage to the coast. As we basked in the sun little did we realize what lay in store for us. . . .

XII

The Lost Metropolis

It had been my plan to go from Tankah to the village of Tulum and from there to make my way inland to the great lagoon of Muyil and that of Chunyaxche. I believed, from what I had seen three years previously, that the center of the coastal trade of the Mayas might have been there. For this trip I planned to meet Canche again and use him as a guide. In Mérida I had purchased various presents for him and his wife, and I counted greatly on his assistance in making a more thorough search of the jungle bordering the lagoons.

When we arrived at Tankah the *Lydia* was greeted by Don Jorge Gonzales; he also remembered my first visit and treated us to his formidable hospitality.

Through him I learned that Canche's brother, Benanzio, was presently employed at Tankah working on the *cocal*. So, without losing time, I was able to make plans for pushing inland to the area I planned to search. Benanzio informed me that his brother Canche was at the family *milpa* in the jungle, felling trees before burning them to make the jungle ready for future crops. We were now in the dry season and two months remained before the rains. With Don Jorge Gonzales' permission we were able to take Benanzio along with us as guide on promising to let him return when we had met Canche.

That evening I spent hours with Don Jorge discussing the present situation on the coast. I learned that since the "tourist rush," boats from Cozumel to the coast had become increasingly frequent, bringing people to see the ruins of Tulum. The airfield, too, had known increased activity and had even been enlarged. In the dry season many small planes landed, staying at Tankah a few hours before flying back to Mérida or Cozumel with their tourists. Tankah had become quite a center of activity and Don Jorge had even erected a guest house for the occasional people who would stop overnight.

I also learned that the mighty project of a road down the northern part of the Quintana Roo coast had flopped. This project, which has been promised by politicians since 1900, has remained nothing but a wild dream. Although maps as early as 1905 often go so far as to show the fictitious road along the northern part of the coast, it has yet to be built. On the other hand, Don Jorge had mended and repaired the small jeep track down his *cocal*, past the ruins, and the route was now usable along the coast to Boca de Paila, some twenty-five miles away. As for the Indians of the village of Tulum, they were for the time being in bad condition, being the victims of an epidemic of mumps. This disease, if benign to civilized peoples, was claiming a heavy toll among the Indians—three men at Tulum had already died and many more were in critical condition.

The following morning a plane arrived at Tankah from Mérida carrying three passengers destined for the fishing camp at Boca de Paila. Arriving direct from snowbound New York, the fishermen did not even realize that they were off to an area that three years previously had been inaccessible and unexplored. I felt it was a shame that considerable funds should be expended in the mere quest of amusement while nearby lay invaluable temples undiscovered or unstudied, and even worse, that a whole village should be suffering and many of its inhabitants dying of such an illness as mumps for lack of medical care. Close by, people were spending one hundred dollars a day collecting trophies. Definitely the change in Quintana Roo, if slight, was for the worse.

Toward two o'clock in the afternoon we set off with Benanzio for the village of Tulum. As we trekked down the narrow path, stepping through the damp undergrowth and over the fallen trunks of trees, I felt once again the exhilaration and sense of suffocation that the jungle produces. Through the thick branches the sun hardly filtered down to us and from all around the strange noises of the jungle arose—the laugh of the chachalaka, the croaking of frogs, and the chirping of insects. Barefooted Benanzio advanced as in a half run. Rather timidly, on the lookout for snakes, Marie Claire followed. On the whole she was enchanted by the jungle, having all her life been brought up among the forests of central France, where on her father's estate she had spent much time stag hunting. Soon, however, Marie Claire admitted that she missed her horse. As we progressed we felt as if the bonds that tied us to the outside world were decreasing. How different this flat jungle was from the mountainous jungles of Bengal and that of the lower valleys of Nepal. Here there was nothing in the terrain to break the monotony or destroy the illusion that one was walking in a dark underworld, some sort of a subterranean universe of green hues, dim light, and dampness. This again was the mysterious lost world of the Chacs, the kingdom of the Mayan gods, of another civilization, one dying and forgotten.

With relief we penetrated the clearing around which stood the poor, thatched, oval huts of the villagers. All was still and silent. The healthy men had gone to their *milpas,* not to return for some time, while the others lay sick in their hammocks. From one of the huts a pale-looking creature poked a swollen head out at us. The men were the most affected by the mumps, which brings about infection of the male organs, later causing death or, at best, impotency. Mumps was but one more of the many diseases that had crossed the Atlantic, and which, along with syphilis, scarlet fever, yellow fever, and smallpox, has slowly exterminated millions of

American Indians. Again, the Indian was worse off for civilization, and this was made all the more appalling by the fact that we were no more than two hours, by air, from Cape Canaveral. The Chan Santa Cruz Indians were suffering another defeat. Apparently the epidemic had come from the interior and all the villages inhabited by the Chan Santa Cruz Indians were affected.

There was, unfortunately, little that we could do, our own medical cabinet being completely inadequate. The only thing we could suggest was that the patients be kept warm and given little to drink, advice we had gathered from Don Jorge.

Benanzio immediately took us to his father-in-law, the "priest" of the village, who had entertained me three years earlier and who, with Canche acting as interpreter, had told me about the war of the Chan Santa Cruz Indians.

We spent the evening in his hut and were offered beans with stewed chachalaka as a meal. In Mayan tradition we all ate in turn, so as to get hot tortillas as they were made. While I ate the women of the hut gathered around Marie Claire to look her over. They had never in their lives seen a fair-haired woman and they passed their short brown hands through Marie Claire's hair with amazement. Soon they attempted to teach Marie Claire the elements of Mayan housekeeping, allowing her to try to make tortillas, a process which, I found out from Marie Claire, required far more skill than one would imagine. They are made by throwing a ball of dough adroitly from one hand to the other and gently patting it into shape, a task requiring great dexterity.

When Benanzio and I had eaten, Marie Claire was served a "woman's meal," a rather poorer version of our own with no meat. It took me some time to persuade Benanzio that Marie Claire, although a woman, should eat as well as I. Marie Claire thought this quite amusing although she later raged about a "woman's lot," and she certainly did not approve of the hard life Mayan women lead, eternally crouched beside a fire. That night I hung my hammock in Pablo Canche's hut, where his wife and three children had remained. As we were preparing to rest, two old women came in to pay us a visit, one of whom was Pablo's mother-in-law. They brought presents of fresh eggs to Marie Claire. We turned these over to Mrs. Canche.

The next day was a religious feast day and we attended a ceremony in the small thatched temple directed by the priest of the Chan Santa Cruz religion. After the strange rite was over we were obliged to drink great bowls of blessed *atole*, a task not too easy for me, since for fear of offending Benanzio's father-in-law (the priest), I had not only to drink my own calabash full of lukewarm gluey porridge, but also help Marie Claire with hers, before the eyes of the approving villagers.

It was to take us the better part of the following day to reach the *milpa* of Canche. In the great heat we wound our way through the vines and tall trees, crossing a fairyland of moss, palms, and ferns, through the narrow tunnel-like footpath. Finally we emerged into the *milpa*, which echoed with the blows of machetes as four men, among whom was Canche, felled giant trees and cleared away bushes. Trees were cut at about four feet from the ground, and the vegetation was so thick that once a tree was felled it formed a tangled mass on the ground that often rose six feet above the earth. There the cut jungle growth would lie to dry in the sun until the moment when, according to the traditional Mayan calendar, it would be judged ready for burning.

Canche made his way through the tangle of branches toward us and greeted me with the enthusiasm of a child, his eyes sparkling with pleasure. Like everybody I had seen again so far, he had not forgotten my earlier journey although he never thought I would return. In broken Spanish we exchanged the recent news. Nothing much had happened since my departure, and the only bad news, as I knew already, was the epidemic of mumps. We were led around the *milpa* toward the thatched hut with no walls where I had slept during my first visit, the shelter that was erected on the edge of a *cenote* where the strange, bald idol, with a long neck, who

Canche believed protected the crops and his family while working in the jungle, was still standing. The preceding year's harvest had been good and Canche proudly showed me dried ears of corn he had stored below the roof of the hut.

While I gave Canche the knife I had brought as a present and discussed my plans, Benanzio, untired by the long day's walk, stole out with his shotgun, soon to return with a pair of large chachalakas. They were duly prepared, chopped up with a machete, and thrown into a black pot to simmer in pimento juice and other strong herbs. There were no women at the camp, but great piles of dried tortillas had been brought over from the village and were hung like warped phonograph records threaded on a henequen string from one of the crossbeams of the roof.

As night fell mosquitoes came out in thousands from around the *cenote* and we all hustled near the fire to catch some of the insect-chasing smoke on our faces. The sight was most strange as the small fire lit up the columns of smoke through which one could spot the tanned faces of the Indians, which contrasted with the fair hair and complexion of Marie Claire.

Unfortunately, Canche informed me that he could not come along with us as his father-in-law was ill, and his wife and children were waiting for him to return with a bag of corn which he had "husked" from the store at the *milpa*. Canche's only suggestion was that Benanzio should take us to Chunyaxche and that there we would be put into the hands of his friend Pablo Coba-Cama, an Indian who lived near the ruins. Seeing that nothing could be done to persuade Canche to come along with us, and being faced once more with the impossibility of forcing a Mayan to break a routine or a plan which involved such an important matter as providing the daily food for his children, we resolved that we would set out again the following day with Benanzio for Chunyaxche, and hope for the best there.

It was late when the three of us arrived exhausted at Chunyaxche and were greeted by the barking of dogs. All was dark in the small village save for the low glare of three small fires visible through the spaces between the stakes of the huts. To Benanzio's cry of "U-ugh" came answers from the various huts as we made our way within a stone enclosure toward one of them. There we were greeted by a round-faced Indian with a rather unpleasant, apathetic look. This was Coba-Cama. A few words were exchanged in Mayan between Benanzio and Cama, while a beautiful, petite Mayan woman, Cama's wife, came out to look us over, followed by her two children, a boy six years old and a girl of five. From Benanzio we understood that all had been settled and that we could hang our hammocks in Cama's hut, or, if we preferred, in another hut with no walls that was situated within the stone fence of Cama's home. We both decided to string our hammocks and mosquito nets in what the following day we discovered was nothing less than the village church! It was a sideless hut with an altar on which stood the three wooden crosses of Chan Santa Cruz.

Early in the morning, Benanzio came to say good-by and, despite our insistence, refused to accept any form of payment for his services. As he left he turned toward me and gave me three hand-filled cartridges, saying that I could give these to Cama so that he could shoot some game for us to eat. I could find no way of thanking him, and by the time I had realized the generosity of his gift he was already jogging off down the trail toward the village of Tulum.

With Benanzio gone, we felt a little lost, and Maire Claire, who had looked Cama over, felt very ill at ease. "I'm sure Cama is a crook; I don't like his face." Nor did I, as a matter of fact, but our apprehensions were to prove wrong. Cama was a silent character, and if anything, a lazy fellow. Never did his face light up with a smile, and he seemed to be always on the point of flying into a rage. But this rage never came, and he was to prove most useful, even if it took a great deal of effort to persuade him to assist us in what had been our primary aim, the archaeological survey of the area.

Mrs. Cama was as kind and as attractive as her husband was dull and unsociable. She had the bearing of an Egyptian queen and her manners were both discreet and sophisticated. Marie Claire, who, like most women, had an eye for clothes, counted that Mrs. Cama changed her dress four times a day and thus was always spotless despite the dirt involved in her daily tasks. Like herself, her children often changed their clothes, the Camas' daughter wearing miniature replicas of her mother's *huipiles,* the white cotton Mayan dress adorned with a colorful embroidered hem and neckline. In a thousand ways Mrs. Cama was a strong contrast to her crude surroundings; like an exiled aristocrat she was elegant and poised, but obliged to live in a dingy palm-thatched hut and forced to spend most of her day crouched beside a smoky fire. Every morning Mrs. Cama would go over to a wooden trough and wash the family clothes, which hung like white embroidered banners from a henequen line, little different from the washing of any family of the "civilized" world. One could not help but recall through Mrs. Cama's demeanor that the Mayas were of an ancient and civilized race, the heirs of the New World's most developed culture.

Altogether the small village of Chunyaxche was made up of three families who lived in huts set around a clearing that was planted with orange trees. These trees were all laden with fruit and we picked oranges and began to eat some like starved animals. They were quite bitter but such a delight after our plain diet of tortillas and beans. We had no sooner begun to taste the oranges when Coba-Cama came running out toward us, and in his poor Spanish and with the help of signs made us stop. He then went on to explain that to eat oranges would bring sterility to Marie Claire and that the oranges were only good for pigs. No matter how much we protested or attempted to explain that this belief was wrong, we could not convince the villagers, who for the length of our stay were shocked that we ate the fruit which some erroneous legend had made taboo for them. How foolish are some customs and beliefs such as this one which deprived the inhabitants of a food and vitamin supply they so urgently needed.

To the east of the village clearing the thick mangrove swamps that bordered the lagoon of Chunyaxche began. A little narrow trail led to the shore of the lagoon, an immense lake cut here and there by sand bars and mangrove islands, upon which grew a few tattered and wind-beaten palm trees. To go from the jungle to the edge of the lagoon was like coming out of a cellar into a sunlit desert. Unfortunately the edges of the lagoon were of quicksand and one had to approach by means of a narrow catwalk of rotten trunks that extended into the water, eventually becoming a modest rickety pier upon which lay two small native dugout canoes.

After many hours of arduous trekking in the jungle I would often retire with Marie Claire to the jetty and contemplate the barren, windswept, gray waters of the lagoon upon which the mighty canoes of the ancient Mayas had once sailed, canoes that had carried up to forty people and which must have been navigated up and down the Quintana Roo coast incessantly, linking the towns and cities of the coastal society that was no more. Occasionally large tarpon would break the surface of the lagoon, while flamingos darted overhead, black streaks in the endless blue sky. Here, most probably, the Mayan poets had sought inspiration.

By daylight we were able to examine more closely the hut in which we had set up our hammocks. It had no walls save a small low stockade that served to keep out the chickens and pigs that shared the Camas' compound. At one end of the hut stood a roughly hewn wooden table upon which rested three wooden crosses, the altar of the gods of Chan Santa Cruz. Here, once a year, the procession transporting the original Chan Santa Cruz crosses from Chumpom to Tulum stopped.

Directly behind Cama's house one could see, breaking through the treetops, the summit of the large pyramid I had noticed during my first visit to Chunyaxche. This was the mighty pyramid that the Mason-Spinden expedition had discovered in 1926 and that Charles Lindbergh had sighted from the air more than thirty years before our trip. I now learned from Coba-Cama that a few foreigners had come here since my first visit, arriving at the lagoon by way of the fishing camp of Boca de Paila. This news disappointed me a little, for I had the unreasonable feeling that the ruins were in some way my private property.

No archaeologist, though, had come to visit Chunyaxche since Herbert J. Spinden in 1926, and I felt that it was my duty to record the exact measurements of the structures and temples that I had encountered there. This I thought would be an easy task, having seen only half a dozen buildings when I first came. Chunyaxche had been but one of many sites I had seen, and little did I suspect —nor for that matter did anyone who had been there after me— what lay hidden in the jungle. Chunyaxche was to surpass my wildest dreams. When, ten days later, we left Chunyaxche exhausted, we had uncovered no less than 108 mounds, temples, pyramids, and palaces, the majority of which had lain lost and unknown for centuries beneath the tangle of vines and trees of the jungle. Chunyaxche to all appearances was the largest ancient Mayan city of Quintana Roo, the long-lost center of the Mayan coastal realm, the hub of the maritime civilization of the Mayas. Here was a city more formidable than Tulum, a city that extended for many miles around the tall pyramid that Lindbergh had seen.

For ten days, accompanied by Marie Claire and Coba-Cama, I combed the jungle, returning every night with more ground plans of unknown structures that we had painfully discovered hidden in the dense foliage. Even Coba-Cama, who had spent all his life at Chunyaxche village, was astounded by the number of buildings we found; never in his life had he combed the jungle in such a way and he did not even suspect that he lived within the walls of an immense city.

Our search was made all the more difficult because the site of Chunyaxche, owing to its proximity to the lagoons, was exceedingly damp and covered with a particularly tall and dense jungle. The jungle was a web of giant ceiba trees, immense fan-palm trees, goon trees, and a host of various other species ranging from chicle

Ruins at Chunyaxche

1. Main pyramid. 2. Platform. 3. Small oratories. 4. Mayan *sakbe* (road). 5. Semicircle of pyramids. 6. Small temple. 7. Platform with two oratories. 8. "Pink palace" with underground temple. 9. Great circular wall. 10. Sacrificial platform. 11. Palace with stelae. 12. Platform with rooms. 13. Walk of various structures. 14. Large palace. 15. Small pyramid. 16. High palace on mound. 17. Courtyard. 18. Thick-walled palace. 19. Stairs. 20. Palace. 21. Oratory. 22. Platform with oratory. 23. Pyramids. 24. Large platform. 25. Temple with large idol. 26. Long structure. 27. Oratories. 28. Pyramid. 29. Oratory

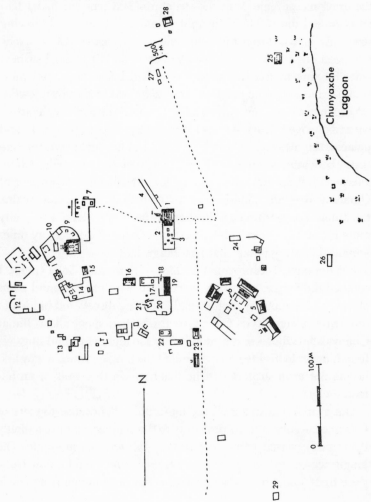

Chunyaxche Lagoon

N

trees to gigantic red-barked fig trees, all these knit together by vines. The undergrowth was but a tangle of roots snaking in and out of shrubs and gigantic ferns. Jungles, I had been told, are measured in feet, a jungle of "ten feet" being one in which an observer cannot distinguish an object more than ten feet away however big it may be. Around Chunyaxche the jungle was often a four-foot one and appeared like an opaque, solid curtain painted by Gauguin. We were frequently within a few yards of a large temple or pyramid without being able to see it or even suspect its existence.

We began by measuring the tall pyramid Lindbergh and the Mason-Spinden expedition had seen. It rose 62 feet above the ground, more than 54 feet above the gigantic platform on which it rested. (Looking at photographs taken of this pyramid by Gregory Mason thirty-five years earlier, we could not recognize it at first, since the entire exterior walls of the temple on its summit had collapsed.) Again from the pyramid's summit I looked out over the lagoons and onto the jungle, but the trees were so closely packed that from our high viewpoint we could not see a trace of another structure. As we searched around the base of the main pyramid in quest of sculptured stones, we made our first new discovery. The gigantic elevated platform on which the pyramid had been erected extended fifty yards south of the base of the steep stairway that rose to the summit of the pyramid. Following the rim of this platform, we cut our way through and took its measurements as best we could. We then set out to investigate the platform itself, and there to our surprise we found, buried in the vegetation, six small rectangular structures like oratories. These oratories resembled small bunkers with no openings except for a low door on one side. The oratories were too small to have admitted human beings with comfort and were once probably minute chapels sheltering idols. Although these structures were closely packed upon the platform and situated within yards of the main pyramid, the jungle was so dense that from none of the oratories could one see the main pyramid or any of the other structures upon the platform. Searching for ruins was like playing blindman's buff with a machete as prodder, and more often than not the clang of steel against stone would be the first indication that before us stood a stone building.

To the west the platform fell two yards to the ground, in gigantic steps resembling the stone seats of an amphitheater. These steps made a right angle with a similar row of seats backed against a wall extending west out from the platform.

Immediately behind the pyramid we encountered a raised causeway some four feet high and six feet wide that extended many hundreds of yards northwestward through the jungle. This most probably had been a *sakbe* (a Mayan road). The Mayas had erected many such roads in Yucatán. Since they had no dray animals, these roads were in fact raised footpaths. This one seemed to lead toward Tulum. Possibly there had been a road all along the eastern coast of the Yucatán peninsula, joining all the towns and villages of the once densely populated Mayan coastal region. Along with the royal Inca roads of Peru and the roads of the Romans, the Mayas had one of the world's best-developed road systems. In central Yucatán the cities of Uxmal, Kabah, and Sayil are all linked by a network of *sakbes*. In my two visits to the coast of Quintana Roo, however, I had not been able to pick out the remains of any coastal road. Here most probably the Mayas preferred the more convenient sea route as a means of communication.

Cutting our way west of the main pyramid, we came upon a succession of other large rectangular platforms made of huge, well-assembled stone blocks. On each of these platforms we encountered other small rectangular structures. Following the rim of the largest of these platforms we came upon the "pink palace," the rectangular pink stuccoed building that I had seen during my first trip, and which Gregory Mason calls "El Centro."

The "pink palace" was composed of a tall rectangular platform, twelve feet high, which one reached by means of a large stairway. The platform was itself covered with large trees and at one end, as previously mentioned, stood a square palace with a columned entrance and gallery, beyond which were three small rooms. As we inspected the palace, Coba-Cama drew our attention to a small hole in the stairway of the platform. Lighting a match, I peered into the hole, which was larger beneath the stairway. I was about to investigate and lower myself into the gap when Cama shouted at me to stop, saying that the cavity was full of snakes. For a moment I hesitated, and then decided to lower myself cautiously. For a moment my feet dangled and then touched the ground. I was in pitch darkness till I managed to light another match. The dim glow then lit up the most extraordinary sight I had seen: a low narrow corridor, with a Mayan V-shaped vault, that ran under the platform into the darkness. I saw something scurrying on one of the walls as my match blew out. Then from above my head came Marie Claire's voice begging me to come up. Gripping the sides of the corridor with my knees, I managed to pull myself out of the narrow entrance back into the eerie greenness of the jungle.

In his book *Silver Cities of Yucatán*, Gregory Mason tells how the Mason-Spinden party penetrated inside this same palace, and reports that in 1926 it was used by the Chan Santa Cruz Indians as a secret meeting place. Now I set about to devise the best way to explore it with Marie Claire. Exhausted by our work of the morning, we decided to leave any further exploration until the afternoon.

As we set off for the village with Coba-Cama, I noticed a great circular wall, a tall mossy cliff of stones, which projected from the "pink palace" and cut an arc through the jungle. We did not stop to investigate this immediately, but hurriedly made our way to the village. In one morning we had already grown certain that we were in for surprises at Chunyaxche.

That afternoon, disregarding Coba-Cama's pessimistic warning as to the dangers of entering the passage, I lowered myself through the hole in the staircase, armed with dried fan-palm leaves for use as torches. As soon as I was in the passage I lit one, and the yellow blaze illuminated the long, narrow tunnel extending straight under the platform. Gigantic beetles the size of small crabs scurried along the walls. From the end of the tunnel, which was in darkness, came strange screeching noises. At first I thought these were the noises of rattlesnakes and while I was wondering what to do my torch burned out. Suddenly something struck my arm. I nearly died of fright only to realize that Marie Claire had just crawled in after me, bringing a fresh stock of dried palms. In the yellow light of another torch, and walking through the smoke, we slowly inched our way along the tunnel. It seemed endless and as if it had just been built. The walls and vaulting were smooth and bone dry, of a light, pinky-yellow stone that glowed all the more for the red glare of our torches. As we progressed our torches cast their glow ever deeper down the tunnel. Half choking from the smoke that filled the tunnel, we emerged into a large room. This also was bone dry and the floor, like that of the tunnel, was flat and free from encumbrances, apart from the tattered remains of a hornets' nest. The screeching noises had increased in volume and finally proved to be nothing more than the cries of thousands of vampire bats which on our entrance into the large room dropped from the roof and flew hectically around our heads, lit by the mysterious glow of our torches. Lighting a new torch, we realized that we were in a subterranean palace. We were standing in a long rectangular room and could see the dark openings of slanted doorways leading to three other chambers.

It was like being in some strange dream as we advanced step by step through clouds of smoke of an orange hue that lit up the barren walls of the palace. There was not a breath of air, and no ventilation. Slowly the quantity of smoke in the underground chamber was increasing. Advancing with our torches to the ground so as to frighten away snakes, we made our way gingerly into one of the other rooms. Our entrance started a panic among the vampire bats which now occasionally struck us as they darted madly about in the confined quarters.

The smoke had now become so unbearable that we made a

retreat toward the corridor. Out in the open again, we could hardly believe what we had seen, all seemed so normal outside. Coba-Cama was still seated where we had left him. It was impossible to imagine that under the trees that grew on the platform lay an underground palace in perfect condition. We told Coba-Cama to gather more palms and sat down to rest before returning to the suffocating bowels of the secret underground structure.

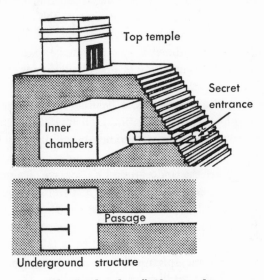

The "pink palace," Chunyaxche

That afternoon we made three successive trips into the underground passage, examining in detail, by the light of our palm torches, the walls and floor of the interior rooms. Apparently, the underground palace had once been an ordinary building which, as happens frequently in Mayan architecture, was later buried and covered with earth and rocks. A tall platform was built over it and a second palace placed on top. The tunnel was later bored under the platform to permit access to the inner rooms. Why the Mayas had buried such buildings, nobody knows. At Chichén-Itzá, the largest pyramid is built in the same manner above a smaller pyramid and, as usual in these cases of superimposed structures, the lower building is in perfect condition and there seems to be no logical or evident reason for covering it up.

The three small rooms of the underground palace at Chunyaxche had against one of their walls small raised altars. To our disappointment, we noticed that someone who had entered the underground chambers before us had broken and dug up the altars, possibly in search of jade objects or pottery idols.

Upon the dry white stuccoed walls of the interior palace, we found the dim green outline of a painted snake that arched itself above the lintel of the doorway of one of the rooms. Apart from this, there were no other frescoes, although it can be presumed that, under the white layer of stucco, lie other layers, some of which may well be adorned with paintings. To investigate this would require the work of an expert who could peel off, layer by layer, the successive coats of plaster.

After looking over the underground palace, we cleared some of the jungle around it and, to our surprise, discovered a square sacrificial platform placed before a small temple. Pushing our search further, we soon found that the "pink palace" was but one structure among a dozen that were encompassed by a tall thick wall, the sustaining wall of a huge platform upon which stood not only the "pink palace" but also a tall narrow pyramid and the remains of an even larger palace with long, narrow corridors and the traces of numerous small square rooms. This second palace and the other structures of the compound were linked by a series of small oratories and larger square buildings, many of which were still in nearly perfect condition. Each machete blow revealed new buildings and we did not know where to begin our survey.

As the sun was setting, we made our way back to the village—and the inevitable tasteless meal of beans and tortillas, the only food we were to eat for ten days, except for bitter oranges.

The following morning we returned to the group of structures we had found the previous day. To perform the reconnaissance of this group of buildings was no easy task. At every step we had to stop and hack at the jungle just to be able to see a few yards ahead of us, and in so doing we were inevitably covered by innumerable ticks, in fact by so many of these insects that, by now, we had learned to dominate our repulsion and allowed them to bury their heads into our flesh and suck our blood until, in the evening, we could cope with the task of getting rid of them.

By the end of our third day, we still had only a small idea of what Chunyaxche had in store for us. With the inspection of the underground palace or temple and the discovery of the large group of buildings around it, we had only begun to investigate the site. We were in such a state of excitement that, had we discovered the moon, we would not have been more delighted. Every tree, we felt, must conceal some structure. And in this we were not far wrong. In an attempt to study the area methodically, we set out the following day to measure and clear more of the structures of the "pink palace" compound.

The buildings there seemed of the Mayapán period. All of them were made of roughly hewn stones mortared together with lime cement. With machetes, it was a hard task to clear the vines and roots and get an exact idea of the contour of the structures; here and there a straight wall would be disrupted by a gigantic tree which had forced a passage right through the masonry; many stones were so imbedded and bound to tentacle-like roots that one had trouble distinguishing where vegetation and natural stones left off and man-built walls began. In many cases, stones had been virtually lifted out of place and carried upward in the tangle of vines. But despite the repeated attacks made by the vegetation, many structures had retained a good deal of their original shape, and on most of the small square buildings the roofs had withstood the inroads of the jungle.

A strange feeling of awe overcame us as we opened up, one after another, the corridors and small rooms of the second palace. Here once had walked the high priests and lords of Mayaluum (the land of the Mayas). Here, Canche's and Coba-Cama's ancestors had ruled among the perspectives of terraces and pyramids; here had rested the gods of the cardinal compass points, the enigmatical Chac Mool, and the fierce rain gods; here also had lived the scholars of Mayan mathematics, whose skill with numbers is still legendary. Now and again a coat of stucco showed the stains of what had been a fresco where the tumbled moss-covered walls had once been alive with paintings. As we cut our way, feeling a path like a blind man and seeing unfold before our eyes the layout of the city, we could not help but feel that only a short distance in time separated us from the ancient Mayas. No one before us had gone through the empty courtyards of this palace. Only the occasional cry of a chachalaka reminded us that we were not in the underworld of the past. The rustle of the damp leaves and the cracking of dead branches were the only noises that accompanied us in our journey in time through the undergrowth that now slowly revealed the outlines of the great city it had hidden for centuries.

As we were about to complete the census of structures set within the bastion that started from the "pink palace," we strayed a little deeper in the jungle to the west, and there we came upon the remains of a wall that led us to a series of alcoves flanked by large stones standing upright in the manner of stelae. The following day we spent all morning clearing this second find. It proved to be the wing of a large structure that itself stood on a huge, oddly shaped terrace studded with structures and the remains of intricate walls. These we followed until, exhausted, by midday we made our way back to the village and Mrs. Cama's inevitable beans.

The strenuous exercise of cutting one's way through the jungle amid the ticks and mosquitoes displeased Coba-Cama considerably, and after each excursion in the jungle, it was necessary for us to plead with him to return with us again. Although the buildings that we were now charting had never been seen by Cama, who regarded them with disgust as "piles of rubble," his company was

essential to us in that, if we went even a few hundred feet alone in
the jungle, we were sure to get lost, and each time we would
marvel at how Cama, after having turned around in circles all day,
would immediately set off for home, cutting a path between and
around trees and mounds toward the village, while I felt con-
vinced that we were going in the opposite direction. Many people
have been known to go astray and get lost within calling distance
of a camp. Furthermore, Coba-Cama was indispensable in that he
could clear more jungle in two strokes of his machete than I could
in twenty. It is quite an art to pick out the right vine that will open
up a net of vines, or to distinguish the exact obstacle to cut when
this is shielded by a tangle of leaves or when creepers are ever
ready overhead to catch a raised machete and make it glance
dangerously in an unexpected direction.

Every evening upon returning, Coba-Cama and I would have to
sit for hours picking the ticks off our bodies, at the same time as we
fought away the swarms of mosquitoes. Even the unpleasantness
of leeches in the Himalayas did not equal that of picking out, one
after the other, the minute insects whose hard heads were buried
deep into our skins. As for Marie Claire, she would retire with Mrs.
Cama to the wharf on the edge of the lagoon where the wind was
usually strong enough to rid the air of mosquitoes, and there the
Indian woman would with nimble fingers rid Marie Claire of
insects. By our fifth day at Chunyaxche, Marie Claire was so
severely bitten that her whole body was infected from the innumerable bites. No repellent could stop the swarms of insects
from covering us as we tramped around the jungle.

After finding the two large compounds of buildings, we encountered a whole new series to the south, beyond the main pyramid. Here were steep platforms with palace-like structures on top
of them and great doorways supported by circular columns. Also
here was a large U-shaped terrace with four thick-walled buildings, and a whole row of structures and small pyramids extended
the entire length of the land that separated the village from the

farthest palace, situated beyond the one with the stele-like stones.

We examined further, in great detail, the majestic courtyard enclosed by five pyramids that I had seen during my first journey. Here had been erected what must have been the most impressive architectural complex of Chunyaxche: a small temple within a semicircle of small pyramids with steep staircases which came down to the edges of the inner temple like the seats of an amphi-theater.

We found many traces of lesser buildings in the same area, and small ceremonial platforms. To the north of this group we en-countered sturdy terraces on which had been erected yet more buildings surrounded by the usual small oratories. By now, the three male inhabitants of the small village of Chunyaxche had joined in with us in our wild hunt for new structures. We were thus able to cover wide areas and discover groups of buildings isolated from the main center of the ancient town.

As days went by, we reached an incredible peak of enthusiasm as, hour after hour, parted leaves uncovered before us more and more mounds and remains of buildings. It became commonplace to sum up in the evening the finds of the day and feel disappointed at having discovered only six new structures. Isolated from the out-side world, we now lived in a world of our own, one of perpetual excitement and discovery. At first, we had cautiously measured every mound, temple, and pyramid with a metered rope. Now this became impossible and we felt crushed by the task that lay ahead of whoever wanted thoroughly to study and measure all the build-ings. It became more and more evident that, again, we could hope to do no more than make a general survey. Chunyaxche was like an archaeologist's dream and we felt more often than not as if we were in the midst of a pleasant nightmare of ticks and visions of strange doorways clustered with vines into which we penetrated to be greeted by vampire bats and swarms of hornets. By now we could already tell that Chunyaxche was a far greater city than either Spinden or Mason had imagined, and even our wildest dreams were overshot by the number of ruins we encountered. Mason had said that there were too many mounds to be able to count them; we were now faced with too many temples, platforms, and palaces to be able to chart them accurately.

At first, Marie Claire and I had found it amusing to give names to the structures which we found, but now we were content with giving numbers, as little by little the charts we drew up had to be enlarged, recopied, and adjusted to allow room for the new discoveries that each passing day brought along.

We had little or no time to search in likely spots for idols, fragments, or even for architectural details. Carved stones must have lain by the thousands at the foot of the ruins, but we neither had the time nor the energy to search among the moss and overturn each of the innumerable stones that were strewn all over the floor of the jungle around Chunyaxche.

On our tenth day at the site, we pushed our search toward the edge of the lagoon through the mangrove marshes and tall grass savannas. We went guided either by what we thought were mounds or by recollections of the villagers. Thus we stumbled upon a solid rectangular building the roof of which had partly crumbled. Its doorway had been supported by huge circular pillars; inside the temple, the stuccoed walls showed numerous remains of frescoes done on several coats of the crumbling limestone plaster. Turning a stone over, I noticed that it bore signs of having being sculptured. Carefully wiping off moss and earth, to my surprise I was soon looking into the dull eyes of a large sculptured head with protruding slit eyes: those of a strange idol, the most beautiful piece of sculpture that I had yet discovered on the coast. About three feet high and one foot wide, the idol was too heavy to be transported. With the reluctant help of Coba-Cama, we therefore made a shelter for it under large blocks of stone. It was only upon the discovery of the large idol that Coba-Cama became interested in the ruins. The idol having confirmed to him what we had told him about the ancient Mayas, he now became even enthusiastic and helped us with great energy to dig for pottery and hunt for new buildings.

Later, we came upon a group of three small oratories perched upon ten-foot-tall pyramids, situated about five eighths of a mile from the village. As we crouched down searching for pottery, a gigantic tarantula crawled away from under Coba-Cama's hand and made us a little more cautious. As for Marie Claire, after having been for three weeks on the lookout for snakes, she had only just gained confidence and forgotten about them when she stepped on a log from under which slithered away a deadly coral snake.

There seemed to be no end to the dimensions of Chunyaxche and we soon were faced with the fact that, alone, we could not cope with all that we had found and with what certainly must have remained still hidden around the core of the city.

By our tenth day at the ruins, we had run out of film and were beginning to feel the effects of our diet and of the climate. Fleas that swarmed on the floor of the hut in which we slept had added to the mosquito bites and tick infection in causing our bodies to look like one large raw blister. Marie Claire, in particular, suffered to such an extent that she could no longer sleep from itching all over. Her spirits, however, were in no way dampened and she refused to let me go on a scouting tour for ruins without her coming along. As for our diet of beans, only once was it broken when Cama shot a giant black pheasant.

We had made rather vague arrangements for the guide of the fishing camp at Boca de Paila to pick us up on the edge of the Chunyaxche lagoon with a flat-bottomed boat, but he had not appeared and three days had passed since the appointment with no sign of anyone coming. We feared that possibly the boat from Cozumel to the coast of Boca de Paila had not been able to make its way through the reef. Coba-Cama had a dugout canoe, but unfortunately it was so small that we could not hope to fit all three of us into it. Being exhausted, we hesitated to go back by foot over the fifty-five miles of jungle trail to Tankah. Coba-Cama came up with an unexpected suggestion: "I make a bigger canoe." The building of the canoe, we learned to our pleasure, would be only a matter of four days once a tree had been felled. The proposition seemed both highly interesting and feasible till Cama explained that it would take at least ten men to launch the dugout canoe, which would weigh several thousand pounds. Short of time and strength, reluctantly, we abandoned this project for that of going back to Tankah on foot.

The evening before our departure, we counted on our charts 108 structures, among which were twelve pyramids, five large palaces, nine temples (single- or double-room buildings, mostly with columned entrances), a dozen platforms, more than twenty small oratories or shrines, most of which were still standing, many mounds, and over half a dozen crumbled buildings with still apparent intricate floor plans. Chunyaxche now spread over an area of close to one square mile. This extent seemed incredible, especially when one considered that we had been the first to see the majority of these buildings. Incredible also that a town as large as Chunyaxche should have become lost and forgotten for some four hundred years. I could explain this only by the thickness of the jungle and by recalling that, upon my first visit, I had not even been able to guess the existence of so many ruins at Chunyaxche. Even those who had been there before me had seen only twelve buildings in the dense growth, and numerous mounds. But what was still more intriguing was the thought that, possibly, the jungle still held the secrets of dozens more in the one-time largest city of the Quintana Roo coast.

When one considers that the majority of the structures we had found were religious or governmental buildings and that the city must have had thousands of wooden huts in which the poorer classes lived and which today have disappeared, one gets but a first approximation of what must have been the population of the town in ancient times.

Chunyaxche was, it appeared, a city of the Mayapán era and

had flourished between the thirteenth and the fifteenth centuries A.D. Why it had become lost and gone unnoticed by ancient Spanish chronicles or later surveys until 1926, no one knows. Perhaps, like many Mayan cities, Chunyaxche had been abandoned for unknown reasons before the Spanish conquest, and thereafter its location had been kept secret by the fiercely independent Indians, whose descendants still today venerate the place as sacred.

Exhausted, we finally left Chunyaxche on foot for Tankah. As we snaked our way through the jungle, every step, we felt, was a step in time through the centuries. Chunyaxche soon seemed to us like an incredible dream from the past, a dream that we would never forget, and that our charts and photographs reminded us was in fact reality.

We left behind in Chunyaxche many riddles unsolved, although now we were certain that it was the largest of the coastal sites of Quintana Roo. Much further study will be necessary to steal away from the vines the last of the many secrets of that long-lost city.

Archaeologists will eventually one day take over Quintana Roo, and study to the core the temples, the pyramids, the palaces and oratories that I have found, but till then they will remain in a way my own, and Quintana Roo the mysterious land of the last independent Mayas.

Unfortunately, Quintana Roo is changing rapidly and civilization will soon precipitate the extinction of the last rebellious Indians, thus hastening the end of the long history of the Mayas, who for such countless centuries have reigned as masters over the jungles of Yucatán. And the day will come when only the chachalaka will remain to call up the gods of the East, the North, the West, and the South who rule the windswept lagoons, the endless jungles, and the sun-scorched beaches of Quintana Roo.

Florence and Cadaques,
1962

Index